The .... tics
of Natural Resources

Written under the Auspices of the Center for
International Affairs, Harvard University

By the same author

*The Community of Oil Exporting Countries: A Study in Governmental
Cooperation*

A Financial Analysis of Middle Eastern Oil Concessions, 1901–65

*An Analysis of World Energy Demand and
Supply, 1974–1985* (coauthor)

The Economic Development of Libya (coauthor)

Continuity and Change in the World Oil Industry (coeditor)

To Robert Mabro

my esteemed colleague and

friend,

Zuhayr Mikdashi

Sept 20, 1976

The International Politics of Natural Resources

ZUHAYR MIKDASHI

Cornell University Press Ithaca and London

First published 1976 by Cornell University Press.
Published in the United Kingdom by Cornell University Press Ltd., 2–4 Brook Street, London W1Y 1AA.

International Standard Book Number 0–8014–1001–0
Library of Congress Catalog Card Number 75–38002
Printed in the United States of America by Vail-Ballou Press, Inc.
Librarians: Library of Congress cataloging information appears on the last page of the book.

To UN Ideals

Contents

Tables

Figures

Preface

Business enterprises and governments have used various individual or collective approaches to exploit market opportunities in the natural resource industries. This book investigates these approaches by selecting examples which illustrate the policies, strategies, and relationships of the protagonists in these industries under various market and environmental conditions. It also suggests specific cooperative actions which could serve the needs of the less developed areas as well as promote international harmony.

The first chapter reviews the broad objectives and strategies of the major protagonists: the exporting governments, the importing governments, and the transnational enterprises. It also discusses the costs and benefits of foreign investment for the various parties. The second and third chapters scrutinize existing multilateral approaches aimed at influencing the markets in various commodities. The cases discussed cover exporter cooperation (notably in petroleum, copper, iron ore, bauxite, and other primary commodities) and exporter-importer cooperation (chiefly in tin). The fourth chapter analyzes policy issues and proposes certain collective measures at the regional and interregional levels. The book concludes with reflections on sharing the gains from the resource trade, and an evaluation of the effectiveness of group action.

In using the term "transnational," I mean to describe a vertically integrated enterprise with spread in several countries; "independent" characterizes a nonintegrated enterprise with limited spread. (A company which is vertically integrated owns the successive stages of activity from exploration through marketing.) Transnational is used in preference to "multinational" or "international" because the latter could imply businesses owned by several nations, whereas in fact most transnational companies are owned by stockholders in a single or a few developed countries.

This work addresses itself to all persons interested in and concerned with natural resources, international trade, and development. The information has been gathered from many sources, including visits to major resource-exporting and importing countries in Africa, the Americas, Asia, Europe, and Oceania, both developed and developing, market-oriented and centrally planned. I have also greatly benefited from discussions with officials of several international organizations, notably the United Nations Secretariat, the United Nations Conference on Trade and Development (UNCTAD), the United Nations Organization for Industrial Development (UNIDO), the International Bank for Reconstruction and Development (known as the World Bank), the International Monetary Fund (IMF), the Organization of Petroleum Exporting Countries (OPEC), the Intergovernmental Council of Copper Exporting Countries (CIPEC), and the International Tin Council (ITC).

It is impossible to name all those who have assisted me in this research, but I am thankful for the friendly and helpful attention they gave to my numerous queries. Grateful acknowledgement for research facilities is due to the Ford Foundation, the Harvard University Center for International affairs, Resources for the Future in Washington, the Institute of Developing Economics in Tokyo, and the Centre d'études industrielles in Geneva. The author's family sustained his efforts, and bore graciously the multiple and extensive sojourns abroad that made the research possible.

ZUHAYR MIKDASHI

Geneva, Switzerland

Abbreviations

BP	British Petroleum Company
CFP	Compagnie Française des Pétroles
CIPEC	Conseil Intergouvernemental des Pays Exportateurs de Cuivre (Intergovernmental Council of Copper Exporting Countries)
ECOSOC	Economic and Social Council (UN)
IBA	International Bauxite Association
IBRD	International Bank for Reconstruction and Development (also known as World Bank)
IMF	International Monetary Fund
ITC	International Tin Council
LDC	less developed country (also called developing)
LME	London Metal Exchange
MEES	*Middle East Economic Survey* (Beirut)
MITI	Ministry of International Trade and Industry (Japan)
OECD	Organization for Economic Cooperation and Development
OPEC	Organization of Petroleum Exporting Countries
Shell	Royal Dutch–Shell Group
UNCTAD	United Nations Conference on Trade and Development

The International Politics
of Natural Resources

Charter of Economic Rights and Duties of States

ARTICLE 1

Every State has the sovereign and inalienable right to choose its economic system as well as its political, social and cultural systems in accordance with the will of its people, without outside interference, coercion or threat in any form whatsoever.

ARTICLE 2

1. Every State has and shall freely exercise full permanent sovereignty, including possession, use and disposal, over all its wealth, natural resources and economic activities.

2. Each State has the right:

(a) To regulate and exercise authority over foreign investment within its national jurisdiction in accordance with its laws and regulations and in conformity with its national objectives and priorities. No State shall be compelled to grant preferential treatment to foreign investment;

(b) To regulate and supervise the activities of transnational corporations within its national jurisdiction and take measures to ensure that such activities comply with its laws, rules and regulations and conform with its economic and social policies. Transnational corporations shall not intervene in the internal affairs of a host State. Every State should, with full regard for its sovereign rights, co-operate with other States in the exercise of the right set forth in this subparagraph;

(c) To nationalize, expropriate or transfer ownership of foreign property, in which case appropriate compensation should be paid by the State adopting such measures, taking into account its relevant laws and regulations and all circumstances that the State considers pertinent. In any case where the question of compensation gives rise to a controversy, it shall be settled under the domestic law of the nationalizing State and by its tribunals, unless it is freely and mutually agreed by all States concerned that other peaceful means be sought on the basis of the sovereign equality of States and in accordance with the principle of free choice of means.

UN General Assembly Resolution 3281 (XXIX), December 12, 1974.

1. The Protagonists

Participants in the international commodity markets can be broadly grouped into three main categories: resource-exporting governments and their national agencies, resource-importing governments and their agencies, and transnational enterprises. One should, however, guard against the assumption that members of each group are homogeneous, have identical interests, or concur in their "optimal" strategies. Differences in size, command over resources, level of development, institutional organization, needs and priorities, or styles of action are bound to lead to disagreements and to rivalry in international markets. Nevertheless, a useful general analytical framework for interpreting the behavior and performance of the parties in resource markets is that of exporters versus importers. One should of course keep in mind that there are important departures from the foregoing framework—for example, explicit or tacit coalitions across these groups to improve or dilute terms payable by transnational companies to producing country governments, with acquiescence or even support from some consuming country governments.

Exporting Governments

Resource-exporting governments share in common the objectives of maximizing gains from exports of natural resources, protecting the country's consumer interests and safeguarding resources for future needs, and encouraging resource-based industrial development.

In order to fulfil these goals, most states in the 1970s are attempting to gain sovereignty over their key economic sectors. Such control is perceived to be more readily attainable through the promotion of national enterprises, private or public. These enterprises are considered more responsive to the needs and priorities of their governments.

Governments of developing or less developed countries (LDCs) have on several occasions expressed this opinion. At their Dakar meeting of February 1975, LDC representatives were "convinced that the only way for them to achieve full and complete economic emancipation is to recover and control their natural resources and wealth and the means of economic development in order to secure the economic, social and cultural progress of their peoples." [1]

This objective is not only common among developing countries. Leaders of developed countries have increasingly voiced concern over the dominant role of foreign companies. All favor having national capital and management increase their shares of ownership and control in key sectors of the domestic economy. [2]

Among developed countries with sizable natural resources in excess of domestic requirements, Canada and Australia have taken active steps to encourage this. Domestic enterprises are helped to repurchase foreign investments or to preserve key domestic enterprises for national ownership and control. [3] The British, Scandinavian, and Dutch governments have also acted to promote national operators—including state owned—in the development of oil and gas in the North Sea. In particular, the British,

---

[1] The Dakar Declaration of the Conference of Developing Countries on Raw Materials, February 3–8, 1975, reprinted as UNCTAD document TD/B/C.1/L.45.

[2] See Declaration on the Establishment of a New International Economic Order, UN General Assembly Resolution 3201 (S-VI), May 1, 1974, and the proceedings of the UN General Assembly's Sixth and Seventh Special Sessions on Problems of Raw Materials and Development, April 1974 and September 1975 respectively. See also Joseph Grunwald and Philip Musgrove, *Natural Resources in Latin American Development* (Baltimore: Johns Hopkins Press, 1970); and T. H. Moran, *Multinational Corporations and the Politics of Dependence: Copper in Chile* (Princeton: Princeton University Press, 1974).

[3] This is done through government agencies such as the Canada Development Corporation (CDC) and Australia's Industry Development Corporation (IDC). For Canada, see, for example: "Canada: Mineral Policy Objectives," *Mineral Trade Notes* (U.S. Bureau of Mines), October 1973, p. 18; "United States and Canada: Good Neighbors, but—Interview with Pierre Elliott Trudeau, Prime Minister of Canada," *U.S. News & World Report*, July 3, 1972, pp. 32–35; "Exclusive Interview by Charles Lynch with Prime Minister Trudeau," *Ottawa Citizen*, October 29, 1971, p. 7; and "Trudeau: Canada Moving to Wean Itself from U.S.," *Washington Post*, November 2, 1971, p. A23. See also Canada, Department of Energy, Mines, and Resources, Mineral Resources Branch, *An Approach to Mineral Policy Formulation*, by W. Keith Buck and R. B. Elver (Ottawa, 1970), p. 2; John Fayerweather, "Canadian Attitudes and Policy on Foreign Investment," *Business Topics* (Michigan State University), Winter 1973, pp. 7–20; and "C.D.C. Wins Right to Buy Shares in Texasgulf Bid," *New York Times*, September 6, 1973, p. 51. For Australia, see the annual reports of the state-owned IDC based in Canberra; and Committee for Economic Development of Australia, *The Minerals Industry in Australia*, Melbourne, October 1972, pp. 25–27.

emulating the Norwegians, offered financial incentives and protection to British operators and required 51 percent state participation.[4]

Even resource-importing developed countries restrict foreign capital, including Japan,[5] the United States, and European countries. Although not reflecting official U.S. policy, a· government source referring to developing countries' susceptibilities acknowledged that "massive foreign investments, especially if originating mostly from one nation, may mean that essential decisions relating to the well-being of the economy will be made elsewhere. Foreign control of key industries could encumber military and diplomatic policy." [6]

According to one U.S. official, exceptions to its open-door policy apply to "certain sectors of the economy which have a fiduciary character, which relate to the national defense or which involve the exploitation of natural resources." This covers domestic transport and communication, hydroelectric and atomic power, and the exploitation of federal mineral lands. Political leaders and executives in developed Western economies have furthermore been supporting legislation and other measures aimed at curbing foreign control of their enterprises.[7]

Besides national control of their key resources, another leading objective generally sought by host governments is resource-based industrialization. Their general aim is to convert foreign-owned "enclave-type" ventures, which produce raw materials for export with relatively

[4] See "When Are the British like the Arabs? When It Comes to Developing a Major Natural Resource," *Forbes,* June 15, 1973, p. 88; and "UK Offshore—The Bill for State Participation," *Petroleum Economist* (London), August 1975, pp. 296–97.

[5] See, for example, Yusakee Furuhashi, "New Policy Toward Foreign Investment? Issues in the Japanese Capital Liberalization," *Business Topics,* Spring 1972, pp. 33–38.

[6] U.S. Department of State, Bureau of Intelligence and Research, *The Multinational Corporation and National Sovereignty,* Research Study no. 1, 1971, p. iii; see also "Increasing Investment in U.S. by Foreigners Irks Many in Congress," *Wall Street Journal,* January 22, 1974, p. 1.

[7] See Peter M. Flanigan, presidential assistant and executive director of the White House Council on International Economic Policy, testifying before the Subcommittee on International Finance of the Senate Finance Committee on January 23, 1974, quoted in the *Bulletin of the American-Arab Association for Commerce and Industry* (New York), February 1974, p. 3; "Regulating the Multinationals: Fair Play or Anarchy," *New York Times,* August 26, 1973, p. 11; and "Iran Bid for Daimler Stake Blocked" and "Mannesmann Fights Arab Intrusion," *International Herald Tribune,* January 6, 1975, p. 9, and February 6, 1975, p. 7. However, company officials of a large U.S.-based natural resources company, whose major portion of income comes from operations within Canada, could not block the purchase of company stocks by the CDC, a wholly owned agency of the Canadian government. See "C.D.C. Wins Right to Buy Shares in Texasgulf Bid."

little dependence on domestically produced goods and services, into national industries exporting and selling domestically processed or manufactured products, and to rely as far as possible on domestic factors, notably labor.

The objective of resource-based industrialization as a means of increasing employment opportunities and skills is held by governments of both developing [8] and developed primary exporting countries. For example, Canada's minister for external affairs remarked: "Suggestions from responsible authorities in the United States that Canada should reduce its secondary manufacturing industry and concentrate on the exploitation and processing of natural resources are as insensitive as they are uninformed. We have the fastest growing labor force in the world. Extractive and processing industries could not begin to absorb the labor force we have today, let alone provide the new jobs we need now and in the future." [9] This concern applies with greater force to LDCs which have been faced with relatively high population growth rates and low per capita income. Although several resource-processing industries are relatively capital-intensive, they may still be the most economical sectors to develop, as compared to some labor-intensive industries for which the resource-exporting countries may not have a comparative advantage.

Industrial development is also sought by most resource-exporting countries in order to broaden and diversify their economic structure and to increase their trading partners. The attainment of these objectives would reduce their economic instability and political insecurity, which derive from a state of dependence on a few commodities and a few partner countries or companies, and the vicissitudes of the primary commodity markets. Industrialization based on primary commodities and the development of manufactures for internal consumption or export—comparative economic advantage permitting—appear therefore to be their general approach. This can widen the range of commodities produced and promote a stable but rising level of export proceeds, on which these countries' well-being rests.

[8] See, for example, "Industrialization: Key to Future OPEC Policy?" *MEES Supplement,* March 23, 1973, pp. 1–4; and the Declaration and Plan of Action of the General Conference of the United Nations Industrial Development Organization (UNIDO), Lima, March 27, 1975. This document called for raising LDCs' share of world industry from 7 percent in 1975 to a minimum of 25 percent in 2000.

[9] Mitchell Sharp in a speech in New York on September 21, 1971, quoted in *Washington Post,* October 24, 1971, p. C6.

Given the pressure of socioeconomic problems and the need for quick revenues, "needy" resource-exporting governments are more inclined to exploit the short- or intermediate-run inelasticity of demand for their commodities. (Inelastic demand means that a change in price will lead to a proportionally lower change in demand.) By pushing for higher prices, however, these governments may accelerate the substitution process for their commodities. Nevertheless, this pricing policy reflects the fact that the social discount rate, or the urgency of the need for financial resources, of these governments is higher than that of private enterprises. As revealed in a study of the copper industry:

> The [private] producers feel that high prices and rapid exploitation are not the proper long-term policy, and at the discount rates appropriate for producers this is an entirely possible assertion. But an underdeveloped nation, with very large needs for foreign exchange and capital for investment and critical shortages of both, is unlikely to agree that this is the optimal policy. It is not necessarily irrational for an underdeveloped country to prefer very large returns per year for a shorter period to somewhat smaller returns for a longer period.[10]

If, however, resource-exporting governments feel that future prices (in real terms) are likely to be higher, and assuming that they have no immediate profitable use for funds, they may prefer to defer production. The Saudi minister of petroleum and mineral resources expressed this view: "Most of the oil producing countries with large [monetary] reserves are likely to reach a stage of financial saturation where it will be impossible to increase internal expenditure without running a grave risk of inflation. These producing countries realize that the appreciation in the price of a barrel of oil in the ground is greater than the increase in the rate of interest on the unused portion of their revenue." [11]

It is important to add that the LDCs' demand for revenue is as much a result of the internal political process and the impact of external influences, as it is a consequence of the social discount rate and the developmental opportunities in the domestic economy.

Besides national control and resource-based industrialization, a third strategy resource-exporting countries have used is that of collective ac-

---

[10] Charles River Assoc., *Economic Analysis of the Copper Industry,* prepared for the General Services Administration (Cambridge, Mass., 1970), p. 174.

[11] "Yamani on Participation," *MEES Supplement,* September 22, 1972, p. 4.

tion. This approach will be discussed at length in the following chapters.[12]

Importing Governments

Preoccupied with balance of payments problems, inflationary pressures, and concern over availability of supplies, resource-importing governments have generally aimed at lower disbursements for raw material imports, consistent with their perceived objective of "security" of supplies. The latter usually refers to uninterrupted availability of material at "reasonable" prices. Security of supplies can be satisfied through diversifying sources of imports and developing competitive domestic production of the same or of substitute products (see pp. 171–84).

The United States, the world's largest consumer of natural resources, does not have a centrally formulated policy with a comprehensive coverage. U.S. policy-makers have admitted that their country has yet to develop a coherent and coordinated resource policy, although the declared objective, according to one official, is to have "adequate, dependable, and hopefully low-cost supplies." The same official attributed this situation to the diversity and complexity of the forces involved, some of which work in different directions:

In pursuit of this objective, we have adopted certain public policies addressed to mineral imports, public land use, taxes, conservation, direct subsidies, stockpiling, production, antitrust, and research and development—all in an effort to coax, encourage, cajole, and otherwise induce the private sector to take the actions required to make these desired mineral commodities available. And along with these policies specifically addressed to minerals are others, adopted with other purposes in mind, but which impinge, lightly or heavily, upon the production and use of minerals. Environmental policy is a conspicuous recent example. Human health and safety is another. Foreign policy another. To some degree, perhaps as many as half a hundred discrete influences deserving to be called government policy exert some effect upon the operations that have to do with mineral supply and demand. The pulling and hauling that goes on between these varied and often conflicting aims; the manoeuvering, the bargaining and the trade-offs that finally materialize over specific issues form the broth in which our mineral policies are steeped, and they often come out with quite a different flavor and smell than the cook intended them to have. Thus, policy states what our actions should be; politics determines what they are.[13]

[12] Also see H. W. Arndt, "Australian Resources Diplomacy," *Aluminium* (Comalco), September 1974, pp. 6–11.
[13] Hollis M. Dole, assistant secretary for mineral resources, U.S. Department of Interior, "Mineral Policy: The Art of the Possible," *Mining Congress Journal,* vol. 58, June 1972.

In recent years there have been attempts in the United States to formulate a central resource policy. On December 31, 1970, the U.S. Congress enacted Public Law 91-631 for that purpose. This legislation states that the policy of the federal government at the domestic level is

to foster and encourage private enterprise in (1) the development of economically sound and stable domestic mining, minerals, metal and mineral reclamation industries, (2) the orderly and economic development of domestic mineral resources reserves, and reclamation of metals and minerals to help assure satisfaction of industrial security and environmental needs, (3) mining, mineral and metallurgical research, including the use and recycling of scrap to promote the wise and efficient use of our natural and reclaimable mineral resources, and (4) the study and development of methods for the disposal, control, and reclamation of mineral waste products, and the reclamation of mined land, so as to lessen any adverse impact of mineral extraction and processing upon the physical environment that may result from mining or mineral activities.

At the international level, the focus of the U.S. law is on devising "measures necessary to maintain an adequate flow of minerals for America's future growth." This is of course quite general, but later governmental statements reveal a sharper focus.[14] One notices a heightened awareness of U.S. authorities concerning the country's dependence on imports of certain key materials, especially in the absence of suitable, sufficient, or competitive domestic substitutes (see Tables 1 and 5). The

Table 1. U.S. import dependence on major minerals

	Imports as a percent of consumption in 1973
Bauxite	84
Chromium	100
Cobalt	100
Copper	8
Iron ore	29
Lead	19
Manganese	100
Mercury	82
Nickel	92
Tin	100
Tungsten	56
Zinc	50

Note: For U.S. oil and gas dependency, see Figure 1.
Source: "Foreign Raw Materials: How Critical Are They?" *Morgan Guaranty Survey,* March 1974, p. 10.

[14] Statement of Hollis M. Dole, in U.S. Senate, *Interior Department Mines and Mining Orientation Briefing,* Hearings before the Subcommittee on Mines and Mining of the Committee on Interior and Insular Affairs, 92nd Cong., 1st sess., May 17, 1971, p. 7. For later

growth in potential world demand and the finiteness of resources are such that the United States, along with other major industrial countries, has become increasingly worried about assuring the regular availability of raw materials over the long term at competitive prices. As U.S. Department of Commerce Secretary Maurice Stans explained: "If the U.S. is pre-empted from the use of key resources, our society can be jeopardized in many ways. Even discounting needs for national defense and for energy, shortages of key raw materials would inevitably lead to higher prices, and jeopardize the capacity of the U.S. to produce goods for export. In addition, it could put the U.S. at a severe disadvantage in domestic production—leading to a weakening of national security." [15]

In the energy field, the U.S. government opted in 1974 for "independence" (for U.S. import dependency, see Figure 1). President Ford de-

Figure 1. Energy import dependence of Western Europe, Japan, and the United States.

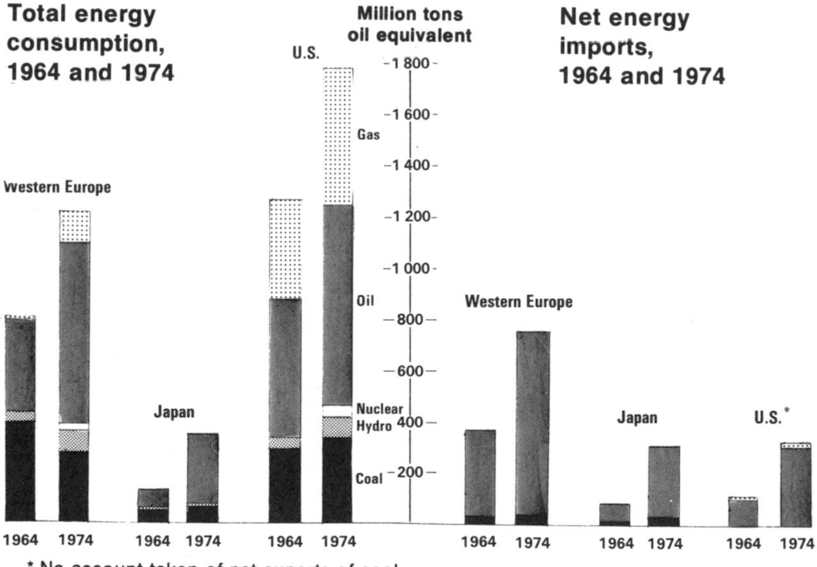

* No account taken of net exports of coal.
Source: BP Statistical Review of the World Oil Industry, 1974 (London, [1975]), p. 16.

statements, see President Nixon's Energy Message, submitted to Congress April 18, 1973, reprinted in Petroleum Intelligence Weekly (PIW), Special Supplement 2 (New York), April 23, 1973; and U.S. Congress, Joint Committee on Defense Production, Potential Shortages of Ores, Metals, Minerals, 92nd Cong., 1st sess., September 22 and 23, 1971, vol. 2.
[15] "Tin in the U.S. Economy," Tin International (London), May 1971, p. 121.

clared before the ninth World Energy Conference on September 13, 1974: "We will take tough steps to obtain the degree of self-sufficiency which is necessary to avoid disruption of our economy." President Ford's Project Independence called for an increase in energy efficiency, an increase in domestic supplies, enlarging investments in research and development, and improving the government energy administration. The formulation of specific plans for achieving energy independence has been a source of dispute within the U.S. administration and between it and the legislature.[16]

Governments have also followed more devious means to achieve their national goals. Some of these means have lately been aired in the United States, which has had congressional hearings and various investigations by federal agencies, especially concerning the CIA. Valuable information was disclosed, some of which was effectively used in the developing, resource-exporting countries—a subject which merits a separate treatise.[17]

Japan, although third in the consumption of minerals after the United States and the Soviet Union, was the world's second largest raw-material importing country in 1970–1975. In comparison with the United States, it has nonexistent or limited domestic supplies in nearly all the major minerals, such as oil, coal, uranium, iron ore, and copper, and it is heavily dependent on the export of industrial products. This explains the Japanese government's anxious concern for a systematic resource policy aimed at protecting the country's vulnerability (for Japan's energy dependence, see Figure 1).

According to government sources, Japan's natural resource policy objectives are basically four: low prices, stable prices, security of supplies,

---

[16] See "A Global Approach to the Energy Problem," *The Department of State Bulletin,* October 14, 1974, p. 493; and "Energy Mess, Worse and Worse," *U.S. News & World Report,* August 25, 1975, pp. 13–15.

[17] For press references, see, for example, "The CIA's New Bay of Bucks," *Newsweek,* September 23, 1974, pp. 51–52; "CIA Ended Mexico Cover after Angry Agent Quit," *International Herald Tribune,* July 8, 1974, p. 4; "CIA Is Linked to Strikes in Chile That Beset Allende," and "Allende's Fall, Washington's Push," *New York Times,* September 20 and 15, 1974, pp. 1 and 23 respectively; "Destabilization: An Inquiry into Kissinger's Policy of Secret American Intervention in the Politics and Economy of Foreign Nations, and a Case Study of the Policy's First Big 'Victory'—the Destruction of Allende in Chile," by G. Hodgson and W. Shawcross, *Times* (London), October 27, 1974, pp. 15–16; and "Those Charges against the CIA: What the Record Shows," *U.S. News & World Report,* August 25, 1975, pp. 38–41.

and reduction in the level of dependence on overseas supplies, even if such reduction were to be at the expense of growth in the Gross National Product (GNP).[18] The Japanese strategies for achieving security of supplies are essentially three: geographical diversification of sources of imports; acquisition of direct producing rights by Japanese enterprises, thereby reducing their dependence on the hitherto dominant method of importing from non-Japanese transnational enterprises; and bolstering interdependence with governments of resource-rich countries.[19] The strategy of direct rights in effect calls for vertical integration of the resource-using industries of Japan, namely from the fabricating or processing end to the raw materials source.

The instruments the Japanese government has used in support of its resource policy include both financial and administrative measures. Tax incentives are offered for investments by Japanese enterprises in mining ventures. Moreover, the state-owned Metallic Mineral Exploration Agency (created in 1963), and the Japan Petroleum Development Corporation (1967), subsidize the domestic exploration and development of minerals, financing Japanese overseas operations in cooperation with Japanese government agencies such as the Export-Import Bank, the Overseas Economic Cooperation Fund, the Japan Overseas Development Corporation, and the Bank of Japan (BOJ). Assistance is limited to exclusively Japanese firms, and to commodities produced for the Japanese market.[20]

The Japanese government can furthermore resort to moral suasion or use "administrative guidance" by the Ministry of International Trade and Industry (MITI) to influence Japan-based enterprises. This was the case in the creation of Kyodo Sekiyu, a domestic oil refining–marketing venture, out of the guided merger of five small companies. The new company has also become eligible for cheap credit through the Japan Development Bank. On March 5, 1973, MITI established guidelines for the direct purchase of crude oil from exporting countries. These guidelines are ap-

---

[18] OECD, *The Industrial Policy of Japan* (Paris, 1972), p. 58; also Hideo Suzuki, Mining Policy Section, MITI, "National Minerals Policy," *Mining Magazine* (London), vol. 125, no. 5, November 1971, pp. 455–56; "Rising GNP Must be Reduced to Overcome 'Energy Crisis,' " *Japan Times,* September 26, 1973, p. 10; and R. P. Sinha, "Japan and the Oil Crisis," *World Today* (London), August 1974, pp. 335–44.

[19] "New Order in International Economy Envisaged by MITI," *Japan Times,* June 28, 1975, pp. 1, 11.

[20] OECD, *Industrial Policy of Japan,* pp. 59, 134–35; and Suzuki, "National Minerals Policy," p. 457.

parently generally heeded by Japanese firms. The major objective of MITI is to obtain information, seek coordination of company actions, and avoid excessive competition. Even Australia's minister for minerals and energy noted that the Japanese mineral industry, closely monitored by the Japanese government, used "traditional divisive tactics" to obtain better terms from competing Australian export groups.[21]

Continuous discussion and close cooperation between government departments and private industry are of long standing in Japan. Industrial groups such as the Petroleum Association (Sekiyu Renmei) participate in the discussion of industrial policy issues and assist in the formulation of industrial policy. In many ways the Japanese government is much more involved in corporate decisions than the U.S. government.[22] MITI advises industries on when they should expand, where, and to what extent. It has the authority and influence necessary to back its plans with funds, usually provided by BOJ and other financial institutions under government control. MITI, moreover, constantly confers with manufacturing and trading company representatives about allocation of resources. It sets minimum sizes for industrial plants when it feels economy of scale is vital. The Ministry of Finance, also through BOJ, channels funds to areas with the highest desired growth potential. By backing an extremely high level of corporate debt in order to finance growth, MITI and BOJ play a key part in influencing the pace and direction of expansion.

In view of the size and dominance of large business groups in the nation's economy, it is only natural that the Japanese government should make use of these groups to accomplish its own goals. The close cooperation of these groups is evidenced in the monthly meetings of the fourteen largest trading groups, often with government officials present, to discuss foreign trade and investment tactics. Inevitably, such meetings among competitors lead to gentlemen's agreements, fortify cooperative bonds, and promote consensus in business strategies vis-à-vis "outsiders." In turn the government supports this spirit of cooperation with bank loans,

[21] Shell, *The Japanese Oil Industry* (London, 1971), p. 3; Institute of Energy Economics, *Energy in Japan,* Quarterly Report no. 22, Tokyo, September 1973, p. 3; and speech of R. F. X. Connor to the New South Wales Division of the Securities Institute of Australia, Sydney, August 10, 1973, p. 13 (mimeo.).

[22] Shell, *Japanese Oil Industry,* p. 3; Y. Ojimi, ex-vice minister of MITI, "Basic Philosophy and Objectives of Japanese Industrial Policy," June 24, 1970, in OECD, *Industrial Policy of Japan,* pp. 11–31; and Howard F. Van Zandt, "Learning to do Business with 'Japan, Inc.,' " *Harvard Business Review,* July–August 1972, pp. 83–92.

and to a lesser extent, direct equity interests. In explaining the close business-government relations in Japan, a U.S. official source invoked cultural factors peculiar to Japanese society:

The acceptance, to a greater or lesser degree, by Japanese businessmen of the government's goals and priorities is based on two all-important factors:
—a reluctance on the part of both business and government to unilaterally adopt policies or undertake major moves in the high priority sectors of the economy without consulting each other;
—a propensity, which all Japanese share, for a consensual approach to harmonizing differences that may exist within as well as between each group.[23]

One should not exaggerate the impact of "administrative guidance" in Japan. There have been many struggles over the directives of MITI; and more than once MITI has been overpowered by special interest groups. Several times, too, its directives have simply been disregarded, and MITI has no power to impose sanctions in such cases. As acknowledged by the above source, "the interaction between business and government in Japan can be terribly effective in some cases, virtually impotent in others." [24]

France, like Japan, offers assistance to national firms searching for natural resources overseas. An early beneficiary of this assistance was Compagnie Française des Pétroles (CFP), established in 1924 and 35 percent owned by the French government, which has, however, a 40 percent voting right. A later one is the 100 percent state-owned ELF-ERAP established soon after World War II. Both have been acting as instruments of French oil policy, including the transnational CFP.[25]

Through the state-owned agency Bureau des Recherches Géologiques et Minières (BRGM), the French government gives financial assistance to French firms exploring for critical materials in LDCs. Prior to 1972, assistance was largely limited to petroleum; since then all minerals have become eligible for such aid. Furthermore, the French government decided in 1972 to offer French enterprises a total of 300 million francs over a five-year period for carrying out overseas mineral prospecting.[26] It

[23] Eugene J. Kaplan, *Japan: The Government-Business Relationship*, A Guide for the American Businessman, U.S. Department of Commerce (Washington, 1972), p. 10.

[24] *Ibid.*, p. 57.

[25] Statements of CFP's chairman in answer to questions at the ordinary general shareholders' meeting of June 27, 1975 (text published in English).

[26] *Le Monde*, May 12, 1972, p. 19; "French Plan for Metals Stockpile," *Financial Times*, May 12, 1972, p. 29; "France: Our Very Own," *Economist*, May 6, 1972, p. 98; "Matières premières: Un Conseil interministériel met au point un plan d'approvisionnement

considered as nationally desirable the vertical integration of French enterprises, including raw material sources, in the hope of providing at least one-quarter to one-third of the country's domestic requirements.

Some resource-importing governments have offered extensive help for domestic exploration. Through the Office of Minerals Exploration (OME) and the Defense Minerals Exploration Administration (DMEA), U.S. private enterprises are eligible for government aid when exploring for strategic or critical minerals and metals. Other countries have offered financial support to ventures exploring for minerals in their territories regardless of company nationality. For example, tax concessions, subsidies, or technical assistance provided by the Australian government to petroleum exploration ventures amounted to about $419 million from 1959–1972, excluding assistance from state governments in Australia. In general, resource-importing countries—developed or developing—have encouraged their national enterprises to search for and develop alternate sources of minerals. They thereby hope to either cut the transnational middleman's profits, or to negotiate deals or exchange operations so as to reduce prices.[27]

It is difficult to assess and compare the various incentives or protections offered by countries to their natural resource ventures. The nature, conditions, and range of measures of aid or protection vary widely. Moreover, the period of benefits and the fiscal treatment (for tax purposes) of aid vary considerably. A comparative study of West European aid regimes showed that in 1972 Italy, Ireland, and Great Britain generally outpaced other European countries in global aid to their national enterprises.[28]

In a period of greater awareness of supply constraints, industrial powers have underlined the need for security of supplies, for "reasonable" or

de la France," *Le Monde,* May 12, 1972, p. 19; and "La France consolide sa politique d'approvisionnement en matières premières à usage industriel," *Les Echos,* April 19, 1972, p. 16.

[27] U.S. Congress, *Twenty-First Annual Report of the Activities of the Joint Committee on Defense Production,* 92nd Cong., 2nd sess., H. Rep. 92–843, February 21, 1972, p. 282; statement by the minister for minerals and energy, Canberra, June 4, 1973; "Oil: Governments Try to Bypass the Majors," *Business Week,* December 7, 1974, pp. 43–44; and "India Replacing Majors' Crude with Its Own Imports," *Petroleum Intelligence Weekly,* June 2, 1975, pp. 5–6.

[28] Secrétariat Général du Gouvernement, La Documentation Française, "Les Aides à l'expansion industrielle régionale dans les pays du Marché Commun," *Notes et études documentaires,* September 11, 1972, p. 14.

competitive prices, and for individual countries' refraining from outbidding, foreclosing, or pre-empting supplies. Such concern was articulated in the United States by the chairman of the Joint Committee on Defense Production:

We appear to be faced with diminishing domestic reserves of raw materials, lower grades of ore, potential shortages of fuels and energy, an increased dependence on foreign sources of supply, greater competition in purchasing metals and minerals in foreign markets, a reduction in training programs in colleges and graduate schools for highly qualified personnel for the minerals industry, estimates of continuing increases in population as well as increases in the gross national product, and greater per capita consumption of raw materials, while attempting to meet challenges which relate to the environment in the mining and processing of raw materials. Yet, metals, and fuels and energy, are essential to the operation of our assembly lines and to our future growth.[29]

It is not inconceivable, however, that a resource-importing government would support or tolerate efforts of individual exporting governments to raise prices within acceptable limits. But for this to happen there must be trade-offs. For example, transnational companies must contribute positively to the home country's balance of payments and gross national product through repatriated profits from worldwide activities and purchases of various commodities from the home country. They must also provide other benefits whose total is deemed to exceed the extra foreign exchange cost of a price hike shifted fully or partially to consumers. Another reason for an importing government supporting a price increase in imports might be a concern for protecting domestic producers against importers; alternately, it might be the expectation that higher prices would spur improved conservation practices, domestic exploration (assuming the importing country has potential reserves), and the search for and development of competitive alternative or substitute products, thereby ultimately reducing dependence on imports. Of course, import restrictions or domestic subsidies could possibly accomplish the same objective. A third reason may be that the mineral-importing government expects trade-offs or compensations from the beneficiary resource-exporting government or governments. Such compensations could occur in economic or noneconomic areas, including security of supplies.

Governments of industrial countries, such as the United States, Britain, France, Belgium, the Netherlands, and Japan, have at times offered sup-

---

[29] U.S. Congress, *Twenty-First Annual Report on Defense Production,* p. 2.

port to their transnational enterprises, both economic and political, against attempts by developing host governments to alter the terms of business contracts entered into with foreign enterprises. With respect to economic support, the United States has enacted legislation (including the so-called Hickenlooper and Gonzalez amendments to the Foreign Aid Act) to withhold aid provided through bilateral or multilateral channels from countries which fail to offer "prompt, adequate and effective compensation" to nationalized U.S. ventures.[30] In the absence of international arbitration, the judge of the promptness, adequacy, and effectiveness of compensation is, of course, the U.S. government or its enterprises. As expressed by a U.S. Department of State source: "The Hickenlooper amendment and investment guarantee programs tend to strengthen the view of close and intimate co-ordination of U.S. corporate and governmental policies. Developing countries are generally more sensitive to the threat foreign investment poses to their national sovereignty than developed countries, owing to their previous colonial experience and their dependence on foreign investment for their economic development." [31]

Transnational Companies

Business executives generally agree that the dominant objective of private enterprises is to maximize the long-run earnings of their stockholders. In this respect, "adequate" rates of return on private investments in developing countries are usually set above those found in developed countries. The difference apparently represents a premium to cover perceived higher risks. But for an enterprise to exact large "risk premia" could prove counter-productive to the extent it might invite the charge of "exploitation" and result in conflict with the host government.

Profit maximization cannot be achieved, executives also generally agree, through a strategy of pushing for growth in quantity sold without

---

[30] These channels include the Inter-American Development Bank, the Asian Development Bank, and the International Development Association; see *Congressional Record,* January 19, 1972, pp. 105–6.

[31] U.S. Department of State, *Multinational Corporation and National Sovereignty,* p. 9. See also Richard J. Bloomfield, "Who Makes American Foreign Policy? Some Latin American Case Studies," Center for International Affairs, Harvard University, April 1972 (typescript); Howard Palfrey Jones, "Oil and Politics in Indonesia," *Pacific Community* (Tokyo), July 1972, pp. 718–19; and "When $25,000 Stood between ITT and Ecuador," *Business Week,* August 11, 1973, pp. 102–3.

due regard for price-cost considerations. The president of the world's largest aluminum producer explained his company's concern for profit and its relevance to choice of strategy in these words: "Growth for growth's sake is self defeating. . . . Pounds of metal shipped and profits earned are no longer synonymous. For Alcoa, we have said, to be first in aluminum is not necessarily to be first in pounds (of weight), but it most assuredly is to be first in profitability." [32]

The objective of profit maximization over the long run was also advocated by another major natural resource company. The president of Noranda said: "We are not much attracted by growing industries as such. Growth is one factor, but many rapidly growing industries have miserable rates of return. We are primarily interested in those industries in which Noranda can obtain a good rate of return over the long term through some competitive advantage." To achieve its objective, Noranda (originally a copper mining company confined to Canada) deliberately broadened its business to include other natural resources, and their processing to include the fabrication stage. Besides functional diversification and vertical integration, the company has gone into geographical diversification by exploring, producing, and processing minerals abroad. In seeking to maximize its long-run rate of return, company management hopes to exploit the comparative advantage of its resources. Noranda's leader stated the company's competitive advantage to be the potential of its land, in addition to its expertise in exploration, mining, metallurgy, marketing, bulk transport, and finance. [33]

Profit maximization through economies of size, diversification, and vertical integration can come through the creation of additional capacity, as well as through the merger of competing, complementary, or sometimes unrelated enterprises. It is instructive to note, for example, the stated motives for the 1971 merger of two major French firms, Pechiney and Ugine Kuhlmann. The former firm was largely in minerals-metals, and the latter in chemicals-metals. In seeking the merger, the chairman of Pechiney stated that he was not after "systematic gigantism," although the merger gave the new company quasi-monopoly power in France in

[32] W. H. K. George, "The Aluminum Industry: Strategy for Profit," address to the Organization of European Aluminum Smelters, London, September 10, 1971, p. 5 (typescript).

[33] Afred Powis, "The Scope and Diversification of the Noranda Group of Companies," *Western Miner* (Toronto), January 1971, p. 22.

such commodities as aluminum. Through larger size the new company can achieve diversification, exploit a larger number of options, rationalize management, institute economies of scale, and support greater research and development. All these advantages, the chairman of Pechiney argued, would be in the interest of stockholders:

—The merger will permit us to complete rationalizations already commenced in the fields of aluminium, ferrous alloys and the nuclear industry.
—The increased turnover will allow us, without a corresponding increase in cost of goods sold, to reinforce our research in mining prospection as well as in manufacturing and in new uses.
—The merger will enable us to develop the diversification of a powerful industrial group which generates a cash flow of 1,500 million francs per year.
We are certainly not aiming for mammoth size for its own sake, but an increase in size and diversification should result in a more reliable and more efficient management of resources and give us a greater freedom of action.[34]

To strive for size, diversification, and vertical integration is common among resource enterprises, be they Western or Eastern. This was clearly put by the chief executive of an Australian resource enterprise: "We believe your Company derives considerable strength from the diversified and integrated nature of its operations. Integration provides maximum access to research, development and financing resources. Diversification protects shareholders from sole dependence on the short-term success of a particular product or activity." He admitted that size and strength could bring disadvantages in the form of criticism (bigness being occasionally equated with badness); but commercial advantages and opportunities would more than compensate.[35]

In their endeavor to maximize long-term returns, it is not uncommon for transnational corporations to set prices for transactions among affiliates so as to reduce the global tax burden. This can be done, within limits, by splitting their vertically integrated profits and declaring comparatively lower taxable profits in high-tax countries, while declaring higher taxable profits in low-tax countries.[36]

---

[34] Pierre Jouven, *Annual General Meeting* (Paris, 1971). Similar views were expressed by the chairman of Ugine Kuhlmann, Pierre Grezel, *Annual General Meeting* (Paris, 1971, English text).
[35] The Broken Hill Proprietary Co., *Chairman's Address at Annual General Meeting* (Melbourne, 1971), p. 8.
[36] See Zuhayr Mikdashi, *The Community of Oil Exporting Countries: A Study in Governmental Cooperation* (London: Allen & Unwin; Ithaca: Cornell University Press, 1972),

In setting interaffiliate transfer prices, transnational enterprises furthermore endeavor to minimize "assignable" returns on those functions which are readily accessible to potential or actual competitors, in order to discourage their entry into the market or their competition. By comparison, they will attempt to show highest returns on those functions most inaccessible, for reasons of technology, size, or other barriers, to competitors.[37] However, many of the transnational enterprises are conscious of the need to be able to justify their transfer prices by market criteria, since in every country in which an affiliate operates, that affiliate has become subject to surveillance (increasingly close and penetrating) by the domestic fiscal authorities.

It is of course an oversimplification of a complex reality to assume that profit-making is the sole objective of a private transnational corporation. While researchers generally acknowledge the dominant role of that objective, one should add others: concern for growth of sales, for raising market shares, and for reducing uncertainty in the business environment.[38]

In their efforts to satisfy these objectives, transnational companies have had command over or access to vast resources and wide opportunities as compared with a large number of host country governments, and notably the LDCs. The strength of transnational companies is based on not only their size and resources, but also their capacity to exploit economies of scale, advanced technology, and know-how; their superior organizational and managerial ability and their unity of command; their extensive market outlets; their close interrelatedness in partnerships and in other respects; and their negotiating skills. Historically, these factors have favored the transnational companies in bilateral negotiations with resource-exporting LDCs. Referring to bargaining skills, one scholar commented:

In negotiations between companies and (LDC) governments, there is a great disparity in technical ability. The company representatives earn perhaps ten or even twenty times as much as those on the official side; they can devote much more time to advance study; they are cosmopolitan and sophisticated enough to exploit differences in temperament and attitude among their opponents, using flat-

---

p. 42, and the statement of Emilio G. Collado, executive vice president, Exxon Corporation, in UN, ECOSOC, *The Impact of Multinational Corporations on the Development Process and on International Relations,* New York, September 11, 1973, p. 21.

[37] Raymond Vernon, *Sovereignty at Bay: The Multinational Spread of U.S. Enterprise* (New York: Basic Books, 1971), p. 138.

[38] *Ibid.*

tery and mild ridicule; above all, they can draw on the experts of their whole organization (in law, accounting, engineering, etc.). The atmosphere is that of bargaining between two nations, of which the foreign company is much the stronger.

Indeed, one transnational enterprise has admitted that it has command over more information than many LDC host governments, and consequently has an advantage over these governments.[39]

Some LDC government negotiators have recently come close to matching in competence and skill the negotiators from transnational companies. Moreover, transnational companies have on various occasions exercised restraint in bargaining lest they give scope to future resentment and retribution, probably ending in nationalization. The existence of real competition between companies, which could be created by able negotiation, could offer attractive options to a host government and provide it with useful data. This assumes, however, that the host government has the ability and willingness to take advantage of that competition—which is not always the case.

Even the government of a developed country like Australia, when confronted by a few large transnational companies bidding for mineral rights, has acknowledged their strong bargaining power; it resulted in the companies capturing large economic rents.[40] An official document stated:

[39] Dudley Seers, "Big Companies and Small Countries: A Practical Proposal," *Kyklos* (Basel), vol. 16, fasc. 4, 1963, p. 602; and Shell, *Multinational Enterprise,* a background paper prepared for Shell management (London, 1972), p. 4.

[40] More specifically, the size of economic rent accruing to a given mineral deposit is equal to the difference between the cost (including normal return on the required capital, but not including "user cost") of producing that deposit and the cost of producing a marginal deposit. "Economists use the concept of 'user cost' to help measure the consequences of the non-renewability of a resource. The user cost of a particular resource is the amount that we ought to charge ourselves now, when determining output, to take into account that the resource used now will not be available in the future. For example, if we have crude oil costing $1 per barrel to develop and transport, and there is enough of that oil to last ten years, but thereafter crude oil, though available in unlimited amounts, will cost $10 (presently valued) per barrel, and is expected to sell at that price, the user cost of a barrel of oil today is equal to $9 (i.e., $10 − $1) discounted back ten years. Thus when we are using crude oil, we should be treating it not as a $1 resource, or as a $10 resource, but as a resource worth slightly less than $10 because it is possible to defer until some future period the requirement to spend $10 to develop a barrel of oil or its substitute ($10 discounted to present by i). The appropriate value for oil is thus equal to the direct costs of extraction plus the user cost." See John Helliwell, "Extractive Resources in the World Economy," *International Journal* (Canadian Institute of International Affairs), vol. 29, Autumn 1974, p. 594. The "i" stands for the hypothetical discount rate.

In practice, as distinct from theory, foreign companies in many cases have sufficient power to prevent the resource owner, whether private or public, from reaching an agreement which would succeed in capturing all forthcoming rents. The importance of the overseas investor in the mining industry results in part from the large quantities of development capital usually required to exploit mineral resources, and in part from the importance of securing adequate market outlets. The bargaining power of the foreign company derives therefore from the limited number of potential bidders and the uncertainty this engenders. These considerations notwithstanding, the available evidence suggests that contracted royalties could have been higher without reducing investment incentives beyond the critical point where the investment does not occur at all.[41]

Under some circumstances it appears that the power of the giant transnational enterprises transcends national boundaries, and they come close to forming autonomous supranational entities. For an illustration one could refer to the international prorating implemented by transnational oil companies following the reduction in Arab oil exports to selected destinations in late 1973. In fact, the international oligopoly partially thwarted Arab action by diverting non-Arab oil supplies from countries not affected by Arab cutbacks to the affected countries. This redistribution of world oil supplies was made in accordance with what the transnational companies ostensibly deemed "equitable." [42] Actually, the redistribution was designed to protect their assets and markets in the countries affected by the cutbacks.

Some authors have argued that the "supra-national" aspect of transnational business does not offer an accurate description of a world of nation-states with a rising sense of national consciousness. The above evidence supports the view that the supranationality characteristic of transnational firms is not always exaggerated.[43] Moreover, it is reason-

[41] Australia, Commonwealth Treasury, *Overseas Investment in Australia,* Canberra, May 1972, p. 92.

[42] See the statement of Shell official Geoffrey Chandler, reprinted in the *Guardian Weekly* and *Le Monde,* December 15, 1973; "Oil Companies Warn France of 10 to 15% Cuts Next Month," *International Herald Tribune,* November 23, 1973, p. 2; and "France Tells Oil Groups They Face Marketing Nationalization If Cutbacks Are Too Drastic," *Times* (London), November 22, 1973.

[43] See, for example, witnesses, statements, and submissions in U.S. Congress, Joint Economic Committee, *A Foreign Economic Policy for the 1970's,* p. 4, *The Multinational Corporation and International Investment,* Hearings before the Subcommittee on Foreign Economic Policy, 91st Cong., 2nd sess., July 27, 28, 29, and 30, 1970; also U.S. Senate, *The International Telephone and Telegraph Company and Chile,* Hearings before the Subcommittee on Multinational Corporations, 93rd Cong., 1st sess., 1973.

able to generalize that transnational companies (mostly based in the United States, Western Europe, and to a lesser extent Japan) have enjoyed and exercised a large measure of discretionary power, subject, on balance, more to the influence of the industrially advanced parent countries where their leaders and a major portion of their assets are. This was recognized by an official Canadian source which said that "the investment decisions of foreign-controlled corporations tend to reflect the laws and industrial priorities of foreign governments and economies." [44]

In protecting their interests, transnational companies have resorted, among other tactics, to the "payoff" strategy. One company, Exxon, paid to political parties in a single country, Italy, about $51 million from 1963–1972. The payments were tied to particular corporate objectives such as reduction in manufacturing and excise taxes, the interest-free use for three months of the proceeds of petroleum excise taxes collected in Italy, and "special" fuel oil supply contracts to power plants. The gifts were camouflaged through such means as the issuance of vouchers for goods that were never bought, partly to enable the company to deduct them for its Italian income tax purposes. Senator Frank Church, presiding over hearings of the Senate Foreign Relations Subcommittee on Multinational Corporations, declared that "the company was practicing a fraud on the Italian Government." Mobil's declared gifts to Italian political parties from 1970–1973 amounted to $2.1 million, and were disguised in the company's books as advertising, research, and other expenses. Gulf Oil Corporation admitted spending $5 million between 1960 and 1973 for illegal political purposes, mostly in South Korea, and another $5.3 million in the United States, also for political purposes, some illegal. Exxon's Canadian subsidiary (Imperial Oil) contributed in 1970–1974 an annual average of $236,000 to Canadian political parties favoring Exxon's "political philosophies." [45] Other illegal contributions were disclosed by Ashland Oil.

The practice of offering multimillion dollar illegal gifts has been of

[44] Canada, *Foreign Direct Investment in Canada,* Ottawa, 1972, p. 5.
[45] See "How U.S. Firm Bribed Italy's Left and Right," *Times* (London), July 17, 1974, p. 5; "Exxon Italian Payments Tied to Specific Benefits," *New York Times,* July 17, 1975, pp. 1, 47; "Exxon Chiefs Knew of Italian Payments," *Financial Times,* July 17, 1975, p. 4; "Mobil Italy Gifts Put at $2 Million," *New York Times,* July 18, 1975, pp. 39–42; "Mobil's Italian Unit Donated $2.1 Million to Political Parties, Senate Panel Is Told," *Wall Street Journal,* July 18, 1975, p. 19; *New York Times,* July 13, 1975, p. 22; and "Exxon Canada Gift $234,000 Each Year," *New York Times,* July 16, 1975, pp. 51, 61.

long standing. Transnational enterprises have defended this approach "as the only way they can compete effectively abroad." It was reported that "some such payments are officially sanctioned by the United States Government."[46]

There are also instances where host governments were misled by company negotiators. Such a situation need not only happen with less developed countries. For example, an Australian government team, negotiating on behalf of Papua New Guinea (PNG) with the British-based transnational company Rio-Tinto Zinc (RTZ), was misled by company projections of output and profitability which conveyed the impression that the concession applied for, namely Bougainville, would be a marginal operation.[47]

The extent to which a private transnational enterprise heeds or influences government objectives varies from one country to another. In several developed countries, governments have on several occasions responded to the wishes of their firms. The official reason usually adduced is service of national interest. For example, in January, March, and October 1971, the U.S. Department of Justice waived antitrust provisions so that U.S. and other Western petroleum companies could join forces to bargain collectively for production, tax, and price matters vis-à-vis oil exporting governments. The stated reason for permitting collective company action, according to spokesmen, was the U.S. government's desire to have an oil company bloc face OPEC (Organization of Petroleum Exporting Countries) in order to moderate oil price increases to Western consumers. Shell was apparently the prime mover behind the creation of a company bloc. Its purpose was to establish a mutual assistance program calling for the sharing of oil supplies from various sources to counter any move by a single OPEC government—such as a production cutback affecting one or more companies.[48]

[46] "U.S. Company Payoffs Way of Life Overseas: Such Activities Are Often Sanctioned by Washington," *New York Times,* May 5, 1975, pp. 1, 52; see also "Why Americans Pay Bribes to Do Business Abroad," *U.S. News & World Report,* June 2, 1975, pp. 57–58.

[47] See Stephen Zorn, U.S. consultant to the Papua New Guinea government, "Renegotiating Mining Agreements: The Case of Bougainville Copper," UN Training Workshop on Negotiation and Regulation of Foreign Investments, New Delhi, 1975, Document no. ND-6, pp. 25–26 (typescript).

[48] See documents in U.S. Senate, *Multinational Corporations and United States Foreign Policy,* Hearings before the Subcommittee on Multinational Corporations of the Committee on Foreign Relations, 93rd Cong. 2nd sess., August 30, 1974, pt. 6, especially pp. 248–250ff., and pt. 5, pp. 80–81, 116–17.

In another instance, U.S. Secretary of the Interior Rogers C. B. Morton explained in a statement to the petroleum industry in August 1973: "Our mission is to serve you, not regulate you. . . . I pledge to you that the Department is at your service." [49]

Besides these examples, one can point to a general tendency among the transnationals and their parent governments to establish symbiotic relationships as a means of protecting gains or improving on them. For example, such a symbiosis arose in reaction to OPEC. The chairman of the Committee on U.S. Energy Outlook of the National Petroleum Council said early in 1972: "To meet this growing collective effort among major oil supplying countries, we must marshal massive countervailing power on the consumer-country side of the table. We urgently need a strong framework for collective action at top diplomatic levels on behalf of the consuming nations." And in 1974 the U.S. government led in the formation of such a framework, the International Energy Agency (IEA), compromising major Western energy-consuming countries. The chairman of British Petroleum (BP), among other oil executives of the West, "warmly welcomed" IEA's establishment.[50]

This antagonism is not necessary, however. Resource-exporting governments and international oligopolists could have parallel interests; for example, in obtaining higher product prices under "sellers' market" conditions, in barring entry of alternative sources or substitutes, in maintaining business stability, and possibly in growth of sales. Among the advantages which transnational corporations can offer resource-exporting countries is the acquisition of technology and managerial know-how. The transnationals can also lobby in favor of relaxed trade barriers with their home country authorities. Their lobbying is likely to be more intense the greater their business interests in the host countries. This was apparently the case of Anaconda, with Kennecott helping, in successfully fighting in the 1950s for the suspension of import tariffs on copper, which were

[49] *Business Week,* July 13, 1974, p. 8. For additional evidence on the transnational oil companies' close relation to their home governments, see Michael Tanzer, "The International Oil Companies and Their Home Governments," in his *Energy Crisis: World Struggle for Power and Wealth* (New York: Monthly Review Press, 1974), pp. 38–53; and Mikdashi, *Community of Oil Exporting Countries,* pp. 58–61.

[50] John G. McLean, late president and chief executive of Continental Oil Company, "Energy Users Must Unite," *New York Times,* January 9, 1972, sec. 3, p. 14; and address by Sir Eric Drake to the American Petroleum Institute, November 11, 1974, reprinted in *Petroleum Information Foundation* (New York), January 1975.

clamored for by a majority of U.S. domestic producers and favored by the U.S. administration.[51]

In the above review of the major parties to resource industries, emphasis has been put on the dominant objectives and strategies. Furthermore, it would be unrealistic to leave the impression that objectives and interests are uniform or necessarily consistent for all members of each group. Variances have existed and continue to exist among firms, as well as among exporter or importer governments. In particular, sharing the rewards and costs among the parties concerned has been a crucial problem of contention. The split can be that of a zero-sum game, meaning that the loss of one party is exactly the gain of the other. Alternately, both parties can lose or gain simultaneously.[52]

Costs versus Benefits

The main indicators of performance for a private enterprise are usually expressed in terms of return on invested resources, growth of sales and income, and overall business stability. By comparison, a country's performance in certain areas, for example the hosting of foreign investments by transnational firms, is much more difficult to measure. In this case, it should be assessed in terms of benefits accruing to labor and management, in the form of technology transfers and improved efficiency, larger employment, higher real wages, and more equitable income distribution; consumers and industrial users, in the form of lower prices, better quality, and new products; government, through higher revenues; the country's international position, through growth in the level and diversification of export earnings and through increased self-reliance in key activities; and the country's domestic conditions, through efficient use and conservation of resources, protection of the environment, and realization of external economies (external to the investing firm). External economies can show up in the form of improved technical, managerial, and organizational ability, improved methods of production, development of the country's infrastructure, and the creation or expansion of domestic industries. These in turn supply inputs to investing firms, make use of domestic output, produce complementary products, or provide goods and services for the now higher real income of the population. Additional

---

[51] James L. McCarthy, "The American Copper Industry, 1947–1955," *Yale Economic Essays,* no. 4, Spring 1964, pp. 92–93.

[52] See Mikdashi, *Community of Oil Exporting Countries,* p. 194.

economic benefits can accrue in the form of encouragement of domestic savings available for investment, and more generally through optimal industrialization and diversification leading to self-sustained, steady, and balanced development.[53]

As for the social costs of direct foreign investment by transnational firms, though difficult to identify and gauge, they should be approximated in the light of national goals, priorities, and planning horizons. Such costs may consist of: stifling local entrepreneurship by pre-empting growth sectors of the national economy, by attracting local talents and financial resources at the expense of domestic firms, or by supplanting nationals with expatriates; having important decision-making powers (with respect to transfer pricing and allocation of overheads, procurement, nature and size of production, destination of exports, research and development, sources and flows of financing) which affect socioeconomic conditions made outside a host country and with disregard to its needs; and having a transnational enterprise use its home country government to promote and protect its interests, or be used by the latter in the extraterritorial extension of home country laws, policies, and regulations.[54] It has also been argued that direct foreign investments can increase the risk of occasional instability in a host country's foreign exchange position, because of the large size of the transnational firm's transactions and its capacity to shift financial and productive assets across national boundaries in response to its own private interests.[55]

Perception of costs vary from one government to another. A host gov-

[53] For a review of the literature on this subject, see G. M. Meier, *Leading Issues in Economic Development: Studies in International Poverty*, 2nd ed. (New York: Oxford University Press, 1970), pp. 298–302; also, *Private Foreign Investment in its Relationship to Development*, Report by the UNCTAD Secretariat, Geneva, November 17, 1971 (TD/134).

[54] Notable among these are U.S. antitrust legislation, requirements for repatriation of profits and limitations on capital export, and U.S. Export Control and Trading with the Enemy acts limiting the exports of U.S. overseas affiliates to Communist countries. See also C. N. Ellis, "United States Multinational Corporations: The Impact of Foreign Direct Investment on United States Foreign Relations," *San Diego Law Review*, vol. 11, no. 1, November 1973, pp. 1–26; and A. E. Safarian, *The Performance of Foreign-Owned Firms in Canada* (Montreal: Canadian American Committee, 1969), pp. 1–6; and R. A. Matthews, "The International Economy and the Nation State," *Columbia Journal of World Business*, November–December 1971, pp. 51–60.

[55] For a review of these arguments, see, for example, William R. Weinberg, "The Costs of Foreign Private Investment," *Civilizations*, vol. 21, nos. 2 and 3, 1971, pp. 207–19; *Revue économique et sociale* (Lausanne), special issue on "L'Entreprise multinationale," March 1973; and Bank of Nova Scotia, "Foreign Investment in Canada," *Monthly Review* (Toronto), April–May 1971.

ernment may consider as the costs of direct foreign investment being "locked into accepting a pattern of innovation and technological development which has its origins abroad," or having "truncated" enterprises "in which many important activities are performed abroad by the parent or other affiliated firms." In an official Canadian view, "this reliance on external sources for many of the inputs of industrial activity has meant a lesser development of Canadian capacities—and perhaps even a stultification of these capacities." [56]

In the economic—as distinct from sociopolitical—evaluation of foreign investment costs from the standpoint of the hosting government, the guiding test is normally the net contribution to national income, or put differently, to the goods and services available for the country concerned, as compared with alternative courses of action.[57] This view is common among most economists. One economist, however, adds to the objective of increasing "aggregate consumption benefits" other objectives, notably the "redistribution of benefits" and the fulfillment of "merit-want" and "self-sufficiency benefits." He argues that the relative importance of objectives can be conceptually and operationally weighted, but he offers no empirical calculations.[58]

A United Nations seminar which brought together representatives of countries with disparate socioeconomic conditions "recognized that the importance attached to each objective by a Government will depend on (a) the size of the country and its population; (b) its human, natural, mineral, and financial resources; and (c) the stage of economic and industrial development reached." [59] One should add the country's sociopolitical conditions as another important factor. In an earlier book, I identified the policy objectives of the oil exporting governments.[60] There were many

[56] Canada, *Foreign Direct Investment,* p. 6; and speech by the Canadian minister of industry, trade, and commerce to the Economic Club of Detroit, "Canadian Policy Initiatives: Unamerican Activities," February 11, 1974.

[57] See D. M. Schydlowsky, *Benefit-Cost Analysis of Foreign Investment Proposals: The Viewpoint of the Host Country,* Development Advisory Service, Harvard University Center for International Affairs Report no. 170, 1970, p. 6.

[58] Stephen A. Marglin, *Public Investment Criteria: Benefit-Cost Analysis for Planned Economic Growth* (Cambridge: MIT Press, 1968), pp. 40–47, 23–39; see also P. Dasgupta, S. Marglin, and A. Sen, *Guidelines for Project Evaluation* (New York: United Nations, 1972), pp. 247–56.

[59] United Nations Industrial Development Organization (UNIDO), *Seminar on Selected Aspects of Industrial Policy,* Beirut, 1971 (ID/66, ID/WG.86/10).

[60] Mikdashi, *Community of Oil Exporting Countries,* pp. 62–68.

hurdles, however, which prevented my weighting these objectives, or ranking them. It was especially difficult to determine whether the weighting or ranking should be done from the standpoint of the collective interest as viewed by the OPEC Secretariat, or from that of an individual member government.

Social objectives, it is important to bear in mind, are not necessarily additive or consistent. They may indeed be competing: for example, national control could be at the expense of economic growth and this would therefore invite trade-offs. Moreover, in the calculation of net social benefits accruing from an investment, market prices cannot be generally used because of imperfections and rigidities domestically or internationally. The market price of a commodity is not representative of the social cost of producing that commodity. Corrections have to be made by devising "shadow" prices (which show the true social cost), a complex undertaking with many pitfalls.

One should therefore question the conceptual validity and the computational practicality of weighting benefits. One scholar argued that " 'weighting' such measurements in any formal sense . . . is dangerous and suppresses useful information." In his judgement, "the intangibles are probably the most important assets of all: information on production and marketing techniques; a commitment to the creation of a local organization; a capacity efficient or otherwise, to search out needed inputs in the local economy or abroad." [61]

Another scholar also criticized those who contend that the direct and indirect benefits and costs of development projects can be measured, aggregated, and ranked. He even doubted that the properties of projects can be properly ascertained or compared: "Earlier I have argued in favor of abandoning the search for a ranking device that would presume to aggregate the direct and indirect effects of projects. It is now seen that the project analyst must be still more modest: he cannot even pretend to classify uniformly, for purposes of decision making, the various properties and probable lines of behavior of projects, as either advantages or drawbacks, benefits or costs, assets or liabilities." [62]

[61] Raymond Vernon, *Some Notes on Concessions Policy,* Development Advisory Service, Harvard University Center for International Affairs Report no. 117, September 1968, p. 171.
[62] Albert O. Hirschman, *Development Projects Observed* (Washington: Brookings Institution, 1967), p. 188.

As a practical alternative to the approach of ranking and weighting benefits, advising economists should restrict their efforts to identifying and assessing individual benefits or costs. The exercise of identification and assessment is in itself challenging, and there is no need to compound difficulties by offering weights. Economic advisers should then present government leaders with a collection of packages of benefits—a cost mix, each package representing an alternative course of action. It is up to the responsible leader or group of leaders to choose, and the choice will then reflect implicitly the weights they assign to individual elements in each package.

For LDC primary exporters, one can plausibly assume that a major benefit derived from the exploitation of their natural resources is foreign exchange; it is estimated that 90 percent or more of the total foreign exchange receipts accrue to the host government. It is conceivable that a government with a pressing need for hard currency would support the production of a commodity for which there is a ready export market, even if that commodity were to be produced at no or little commercial profit.

For illustrative purposes, one can review the balance of payments impact of transnational investments. For example, it was reported that direct U.S. foreign investments in mining and smelting have produced in the period 1960–1967 a net contribution to the U.S. balance of payments of over $2.1 billion:

The mining industry has made very substantial positive contributions to the U.S. balance of payments over the years. If we compute balance of payments flows in a meaningful and realistic way, taking into account royalties, license fees, interest and similar returns, as well as the capital flows which are encompassed within the control program, we find that in the eight-year period immediately preceding the January 1, 1968 Regulations (that is 1960 through 1967) the net contribution of the mining industry was $2.113 billion.[63]

A U.S. Senate study covering the period 1966–1970 reported that ''the most consistent of the conclusions is that the U.S. based multinational enterprises in their transactions with the United States, exert a uniformly large negative impact on the current accounts of balances of payments of

[63] Statement of Frank R. Milliken, director, American Mining Congress, in U.S. House, *Hearings on Foreign Direct Investment Controls,* before the Subcommittee on Foreign Economic Policy of the Committee on Foreign Affairs, 91st Cong., 1st sess., April 24, 1969, p. 176.

the host countries." [64] Conversely, they had a favorable impact on the U.S. balance of payments.

One can also consider the balance of payments impact of direct U.S. foreign investment on a given region, for example Latin America. One source stated that in the 1960s U.S. companies had been withdrawing from that region "$2 in dividends, royalties, and other payments for every new dollar they invest. U.S. private companies exercise a 'double negative impact': at the same time that they decapitalize Latin America by the withdrawal of profits, they plow back a part of their profits to gain increasing control of the mineral assets, industry, and production of Latin American countries." [65]

The interpretation offered by the above source is impressionistic and anecdotal with no decisive value. For systematic attempts at measuring balance of payments effects, one can consult the Hufbauer-Adler and Reddaway reports. Moreover, the often-used term "decapitalization" might falsely convey the meaning of "loss in its net productive resources." The two terms are, however, not synonymous, since the net outflow of funds from one country (in repatriation of principal and profits) does not necessarily mean that the productive capacity of the country has suffered commensurately. It is very likely that U.S. direct investments have increased the productive capacity of Latin American countries and of other host countries, and have consequently improved their balance of payments position worldwide through savings in imports and the expansion of exports. [66]

A capital-exporting country with significant international investments in, for example, oil, can have a substantial net balance of payments benefit. Such was the case of the United Kingdom. One of its two major

[64] See U.S. Senate, Committee of Finance, *Implications of Multinational Firms for World Trade and Investment and for U.S. Trade and Labor*, February 1973, pp. 5, 7, 29.

[65] Senator Frank Church, "Farewell to Foreign Aid: A Liberal Takes Leave," *Congressional Record*, October 29, 1971, p. S17185, using evidence from Gary MacBoin, "Latin America: Who Is to Blame," *Commonweal*, June 25, 1971, p. 331.

[66] U.S. Treasury Department, *Overseas Manufacturing Investment and the Balance of Payments*, Tax Policy Research Study no. 1, by G. C. Hufbauer and F. M. Adler, 1968; W. B. Reddaway, J. O. N. Perkins, S. J. Potter, and C. T. Taylor, *Effects of U.K. Direct Investment Overseas, Interim* and *Sequel Reports*, University of Cambridge, 1967 and 1969 respectively; and Lincoln Gordon, Johns Hopkins School of International Studies, "A Rebuttal to Senator Church's 'Farewell to Foreign Aid: A Liberal Takes Leave,' " *Washington Post*, November 14, 1971, p. B7.

transnational oil firms, BP, contributed to the U.K. balance of payments in 1974 an estimated net amount of £220 million: "Of the £220 million benefit, £200 million resulted from overseas activities, including sale of exports from the U.K., and £20 million represents the estimated saving to the country from the group importing oil for consumption within the U.K. as compared with the foreign exchange cost of buying the same quantity from a foreign based oil company." [67]

The contribution of the French transnational oil companies to France's balance of payments was also substantial. One estimate put the balance of payments contribution of one French group, ERAP-SNPA, at an annual average of $350 million.[68] The contribution of the other larger French group, CFP, should be at least of the same magnitude. The figures exclude other contributions by French enterprises which follow in the wake of the French oil groups, notably the engineering, construction, contracting, and servicing firms.[69]

An analysis of the balance of payments impact of a certain project has to take into account a sufficiently long period to cover the economic life of that project. It should measure, on a presently valued basis, foreign exchange receipts, that is to say, export proceeds resulting from the project, the value of import substitution created, and the export multiplier effect resulting from the increase in savings-investments derived from the increase in income associated with the project. Net foreign exchange receipts should exclude disbursements for capital goods services and other imports associated with the project, for servicing foreign investments, and for the increase in imports resulting from the increase in income associated with the project.

One scholar commented that "there is a great lack of knowledge about

[67] BP, *Annual Report and Accounts for 1974* (London, 1975), p. 11; also Great Britain, Central Office of Information, *Britain's International Investment Position,* Ref. Pamphlet 98, 1973, pp. 24–25.

[68] Société Nationale des Pétroles d'Aquitaine (SNPA) is 55 percent owned by Entreprise de Recherches et d'Activités Pétrolières (ERAP), the latter being 100 percent state-owned.

[69] "Ces activités sont à double titre profitables à notre pays. Sur le plan énergétique d'abord: l'action du group ERAP-SNPA assure une part non négligeable des ressources de la France, sous la forme, la plus précieuse à l'heure actuelle et pour au moins dix ans, de pétrole et de gaz naturel; l'économie de devises qu'elle permet ainsi de réaliser représente chaque année quelque 350 millions de dollars; enfin dans son sillage de nombreuses entreprises françaises d'engineering, de mécanique, d'électricité, de services variés pénètrent à l'étranger." See R. H. Levy and M. G. Rutman, "Le Groupe ERAP-SNPA dans le monde," *Bulletin mensuel d'information ELF,* February 25, 1972, p. 14.

the trade, payment and other financial consequences of multinational enterprises, primarily because there is no reliable model to answer the question 'what would conditions be if these enterprises did not exist?' '' In his analysis of nine industries, this scholar found that direct U.S. foreign investments tended to have a positive effect on U.S. employment and the U.S. balance of payments.[70] This is bound to be the situation, especially with transnational enterprises, in the absence of domestically competitive substitutes.

The Hufbauer-Adler study in the United States, and its counterpart in the United Kingdom by Reddaway, though pioneering attempts in their field, have been the subject of much criticism. The principal criticisms of the first are that the econometric model used oversimplifies complex reality, and that it is static insofar as it assumes fixed basic relationships. The Reddaway study suffers similarly from important shortcomings: a very small number of firms surveyed, reliance on the presumed objectivity of statements made by business executives, and an unverified assumption that if British investments overseas had not been made, rival firms would have necessarily made similar investments.[71]

One investigation found two sets of balance of payments effects impossible to quantify. The first is the size of ''external'' benefits and costs which include effects on domestic skills, tastes, income distribution, prices, entrepreneurship, and government policy. The other set of effects are those which arise from differences in the structure, organization, attitudes, and skills of foreign investing firms as compared with their potential local replacements.[72]

In conclusion, one should recognize that the balance of payments impact is one among several criteria of performance for a country. It is a crucial one for a country heavily dependent on international trade, as

---

[70] Robert B. Stobaugh, ''The Multinational Corporation: Measuring the Consequences,'' *Columbia Journal of World Business,* January–February 1971, p. 64; and Robert B. Stobaugh and Assoc., *U.S. Multinational Enterprises and the U.S. Economy: A Research Study of the Major Industries that Account for 90 Percent of U.S. Foreign Direct Investment in Manufacturing* (Boston, 1972).

[71] U.S. Department of Commerce, Bureau of International Commerce, Office of International Investment, *Policy Aspects of Foreign Investment by U.S. Multinational Corporations,* 1972, pp. 76, 78; and W. A. P. Manser, ''Professor Reddaway's Last Word?'' *National Westminster Bank Quarterly Review,* February 1969, pp. 40–52.

[72] Sanjaya Lall, *Balance-of-Payments Effects of Private Foreign Investment in Developing Countries: Summary of Case Studies of India, Iran, Jamaica, and Kenya,* UNCTAD, April 11, 1972, p. 2 (TD/134/Supp. 1).

judged in terms of the significance of the foreign trade sector in relation to the gross national product. It is, furthermore, imperative to consider simultaneously the other elements of performance before reaching an overall assessment of the role and impact of a foreign investment project on a given host country, on the home country, and on other trading partners.

In the split of benefits and costs, changes in the power relationships among the three major protagonists in resource industries—exporting governments, importing governments, and transnational enterprises—could have crucial effects. Such changes could lead to bargaining, contention, or conflict, and in due course to accommodation and new equilibria. Suggestions as to how accommodation could be facilitated are offered in Chapter 4.

2. Cooperation in Petroleum: The OPEC Approach

> All States have the right to associate in organizations of primary commodity producers in order to develop their national economies to achieve stable financing for their development, and in pursuance of their aims, to assist in the promotion of sustained growth of the world economy, in particular accelerating the development of developing countries. Correspondingly all States have the duty to respect that right by refraining from applying economic and political measures that would limit it.
>
> *Charter of Economic Rights and Duties of States* (Art. 5)

President Carlos Andres Perez of Venezuela directly attributed OPEC's establishment to "the developed countries' use of a policy of outrageously low prices for our raw materials as a weapon of economic oppression." [1] In fact, forces which spurred intergovernmental cooperation among oil exporting countries were more varied and complex. They included a growing sense of insecurity and dissatisfaction among host governments with respect to the existence of a private international oligopoly unable or unwilling to stem the erosion of real export prices of their oil (after adjusting for a world inflation factor), and an unfavorable concession system which transnational companies had established several years earlier during periods of foreign hegemony. Notable among these concession terms was the freedom concessionaires obtained in important matters such as setting and changing posted prices (used for assessing taxable company profits), deciding on investment programs and export volumes, and relinquishing unexplored portions of their vast concessionary areas.

The catalyst which triggered major oil exporting governments' decision to create a collective organization was the oil companies' unilateral reduction of posted prices in August 1960, following on the heels of a February 1959 price cut. Notwithstanding host governments' appeals for

[1] Reply to President Gerald Ford's address to the UN General Assembly Sixth Special Session on Raw Materials and Development, April 1974, reprinted in a special Venezuelan supplement to the *Japan Times,* July 5, 1975, p. 1.

prior consultation, the companies' unilateral reduction of prices was apparently effected in response to a general increase in competition among long-established companies, and between the latter and newer companies. This competition led to a deterioration in open market prices for crude oil traded outside the vertically integrated channels of major transnational companies and representing about 5 to 10 percent of world crude oil trade in 1959–1960. The impact of the 1959–1960 reductions in posted prices was to reduce concomitantly host government income by about 13.5 cents per barrel, under conditions of a relatively inelastic demand for petroleum.[2]

Thus in September 1960, governments of the exporting developing countries—three Arab (Iraq, Kuwait, and Saudi Arabia) and two non-Arab (Iran and Venezuela)—founded OPEC as an intergovernmental interregional organization whose original main purpose was to "study and formulate a system to ensure the stabilization of prices by, among other means, the regulation of production, with due regard to the interests of the producing and of the consuming nations and to the necessity of securing a steady income to the producing countries, an efficient economic and regular supply of this source of energy to consuming nations, and a fair return on their capital to those investing in the petroleum industry" (Res. I-1).

As of late 1975, there were thirteen member countries, with a majority of seven Arab countries (in italics below). Member countries span four continents: six are in West Asia (Iran, *Iraq, Kuwait, Qatar, Saudi Arabia,* and *United Arab Emirates*), four in Africa (*Algeria, Libya,* Nigeria, and Gabon), two in Latin America (Venezuela and Ecuador), and one in Oceania (Indonesia). Their exports accounted in 1974 for about 85 percent of world oil trade and over 50 percent of world oil production (see Table 2 and Figure 2).

Organization

One of the primary concerns of the founders of OPEC was to ensure the continuance of the institution by not limiting its functions to one objective which could turn sterile. They emphasized the need for a continuous exchange of information, consultation, and cooperation in all policy matters relating to the international oil industry. Their concern was that

[2] Abdul Amir Kubbah, *OPEC: Past and Present,* Petro-Economic Research Centre, Vienna, September 1974, pp. 12–13.

Table 2. Interarea oil movements (1974)

From \ To	U.S.	Canada	Other Western Hemisphere	Western Europe	Africa	Southeast Asia	Japan	Australasia	Other Eastern Hemisphere	Destination Not Known*	Total Exports
						MILLION TONS					
U.S.	—	1.7	3.3	4.2	0.2	0.2	1.9	0.6	—	—	12.1
Canada	51.5	—	—	1.0	—	—	—	—	—	—	52.5
Caribbean †	123.0	21.7	7.7	16.3	0.5	—	0.5	—	—	—	169.7
Other Western Hemisphere	6.7	—	6.0	—	—	—	—	—	—	—	12.7
Western Europe	11.7	—	—	—	3.7	—	0.8	—	1.6	4.5	22.3
Middle East †	52.8	18.8	60.8	505.4	24.1	63.9	201.6	13.7	36.0	15.4	992.5
North Africa †	11.4	0.7	6.1	91.2	0.5	—	3.3	—	12.1	—	125.3
West Africa †	40.1	0.7	14.5	63.0	—	1.5	4.8	—	—	—	124.6
Southeast Asia †	15.6	—	2.1	0.2	—	—	47.1	2.1	—	—	67.1
USSR, E. Europe, China	1.6	—	8.2	52.5	3.2	—	6.2	—	1.0	—	72.7
Other Eastern Hemisphere	1.0	—	—	—	—	1.4	1.9	—	—	—	4.3
TOTAL IMPORTS	315.4	43.6	108.7	733.8	32.2	67.0	268.1	16.4	50.7	19.9	1,655.8
					THOUSAND BARRELS DAILY						
U.S.	—	30	60	75	5	5	35	10	—	—	220
Canada	1,025	—	—	20	—	—	—	—	—	—	1,045
Caribbean †	2,320	430	155	320	10	—	10	—	—	—	3,245
Other Western Hemisphere	125	—	120	—	—	—	—	—	—	—	245
Western Europe	240	—	—	—	80	—	15	—	35	95	465
Middle East †	1,025	400	1,265	10,195	490	1,320	4,050	285	715	305	20,050
North Africa †	230	15	130	1,915	10	—	70	—	255	—	2,625
West Africa †	795	15	305	1,300	—	30	100	—	—	—	2,545
Southeast Asia †	315	—	45	5	—	—	990	45	—	—	1,400
USSR, E. Europe, China	30	—	160	1,010	60	—	120	—	20	—	1,400
Other Eastern Hemisphere	20	—	—	—	—	30	40	—	—	—	90
TOTAL IMPORTS	6,125	890	2,240	14,840	655	1,385	5,430	340	1,025	400	33,330

* Includes quantities in transit, transit losses, minor movements not otherwise shown, military use, etc.
† Nearly all OPEC oil.
Source: BP Statistical Review of the World Oil Industry, 1974 (London, [1975]), p. 10.

several objectives should be sought, new ones added, and obsolete ones replaced in order to maintain the relevance and usefulness of the organization.

Among the fundamental common objectives, two interrelated ones stood out: asserting greater control over their mineral resources, and obtaining larger benefits from the production and processing of their oil and gas.

OPEC statutes limit membership to countries with "a substantial" net export of crude petroleum; no exact explanation is offered, except the statement that exporters of only twenty-to-fifty-thousand barrels per day are not qualified.[3] Moreover, an applicant must be accepted by a three-fourths majority of full members, subject to veto power by any of the founding members. In April 1965, an additional requirement was adopted for new applicants: they should have "fundamentally similar interests to those of Member Countries" (Res. VII.56). That restriction was probably ideologically motivated. It was intended to mollify Saudi Arabia's concern about the possible entry of the Soviet Union, a significant oil exporter.[4] An associate member enjoys all the rights and privileges of full members except voting, and can gain full membership when the growth of its production so warrants (for world oil production, see Figure 2).

OPEC's organizational structure is simple. It has four main bodies: the Conference, the Board of Governors, the Economic Commission, and the Secretariat. The Conference is the supreme authority of the organization. It is responsible for formulating general policy and for devising appropriate means for implementing that policy. Composed of one representative from each member country, usually of ministerial rank, the Conference functions according to the principles of unanimity and equal voting rights. Ordinary meetings are held twice a year, one normally at the headquarters of the organization in Vienna and another in the capital of a member country. Extraordinary meetings are held at the request of any member country. Consultative meetings of heads of delegations or their representatives can be called at any time by the president of the Conference; decisions must be approved by the next Conference, unless otherwise authorized by a previous one.

The Board of Governors, also with one representative from each coun-

---

[3] OPEC secretary-general's interview with *Platt's Oilgram,* December 22, 1972, reprinted in OPEC's *Weekly Bulletin Review of the Press,* January 5, 1973, p. 9.

[4] See, for example, Ahmad Zaki Yamani, Saudi Arabian minister of petroleum and mineral resources, "Oil and International Politics," *MEES Supplement,* April 25, 1975, p. 2.

Figure 2. World oil production by OPEC and non-OPEC countries

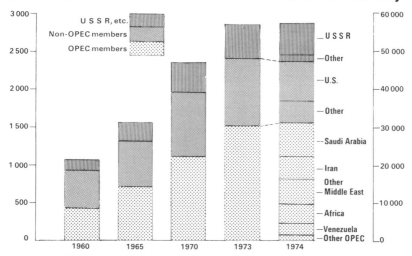

Note: OPEC membership as of December 31, 1974: Algeria, Ecuador, Indonesia, Iran, Iraq, Kuwait, Libya, Nigeria, Qatar, Saudi Arabia, United Arab Emirates, Venezuela—full members; Gabon—associate member.
Source: *BP Statistical Review*, p. 7.

try, is responsible for implementing the decisions of the Conference, drawing up the budget for the Conference's approval, and overseeing the management of the Secretariat. Governors are appointed for a period of two years and the board meets at least twice a year. The Economic Commission comprises experts representing member countries, one from each, and their function is to analyze periodically (usually on a quarterly basis) important economic issues such as prices and other fiscal variables—in close cooperation with the Secretariat's Economics Department.

The Secretariat acts primarily as a research unit, an organizer of meetings, and a forum in which issues are debated and agreements reached. It has been entrusted on several occasions with the preparation of legislation and regulations. Its concern throughout is to harmonize the interests of the major producers in the group.

The headquarters of OPEC were originally in Geneva (1961–1965), but later moved to Vienna because of the many privileges and immunities offered by the Austrian authorities.[5] A European location enables the Secretariat to follow closely the changes in the consumer markets of the

[5] See Kubbah, *OPEC*, pp. 14–15.

world's largest oil importing area. The Secretariat comprises five departments: administration, economics, legal, information, and technical. Its staff is relatively small, 25 to 30 professionals.[6]

The Secretary-General is the legally authorized representative of the organization and the chief officer of the Secretariat. He must be a national of one of the member countries. Until 1970 the secretary-general was nominated by each country in rotation (subject to the perfunctory approval of the Conference) for a statutory period of one year, occasionally extended.

By 1970 member governments realized that the absence of high professional criteria for selecting the secretary-general and the one-year term could not generally attract top qualified talent. Consequently, the Conference agreed in June 1970 to increase the term to three years, subject to renewal for a similar period. The post, beginning in 1971, required the following qualifications: a minimum age of thirty-five, an appropriate university degree, and fifteen years of relevant experience. The nomination must receive the unanimous approval of all members. In the absence of such agreement the post will then be rotated among member countries for two-year periods, while observing the requisite qualifications.[7]

In fact, since 1970 the post of secretary-general has remained on a rotation basis among OPEC countries for two-year periods. The principle of rotation allows each member government to feel that it is sharing the role of leadership in the Secretariat. The setting of high qualifications for the post of secretary-general and the extension of the one-year term of service were important steps in the task of strengthening OPEC through improving the quality of its top management.

The OPEC Secretariat is still faced with certain institutional limitations, such as the absence of a career system with tenure of office, which would give officials security and enable them to resist national influences. The Secretariat staff is appointed for a maximum period of four years. Appointments have averaged less than four years, however, and staff have generally shown little independence of their national governments. A former secretary-general commented forthrightly that "the Secretariat suffers from a serious defect: the impermanence of its leading and professional personnel."[8]

---

[6] Listed in various issues of OPEC's *Annual Review and Record*.

[7] OPEC Res. XX.117.

[8] Fuad Rouhani, *A History of O.P.E.C.* (New York: Praeger, 1971), p. 126.

National feelings, however, would not always be overcome by job security, and it is possible that a permanent secretariat could turn bureaucratic, expansionist, or just lazy. A compromise of a medium-term appointment could be more conducive to efficiency.

The institutional development of OPEC has been hampered by significant differences among member countries. Several decisions of the Conference have failed to be implemented: for example, the decision of March 11–12, 1972, to establish a joint emergency fund. The fund's purpose was to assist member countries which might encounter financial difficulties as a result of measures taken against them by transnational companies because of unanimous Conference resolutions. As of the mid-1970s, though, the creation of such a fund was no longer the top priority it had been, largely owing to the general surge in OPEC countries' income in 1973–1975. Concern then turned toward the formation of a joint development fund for the benefit of other LDCs.

Solidarity

Leaders of the oil exporting countries have learned that their strength in exploiting market conditions lies in their concerted action. On some occasions oil exporting governments have demonstrated a capacity to coordinate their policies effectively; on other occasions, rivalry and antagonism have predominated.

Factors affecting cooperation can be extraneous to the oil issue, for example, the sociopolitical relations between members. Alternatively, they can be endogenous to oil, for example, rivalry among members in expanding their sales. Both groups of factors have been prominent in the rise and ebb of OPEC solidarity.

Oil exporting governments have generally offered a united front in negotiations with transnational companies and have been able to successfully exert their influence. The OPEC-company negotiations of January–February 1971 and the OPEC decisions of October–December 1973 are probably two of the best instances. OPEC governments were able to obtain substantial gains from transnational companies and from Western consumer countries because of their unity of purpose. Their power lay in the threat, explicit or implicit, of withholding oil supplies from those parties which might resist the economic terms they deemed "reasonable." The transnational companies and major oil importing governments perceived, in the absence of substitutes, an imminent oil crisis—with a shortage of tankers and crude—should producer countries' demands be totally ignored.

In its October 1973 resolutions, OPEC took the important new step of placing pricing prerogatives in its own hands, thus doing away with the prior agreement or consent of the major transnational companies. This move, taken in a sellers' market of reduced oil supplies following the October 1973 Middle East hostilities, could not be challenged successfully by the companies. It enabled OPEC governments to raise their oil export prices about fourfold over the October 1973–January 1974 period. Had prior agreement of the transnational companies been required, one would not have expected these substantial price increases to occur over such a short span of time. The transnational companies would have normally protracted, and eventually moderated, increases in crude oil prices.

There are, nevertheless, several instances of intra-OPEC rivalry. It is not uncommon to find an OPEC member soliciting—to no avail—support from fellow members in an encounter with transnational companies or with major consumer countries. This was the case of Iraq, which was faced with a curtailment in the growth rate of its oil exports in 1960–1972 in the course of a series of showdowns with transnational companies. It was especially true following the promulgation of Iraq's Law No. 80 in October 1961 which stripped the transnationals' affiliates of 99.5 percent of their concession areas. As a result, transnational companies favored oil production from neighboring countries—including Arab countries—at the expense of Iraq. Not one single OPEC country among the beneficiaries was interested in countering the company actions. An Iraqi oil minister, addressing a small group of top Arab oil officials at the Fifth Arab Petroleum Congress in 1965, reflected sadly on intra-Arab rivalry: "Unfortunately, I don't think the other Arab states are ready to stand by Iraq against the cartels, even though it is their duty to do so in the common Arab interest." Another Iraqi oil minister held a similar view early in 1972, prior to the nationalization of the Iraq Petroleum Company on June 1, 1972.[9]

However, with the nationalization of June 1, 1972, and the refusal of major companies to take up deliveries from the nationalized venture, the ten member countries of the Organization of Arab Petroleum Exporting

[9] Abdul Aziz Wattari, in *MEES Supplement,* April 9, 1967, p. 2; and Sa'doun Hammadi, "There Isn't Enough Coordination among Producing Countries," *Arab Oil and Gas* (Beirut), May 16, 1972, p. 15.

Countries (OAPEC) came to the rescue of Iraq. They offered in mid-June 1972 to collectively lend Iraq £53.9 million. By the end of 1972, Kuwait and Libya had already contributed £15,175,758 and £9,333,000 respectively.[10] Other Arab oil exporting countries—notably Saudi Arabia, Abu Dhabi, Qatar, and Algeria—later declined to fulfill their promises.

Financial aid to Iraq was not prompted by purely altruistic motives or Arab brotherhood. In fact, a driving force was the OPEC countries' fear that the Iraq government—in desperate need of cash—might be forced to sell its oil at cut-rate prices to independents, while still facing a boycott from the major transnationals. Moreover, Kuwait is constantly worried about its territorial integrity and about Iraq's covetousness of its land, which was publicly made known by Premier Kassem in 1961. Whatever aid Kuwait offered Iraq could well be looked upon as an insurance premium for preserving its sovereignty and territorial integrity. Beginning in 1964, Iraq refrained from pressing forcefully for territorial claims, except for a short lapse in 1972.

OPEC governments often offered Iraq verbal support (Res. II.16, III.18, XI.73, XIII.81, XX.115, XXVIII.146). However, Iraq officials doubtless had hoped that fellow OPEC governments would force their concessionaires to cut down the expansion of oil production in their countries in favor of Iraq. But several oil exporting countries, including Arab ones, were unwilling to cooperate. They had, in fact, little sympathy with Iraq's "revolutionary" leadership and its high-handed actions—taken without prior consultation with them. Finally, in 1973, Iraq reached a compromise with the transnationals.

In a different situation, the OPEC Conference of March 1972 flatly refused to come to the support of another member country, even with a resolution. This was the case of Libya, which toward the end of 1971 nationalized BP's interest in the Sirir concession (producing about 210,000 barrels per day). The Libyan action was prompted by pan-Arab political motives: it was intended as a retaliation against the British government's alleged connivance with Iran. This occurred on November 30, 1971, when the latter seized the island of Abu Musa and the two smaller ones of Tunbs from the Arab sheikhdoms of Sharjah and Ras al-Khaymah in the Arabian-Persian Gulf. Libyan officials, bitter over their failure to gain OPEC's support, suggested privately that they might leave the organiza-

---

[10] *MEES*, July 14, 1972, pp. 5–6, and August 25, 1972, p. 5.

tion. Such a suggestion represented only the disappointment of the moment, and was not taken seriously.[11] In any event, it is unlikely that OPEC would pass any resolution which would imply criticism of a member country (Iran in the above case).

Even unanimous resolutions at OPEC conferences have not been scrupulously observed. One illustration is Resolution XVII.94 of November 1969, asking member countries to refrain from granting new oil rights to the companies of rich industrialized countries (such as Japan) whose governments espouse policies explicitly aimed at reducing oil import prices. Indeed, soon after that resolution was passed, Qatar and Abu Dhabi granted oil rights to Japanese applicants. These countries' rulers claimed that they urgently needed additional oil revenues, and feared that Iran would go ahead and develop adjacent acreage at their expense.

On the subject of participation in the ownership and management of their major oil concessions, there were various differences in 1971–1972. These included the issues of an acceptable percentage of ownership and control, the desirable form of this participation, the compensation to be paid for the government share in participation, and the terms of sales of crude oil to the foreign concessionaire. The so-called moderate governments, under the leadership of Saudi Arabia, accepted an initial 25 percent participation in 1972 rising to 51 percent by 1982. This percentage was vehemently criticized by the "radicals," notably Libya, which demanded an immediate 51 percent participation. The Libyans, moreover, wanted the cost of acquisition to be based on actual net book value, whereas the Saudis agreed to pay for their share on the basis of "updated book value," which was adjusted to account for inflation. The Libyans, furthermore, did not want to be forced to resell part of their participation oil to their "partners," the transnational companies, as the Saudis agreed to do.[12]

There were also differences on the very subject which brought OPEC countries together, namely prices. In 1974 Saudi Arabia, with about a quarter of the world oil reserves outside the socialist countries, argued that prices were too high and should be reduced by $2 per barrel. The Saudi argument was based on two factors: first, that potential supplies were in excess of demand at the 1974 prices, and second, that these

---

[11] *Arab Oil and Gas,* March 16, 1972, pp. 5–6.

[12] See "How Libyan Approach on Participation Differs from Principles of Gulf Agreement," *MEES,* November 3, 1972, pp. 1–2.

prices were damaging Western economies and consequently the OPEC economies which were themselves part of the Western economic system. Saudi Arabia was opposed by nearly all OPEC countries, with various degrees of vehemence. Under Iran's leadership, some OPEC countries were even willing to consider cutting back production should Saudi Arabia contemplate boosting its exports in order to reduce prices. The resulting decision, reached at OPEC's Fortieth Conference of June 1974, was a compromise between production maximizers (and price reducers) and production stabilizers (and price hikers). Prices were kept at their January 1974 level.

Differences in economic conditions among oil exporting countries are very large. Some countries have vast reserves and a relatively small population. This is the case of Saudi Arabia, the United Arab Emirates, and Kuwait. Others have modest reserves compared with their population and their current development needs. This is notably the case of Indonesia, Nigeria, and Iran. Differences also exist in geographical and economic size, including trade (see Figure 3).

To reach a fuller understanding of the formidable obstacles to smooth cooperation, one should bear in mind noneconomic conditions. Indeed, the oil trade is not solely an economic subject, and the student of international relations should investigate how far, given the vicissitudes of Middle East politics, oil increases or decreases solidarity. Divisions among OPEC countries have reflected differences in the internal organization of the states concerned, in their ideological-political objectives, in the pace and direction of change members are willing to undertake or commit themselves to, and in variations in the audacity or conservativeness of their political leaders.

Differences exist, for example, between Iran and its Arab neighbors. The Iranian monarchy is often criticized by other countries' leaders who proclaim themselves "progressive" or "revolutionary" and brand Iran's leadership and regime as "reactionary." Iran's regime, according to the Shah, *is* "revolutionary"; its purpose is to destroy the feudal, oppressive, and antiquated social foundations of Iranian society and replace them "with the most progressive ones in this modern world." [13]

Iran also has had disputes over land and water rights and over the continental shelf, with Iraq and other Arab countries bordering the Arabian-

[13] The Shah's speech to the Majlis (Assembly) on October 6, 1967, in *The Revolution: New Dimensions* (London: Transorient, 1967).

Figure 3. Profile types of OPEC countries (as of December 31, 1974, or in 1974)

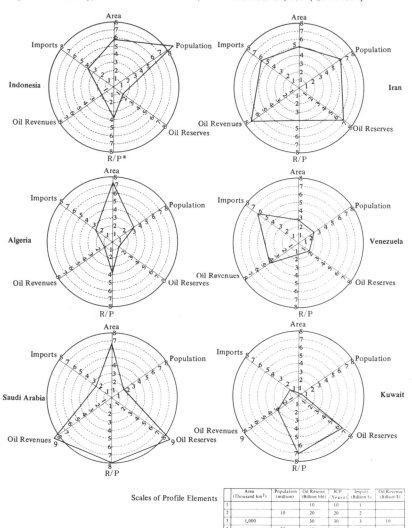

Scales of Profile Elements		Area (Thousand km²)	Population (million)	Oil Reserve (Billion bbl)	R/P (Years)	Import (Billion $)	Oil Revenue (Billion $)
	1			10	10	1	
	2		10	20	20	2	
	3	1,000		30	30	3	10
	4		20	40	40	4	
	5			50	50	5	
	6	2,000	30	60	60	6	20
	7			70	70	7	
	8		40	80	80	8	
	9		40<	80<	80<		30 <

* Reserve/Production

Source: Zuhayr Mikdashi et al., *An Analysis of World Energy Demand and Supply, 1974–1985* (Tokyo, 1975), p. 10.

Persian Gulf. Until 1970, Iran laid claim to Bahrain, a small Arab-ruled oil exporting emirate. Iraq broke diplomatic relations with Iran earlier in 1971 over a dispute on the Shatt el-Arab water rights. Guerrilla actions were also known to have been fostered in Iran by neighboring Iraq,[14] while Iran assisted the Kurdish rebellion in Iraq. These disputes were settled in 1975, through the good offices of Algeria, another OPEC member.

In ascertaining the shifting patterns of alliances, one cannot fail to note the link-up of Iranian-British interests in the early 1970s. Iran's seizure of the three islands in the Arabian-Persian Gulf at the end of November 1971—hitherto part of Arab emirates under British protection—was not incongruent with other apparently unrelated events. Notable among these events was a business alliance between BP (48.4 percent state-owned) and the National Iranian Oil Company, NIOC (100 percent state-owned). The two companies established joint ventures to explore for oil and gas in the British offshore sector of the North Sea in 1972 and in Greenland in 1975. Moreover, they established a joint tanker company in 1975.[15]

The above-mentioned joint ventures satisfied NIOC's desire to grow in expertise and to become a geographically diversified transnational oil producer. The North Sea venture had symbolic value for Iran, in so far as it represented an Iranian stake in the United Kingdom, though the economic significance of the project was comparatively small in relation to BP's interest in Iranian oil. The joint ventures with NIOC satisfied BP to the extent it obtained—implicitly at least—security of oil supplies at comparatively favorable terms. BP's oil supplies from Iran exceeded 2.5 million barrels per day in 1974. NIOC–BP relationships were bound to promote interdependence and cooperation between their respective home countries.

Differences among oil exporting governments are not confined to boundary disputes and regional politics; they also arise over broader issues, such as East-West relations. Iran is formally part of the Western alliance and is an active member of the Central Treaty Organization or CENTO (previously known as the Baghdad Pact), established in 1957 with the support of the United States. CENTO now comprises in one form or another Iran, Turkey, Pakistan, the United Kingdom, and the

---

[14] See the Shah's interview in *Newsweek,* May 21, 1973, p. 20.
[15] *Iran Oil Journal* (NIOC), March 1972, p. 21, and Spring 1975, p. 13.

United States.[16] Although Iran has cooperated in both oil and non-oil affairs with the USSR since the early 1960s,[17] and has played down the military aspects of the CENTO alliance, its formal alliance with Western powers is at variance with the policy espoused by a large number of Arab governments. For example, some Arab governments, notably Iraq, have treaties of friendship and cooperation with the Soviet Union and other socialist countries. Iraq, in particular, has since 1972 had close bonds with East European countries, and has in its government leaders of the local Communist party.

Boundary disputes, regional problems, dissimilar attitudes to East and West, and other political differences (including attitudes toward Israel) are not limited to Iran and certain Arab governments. These difficulties have existed, in varying degrees, among all Arab governments. For example, General Kassem of Iraq claimed sovereignty in 1961 over Kuwait, another Arab state; both Iraq and Kuwait were founding members of OPEC in September 1960. As a result of this dispute, Iraq boycotted OPEC's conference meetings in 1961, although it did not withdraw. Boundary disputes existed prior to 1974 between two traditionalist Arab regimes, Saudi Arabia and the United Arab Emirates, with respect to potentially oil-rich areas.

The student of international affairs can see that, in the rapidly changing conditions of the world, oil and other interests may overlap or clash. The great achievement of OPEC is that it has made some cooperation in oil affairs possible despite deeply rooted differences and serious conflicts among its member countries. The OPEC countries do not therefore constitute a political community, and hardly form a sociopsychological one. But OPEC has generally established itself in the public opinion of member countries as a positive asset, and political leaders, parliamentarians, and government officials keep the objectives of the organization in mind when framing their policies and actions.

To say that OPEC's creation has done away with conflicts or their causes is unrealistic; nevertheless, these conflicts have been moderated.

[16] The United States is a member of several committees of CENTO. Since it did not wish to become a full member of the organization, in 1959 it signed separate bilateral mutual security agreements with Iran, Turkey, and Pakistan. See U.S. Department of State, *The Central Treaty Organization,* International Organizations Series Report no. 1, 1970.

[17] See *Petroleum and Economic Digest* (Dublin), October 1–15, 1970; and Rouhollah K. Ramazani, ''Iran's Changing Foreign Policy: A Preliminary Discussion,'' *Middle East Journal* (Washington), vol. 24, Autumn 1970, pp. 421–37.

Permanent lines of multilateral communication have been established. Moreover, the fact that ministerial level meetings have been held at least twice a year for over sixteen years has led political leaders to become aware of what lay within the scope of common action and what were the opportune moments for action. They became convinced that non-oil matters should not be allowed to wreck common oil interests. Conventional diplomatic methods would have led to serious delays in convening meetings and to the loss of a sense of continuity and regularity in relations, and there would have been no secretariat entrusted with the function of the efficient spreading of information and assisting in the coordination of policies.

OPEC governments have become highly concerned about moves by the industrialized oil importing governments to form a counter-OPEC group. This threat could ironically contribute to a closing of the ranks. A secretary-general of OPEC articulated the impact of such external threats:

Threats of consumer government intervention on behalf of oil companies in support of their position in negotiations with producing countries can only poison the atmosphere of government-company relationships. These threats, recently voiced by such important men as the U.S Secretary of the Treasury, Mr. Connally, can serve no useful purpose and cannot intimidate producing countries. On the contrary, pressure and duress exercised by the great powers on behalf of their companies to discourage or handicap the owners of hydrocarbon wealth from obtaining their legitimate rights would increase the determination and solidarity of producing countries in the face of common danger.[18]

Industry Characteristics

In order to adequately assess OPEC's performance and prospects, a review of the main characteristics of the world oil industry is necessary. Notable among these, especially for the success of OPEC, are three: the growth of demand, the absence of abundant commercial substitutes, and the concentration of the oil industry.

In the last few decades, petroleum has been a relatively high growth industry, growing at an annual rate of 7 to 8 percent. It has increased substantially its share of the energy market, encroaching notably on higher-

[18] See press release by the OPEC Information Department on the Thirty-Second Meeting (Extraordinary) of the OPEC Conference, dated March 17, 1973, reprinted in *MEES Supplement,* March 23, 1973, pp. 3, 4; and Nadim Pachachi, ''The Role of OPEC in the Emergence of New Patterns in Government-Company Relationships,'' lecture delivered at the Royal Institute of International Affairs, London, May 19, 1972, reprinted in *MEES Supplement,* May 19, 1972, p. 10.

cost coal (see Figure 1), and its other uses have also multiplied, especially in the chemical, fertilizer, and synthetics industries. It leads in value and volume among internationally traded commodities. In addition, new competing forms of energy are at an early state of development, notably nuclear power (see Table 3), and are not expected to make a significant contribution to the satisfaction of world energy demand before the late 1980s. And conservation and more efficient utilization are not likely to reduce demand substantially in the near term.[19]

In the energy market conditions of the early 1970s, and given expected technological developments, the demand for petroleum products appeared to be relatively inelastic over significantly wide price ranges.[20] This encouraged oil exporting governments to raise prices in 1973–1974 without fear of massive substitution by other sources of energy in the short or intermediate run. In fact, officials of OPEC member countries have urged energy-importing countries to conserve oil and speed up the development of substitutes—lest OPEC countries' oil reserves be prematurely exhausted.

Consumer countries have also exploited the general inelasticity of demand for oil products by raising tax revenues on sales. The developed world's Organization for Economic Cooperation and Development (OECD) estimated for the first quarter of 1972 that the percentage breakdown on an average barrel of crude oil in eight West European countries was as follows: host governments 16.9, consumer governments 53.9, cost of industry 25.8, and industry margin 3.3. In January 1974, the figures were 39.4, 35.8, 20.7, and 4.1 respectively.[21]

As for concentration, there are eight major transnational companies. Five are U.S. owned: Exxon, Texaco, Gulf, Mobil, and Standard Oil of California; one is British: BP; one Anglo-Dutch: Shell; and one French: CFP. These companies also have several joint ventures. They constitute a major oligopoly, striving for maximum long-run benefits consistent with stability and growth. Stability in this case means that potential competi-

---

[19] See Zuhayr Mikdashi et al., *An Analysis of World Energy Demand and Supply, 1974–1985,* The Research Institute for Overseas Investment–The Export Import Bank of Japan (Tokyo, 1975).

[20] Pre-1973 elasticity figures (generally less than 0.1 or 10 percent) do not apply after the October 1973–January 1974 fourfold price increases. This author estimates that the price elasticity of demand for petroleum products currently varies between 0.2 and 0.4.

[21] OECD, *Oil: The Present Situation and Future Prospects* (Paris, 1973), p. 176; and a World Bank estimate quoted in the *Financial Times,* June 6, 1974.

Table 3. World primary energy consumption (million tons oil equivalent)

	1974						1973					
	Oil	Natural gas	Solid fuels	Water power	Nuclear	Total	Oil	Natural gas	Solid fuels	Water power	Nuclear	Total
U.S.	785.4	560.4	331.9	76.9	28.8	1,783.4	818.0	572.3	335.0	75.6	21.8	1,822.7
Canada	88.1	64.1	15.0	59.4	4.9	231.5	83.7	63.8	16.4	55.5	4.4	223.8
Other Western Hemisphere	178.9	48.0	14.0	31.3	0.3	272.5	169.9	42.5	16.4	28.5	—	257.3
TOTAL WESTERN HEMISPHERE	1,052.4	672.5	360.9	167.6	34.0	2,287.4	1,071.6	678.6	367.8	159.6	26.2	2,303.8
Belgium and Luxembourg	27.5	10.0	11.6	0.1	—	49.2	31.5	8.2	11.0	0.1	—	50.8
Netherlands	35.4	32.9	3.3	—	0.8	72.4	41.3	32.2	3.1	—	0.3	76.9
France	120.1	17.0	27.0	12.6	3.0	179.7	127.3	15.7	26.3	10.6	3.0	182.9
W. Germany	134.4	32.1	82.9	5.0	2.7	257.1	149.7	27.0	87.9	3.0	2.9	270.5
Italy	100.7	15.9	9.2	11.0	0.9	137.7	103.6	14.4	7.6	10.1	0.8	136.5
U.K.	105.8	30.8	68.9	1.3	7.3	214.1	113.4	26.1	78.5	1.2	5.9	225.1
Scandinavia	51.1	—	7.3	36.7	0.4	95.5	55.9	—	7.0	32.6	0.5	96.0
Spain	38.2	1.0	12.3	8.2	1.9	61.6	36.3	1.0	11.7	7.5	1.7	58.2
Other Western Europe	86.0	6.4	39.4	25.4	1.5	158.7	90.0	5.2	38.7	23.6	1.6	159.1
TOTAL WESTERN EUROPE	699.2	146.1	261.9	100.3	18.5	1,226.0	749.0	129.8	271.8	88.7	16.7	1,256.0
Japan	261.1	5.1	58.8	19.0	4.1	348.1	268.3	4.8	59.8	15.8	2.1	350.8
Australasia	33.9	4.1	26.1	2.4	—	66.5	32.8	3.9	29.4	2.2	—	68.3
USSR	341.8	216.6	369.1	38.7	4.0	970.2	317.7	200.4	361.8	36.9	3.0	919.8
Eastern Europe	78.3	43.5	225.1	5.7	0.3	352.9	74.8	39.4	218.7	5.3	0.1	338.3
China *	48.8	4.4	331.5	9.5	—	394.2	41.7	4.0	316.3	9.0	—	371.0
Other Eastern Hemisphere	227.4	42.0	134.8	21.1	1.0	426.3	220.0	37.9	127.5	19.5	1.0	405.9
TOTAL EASTERN HEMISPHERE	1,690.5	461.8	1,407.3	196.7	27.9	3,784.2	1,704.3	420.2	1,385.3	177.4	22.9	3,710.1
WORLD	2,742.9	1,134.3	1,768.2	364.3	61.9	6,071.6	2,775.9	1,098.8	1,753.1	337.0	49.1	6,013.9

* Includes Albania, N. Korea, and N. Vietnam.
Source: *BP Statistical Review*, p. 16.

tors are discouraged from entering the industry in large numbers, that existing operators are dissuaded from any "rocking-the-boat" rivalry, and that governments of producer or consumer countries are not spurred into active antagonism, but rather into tacit or explicit cooperation.[22]

The industry is further characterized by vertical integration. This can be direct or indirect. It is direct when a transnational company owns the successive stages of petroleum activities: exploration, production, transport, refining and manufacturing, and distribution and marketing. It is indirect when the transnational company has long-term contracts with an "independent" (that is, nonintegrated, whether private or state-owned) producer, whereby the latter agrees to supply over a certain period of time given quantities at set terms. In this case the transnational company has tied crude to its system with about the same effect as if it had its own producing subsidiary.

The fact that the international petroleum industry is highly concentrated, that it is composed of giant,[23] diversified, interrelated, and vertically integrated firms has elicited an attitude of challenge in both home [24] and host countries. Moreover, an abundance of oil in surplus of domestic requirements is found in very few countries, thus contributing to a sense of close interdependence among them. And the economic characteristics of the industry generally facilitate the effectiveness of producer cooperation: the high growth rate of demand, the noncompetitiveness of alternative sources of energy, the oligopolistic structure of transnational companies, the small number of major suppliers (five countries), and the formal or informal vertical integration of the industry. Probably the key factor, though, is demand inelasticity and the positive shift of demand—largely owing to the absence of alternative, economically viable sources of oil supplies or substitute forms of energy.

But the split of benefits between host governments and transnational

[22] See Federal Trade Commission, *Concentration Levels and Trends in the Energy Sector of the U.S. Economy,* a staff report by J. P. Mulholland and D. W. Webbink, 1974. On the oligopolistic activities of transnational oil companies operating in France, see French National Assembly, *Report of the Parliamentary Committee Investigating the Activities of Petroleum Companies Operating in France,* vols. 1 and 2, 1974 (Document no. 1280, in French).

[23] Exxon was the second largest transnational firm in the world in 1974 in terms of sales and income. See "The Forbes Sales 500," *Forbes,* Spring 1975.

[24] See, for example, "7 Oil Companies Are Indicted Here in Gasoline Sales: Criminal Conspiracy Seen in Acts Designed to Curb Independent Stations," *New York Times,* September 4, 1974, pp. 1, 31.

companies is not necessarily a zero-sum game split, as many students of the industry have argued. That host governments can increase their take from oil exports should not be looked upon as necessarily having a parallel adverse impact on the companies' return on investments. The latter can raise their product prices (especially for those with relatively inelastic demand), as they have often done. They can thus recover all extra costs, and even improve on their return by raising prices in excess of the level warranted by tax increases.

In comparison, developing oil importing countries are reckoned to have paid the transnational oil companies about 20 percent more for their oil imports than developed ones. The developing countries are handicapped by the smallness of their market which makes them "stand at the end of the consumer line" for supplies and transport facilities; furthermore they lack access to up-to-the-minute information which is crucial in an industry characterized by fast changes and secrecy.[25]

OPEC members, after their take-over of the bulk of their oil production operations, and following their substantial price increases in the early 1970s, have declined to establish a two-tier price system in favor of oil importing developing countries. Their reason is that it is impractical because of the difficulties of sealing markets and the possibility of the emergence of a "black market." OPEC countries have responded, however, by offering easy credit terms, grants, and barter deals. The barter approach suffers from the fact that only a few developing countries (for example, India and Brazil) have sufficiently diversified economies to permit the exchange of oil for commodities needed by oil exporting countries. Oil exporting countries have also offered a few Western developed countries barter deals at favorable prices, if judged by prevailing market conditions. This was the case of Iran's barter deal with Great Britain in January 1974 and Iraq's various barter deals.[26]

It is interesting to note that at the UN General Assembly Conference on Raw Materials and Development of April 1974, India supported the actions of the developing oil exporting countries. India's Foreign Minister Swaran Singh declared: "We fully support the inalienable right and in-

---

[25] "Energy Crisis: Freezing the Poor," *Development Forum* (Geneva), vol. 1, no. 9, December 1973, p. 12.

[26] *Times* (London), January 26, 1974; "Bilateral Deals: Everybody's Doing It," *MEES*, January 18, 1974, pp. 1–2; and "Iraq: Bilateral Oil Agreements," *Arab Oil and Gas*, April 16, 1974, pp. 23–33.

deed appreciate the reasons that prompt the developing countries which export oil principally to developed countries, to demand and secure a remunerative return for their finite resource.'' He said, however, that he had some difficulty in ''appreciating the justification for the enormous increase in the cost of our essential imports from developed countries.'' [27] India's conciliatory position on OPEC's price increases may well be prompted by the desire to mobilize OPEC members' support for favorable oil deals and financial assistance. Moreover, India may need OPEC support for its own endeavors in consolidating the iron-ore exporters' group (see Chapter 3), and in obtaining better terms for the other commodities it exports.

That the value of crude oil has not been readily ascertainable from open markets is largely due to the aforementioned industry features of business concentration and vertical integration. But as vertical integration from production to marketing continues to erode among transnational companies, and as the number of independent buyers and sellers increases, open market prices will reflect with greater accuracy the relative attractiveness of oil for users in relation to other sources of energy.[28] In the absence of a sizeable open market at the crude oil level, one can impute the economic value of crude oil from the open market prices of petroleum products. This approach is known as the ''netting-back'' method, which consists of estimating a weighted average price of refined products per ''standard'' barrel in major consumer markets, and deriving therefrom an export value for a given crude oil after deducting marketing, distribution, processing, freight, and excise taxes. The disadvantage of this approach is that prices of refined products in nearly all consumer markets, even the so-called free ones, reflect the incidence of market imperfections and of restraint to trade due to governmental intervention (for example, fiscal, trade, and administrative barriers), and to the policies and actions of industrial groups (namely labor unions and trade associations).

Another approach to the valuation of natural crude oil is the replacement method. In other words, what would it cost to replace crude with synthetic oil extracted from tar sands or by the destructive distillation of bituminous shale or brown coal.

[27] Address at the UN General Assembly Sixth Special Session on Raw Materials and Development, New York, April 20, 1974. The author was then adviser to the United Arab Emirates delegation.

[28] U.S., British, and Dutch-based transnationals encountered a decline in their share of world oil output from 56.5 percent in 1973 to 40.5 percent in 1974. See the *Petroleum Economist* (London), July 1975, p. 246.

In ascertaining the long-term "replacement" price, the chosen substitute should meet certain criteria: it should yield, if not the same products and benefits, at least a wide range of comparable ones; it should be available in abundance to permit significant market inroads; and it should be available in large quantities within major industrial countries or outside OPEC countries—since alternate energy sources within the OPEC area are bound to follow OPEC crude oil pricing closely. Thus the "replacement" price for OPEC oil is not a point, but rather a range. OPEC's use of the lower level of the price range would postpone or reduce the rate of substitution, whereas the use of the upper level of the price range would speed the rate. Figures on this range vary greatly depending on assumptions with respect to governmental intervention through massive subsidies or effective restrictions in favor of alternatives.

In 1974–1975 some OPEC officials did in fact call for valuing their crude oil in terms of synthetic crude. Simplicity, workability, and conceptual validity were cited in favor of the replacement approach. In one possible formula, the standard OPEC crude Nc could then have the following export value per given unit: $Nc = Sc + Ts - Tc \pm A \pm L$. Sc is the extraction cost (including normal return) of synthetic crude of a quality comparable to the standard OPEC crude; Ts is the transport cost of synthetic crude to a given major oil import market; Tc is the transport cost of Nc to the same major oil import market; A is the tax $(+)$ or financial aid or protection $(-)$ faced by syncrude; and L is the quality differential against $(+)$ or in favor $(-)$ of syncrude.

A third method is the "ability to pay" approach, a standard of pricing which aims at extracting the maximum possible from buyers over a given period of time. A higher price would then reflect a superior bargaining position on the part of sellers. A closely related concept is "willingness to pay." The difference between the two is that the first concept can be defined to apply to an economy where business enterprises have full play, whereas the second concept implies that consumer countries' governments—through political actions and market intervention—assume an active role in deciding on "acceptable" prices.

Achievements

The results of cooperation can be judged in terms of the stated objectives of the parties concerned. The objectives of the major oil exporting governments are embodied in OPEC's statutes, and can be summarily described as aimed at maximizing long-run benefits.

Alternately, evaluation can be made by comparing OPEC's accomplishments with those of similar organizations. The Arab Organization of Petroleum Exporting Countries (OAPEC) is often cited as a control case. This Arab regional organization was created in January 1968 by Kuwait, Libya, and Saudi Arabia. Its membership rose to ten by 1974, and comprised seven other Arab countries: Algeria, Bahrain, Egypt, Iraq, Qatar, Syria, and the United Arab Emirates. OAPEC's achievements have come mainly through the sponsoring of joint commercial ventures, such as a tanker fleet, a dry dock, a petroleum investment company, and an oil exploration and services company.[29] By comparison, OPEC is strictly a policy coordinating group primarily concerned with pricing-cum-tax arrangements, and its scope is interregional. Accordingly, one should view the two groups not as alternatives but as complements, OPEC being basically concerned with international pricing policy, and OAPEC with regional joint projects. For comparison with other producer associations, see Chapter 3.

OPEC's evaluation can also be presented in terms of costs and benefits. In total direct costs, OPEC member governments have contributed about $1.2 million annually to finance the activities of the organization. Additional expenditures have been incurred by individual governments participating in meetings connected with OPEC. For benefits, one can look at OPEC's contribution to its members' gross national products, balances of payments, and governmental income. The latter has been raised through various means: the separate payment of royalty by concessionaire companies, elimination of sales discounts for income tax purposes, increases in posted or tax-reference prices, increases in tax rates, and more recently, host government take-over of, or "participation" in, major concessions before expiration dates.

With respect to OPEC oil revenues, one notes that these hovered around $.75 to $1.00 a barrel from 1960–1970.[30] They rose sharply in the first half of the 1970s, to reach about $2.60 a barrel in 1973 and $9.70 a barrel in 1974 (see Table 4).

[29] See OAPEC, *A Brief Report on the Activities and Achievements of the Organization, 1968–1973* (Kuwait: Al-Qabas Printing Press, 1974); and "OAPEC Nations Plan Billion Dollar Petroleum Investments Company," *MEES,* July 12, 1974, pp. 2–4.

[30] Figures for 1960–1972 are detailed in Zuhayr Mikdashi, "Cooperation Among Oil Exporting Countries with Special Reference to Arab Countries: A Political Economy Analysis," *International Organization* (University of Wisconsin–Madison), vol. 28, Winter 1974, pp. 5, 21, 22.

Table 4. Operational data on OPEC states

	Oil exports (million barrels a day)			Oil revenues ($ billion)	
	1973	1974	Percentage change 1973–74	1973	1974
Saudi Arabia	7.3	8.2	+12	7.2	27.7
Iran	5.9	5.7	− 3	5.6	19.3
Venezuela	3.4	2.7	−21	3.2	9.4
Kuwait	2.7	2.4	−11	2.0	8.3
Nigeria	2.1	2.1	na	2.8	8.0
Iraq	2.0	1.8	−10	1.9	6.9
United Arab Emirates	1.3	1.6	+23	2.1	6.6
Libya	2.2	1.5	−32	1.2	5.8
Indonesia	1.3	1.2	− 8	0.9	4.3
Algeria	1.0	0.9	−10	1.2	4.0
Qatar	0.6	0.5	−17	0.6	1.8
Ecuador	0.2	0.2	na	0.2	0.6
TOTAL	30.0	29.0 *	− 3	28.9	102.7

* Discrepancy in total due to rounding of individual entries.
Note: Gabon was only an associate member of OPEC from November 1973 to June 1975, when it became a full member.
Source: Shell estimates as reported by *Middle East Economic Digest,* June 20, 1975, p. 30.

Obviously the 1973–1974 rapid change in OPEC prices and tax rates brought large wealth to oil exporting countries and serious adjustment problems to oil importing countries. Although one press source recognized that "no country has a responsibility to sell its products for less than the market will bear," it is generally acknowledged that the oil exporters and the wheat exporters (largely the United States) can be charged with making too great a change too quickly with little regard for the effects on customers.[31]

It would appear that the OPEC countries would have been wiser to have increased prices gradually. That might have averted the U.S. government's strong reaction in mobilizing countervailing collective efforts by the major oil importers, and in developing alternative energy sources and instituting conservation measures. But OPEC countries could not effect gradual price increases over the period 1960–1972, largely because pricing of oil exports was the outcome of negotiations between host governments and transnational concessionaires. The latter always managed to

[31] "Oil and Wheat," *Washington Post,* reprinted in the *International Herald Tribune,* January 2, 1974.

protract and whittle down OPEC's demands for price increases. In an OPEC secretary-general's evaluation, the financial achievements of the organization from the date of its creation in September 1960 until September 1973 were "modest, if not derisive." Whatever price increase OPEC governments obtained over this period amounted to mere compensation for loss of purchasing power, the secretary-general declared. Though "unsuccessful in the price field" over that period, OPEC members did, however, manage to gradually assert control over their natural resources either via nationalization or negotiated participation.[32]

It is, of course, not easy to ascertain what proportion of the increase in government revenue gained by these countries can be attributed to the collective efforts of OPEC, or to the individual actions of governments acting on their own initiative, or to favorable market conditions. But certainly some of these gains could not have been realized, and especially not at the rate they have been, had member governments not coordinated their policies and actions within OPEC.

It is true that OPEC's attempts to unify the policies of members (Res. I.2), compile a Code of Uniform Petroleum Laws, and create an Inter-OPEC High Court (Res. V.41) have not yet borne fruit. Nevertheless, a beginning was made in June 1968, when the Conference recommended ten principles to be included in its members' hydrocarbon laws (Res. XVI.90). Understandably, these principles were drafted in very general terms with the intention of accommodating and encompassing wide differences in order to obtain a consensus.

The joint participation of national agencies and transnational companies in some OPEC countries' major concessions represents another OPEC achievement. The participation approach offers an alternative to the ultranationalistic call for outright nationalization. It recognizes that joint enterprises provide a measure of interdependence and stability in operator-government relations, a framework for the investment of private foreign capital and know-how, and a basis for the development of natural resources and export markets. Other host countries, however, are politically allergic to the presence of powerful expatriate economic interests (see Chapter 4).

Most transnational oil companies have adjusted to the new conditions

---

[32] A. Khene, "OPEC and the World Oil Supply," address to the North Sea Oil and Gas Conference, Houston, Texas, November 15, 1973, reprinted as a supplement to OPEC's *Weekly Bulletin Review of the Press,* November 16, 1973, pp. 5–7.

of competition from, or participation with, agencies of host governments. The president of the world's largest oil company, Exxon, informed the company's shareholders at the 1971 annual meeting: "In the future, we will see more of the government oil company, sometimes as a competitor and sometimes as a partner. . . . We recognize this development as an element of changing times. We have learned to live with such government policies and such government entities." [33]

Besides increases in revenue and greater control over domestic oil resources, OPEC can also take credit for providing member countries and their national companies with a forum for the exchange of information and experiences, and with the opportunity for coordination of such policies as joint production programs and joint international marketing.

Joint production and marketing, however, have been bogged down by differences in the conditions, priorities, and outlooks of member countries. Saudi Arabia, with the largest commercial oil reserves in the world, has favored fewer restrictions on production and comparatively lower prices. In the words of the Saudi minister of oil and mineral resources: "The majority of the member countries are being persuaded to adopt a program to limit production. The production program is a relatively old idea which came near to being blessed by an OPEC resolution as far back as 1964. It was Saudi Arabia that used its right of veto to defeat the resolution and has since consistently opposed it for economic and other reasons." [34]

Other OPEC countries, concerned about the finiteness of their reserves, prefer lower production levels and higher prices. These differences have proved a hard test for maintaining unity of purpose and action. [35] In fact, in 1974, aided by their large financial surpluses, most OPEC states reduced their production levels or growth rates in an uncoordinated manner in order to maintain prices.

Other considerations which could prompt OPEC states to restrain production include the desire to conserve finite oil resources and maximize short-term revenues, the preference for oil in the ground over depreciating financial balances, and the desire to index oil prices in terms of infla-

---

[33] *Wall Street Journal,* May 13, 1971, p. 28.

[34] Ahmad Zaki Yamani, "Prospects for Cooperation between Oil Producers, Marketers, and Consumers: The Issue of Participation and After," *MEES Supplement,* October 6, 1972, pp. 3–4.

[35] Belaid Abdessalam, Algerian minister of industry and energy, "OPEC Countries May Cut Back Production to Support Prices," *Arab Oil and Gas,* July 1, 1974, pp. 23–28.

tion. In general, no OPEC member would like to sell its oil at a price below what it perceives to be the future value of that oil discounted to the present (see Chapter 1, footnote 40).

Factors which would encourage OPEC members to expand production in the face of weakening prices include: their judgement that high oil prices would hurt their interests by reducing long-term demand for oil and dampening world economic activity, the desire of individual OPEC countries to maximize their oil revenues at the expense of other producers, and the wish to cooperate with industrial countries.

The contribution of OPEC to members with limited oil experience is especially notable in the areas of analyzing international conditions, offering advice, and training nationals in the technical and economic aspects of the industry. The OPEC Secretariat has also performed useful functions as an organizer of meetings, a forum for exchanging views and selecting negotiators, and a clearinghouse. Detailed, accurate, and increasingly comprehensive information, supplied on a regular basis, assists top officials of OPEC governments in formulating appropriate policies and regulations, whether having to do with the oil sector or with other related sectors of the economy. This is especially important in view of the general unwillingness of their concessionaires to supply them with certain data, for example, information on advanced technology and on markets. Transnational companies often classify such information as trade secrets, bearing in mind that the national companies of their host countries are their active competitors.

OPEC has also endeavored to stabilize its members' price or commodity terms of trade. The first attempt was embodied in the Tehran Agreement of February 14, 1971, between OPEC and the transnational oil companies. The stabilization of terms of trade was done in an admittedly very rough manner. It consisted of raising the level of the oil export tax-reference prices by a world inflation factor of 2.5 percent annually.[36] This factor proved inadequate, and the scheme was abandoned after two years of operation.

OPEC has furthermore encouraged the formation of producer associations among primary exporting developing countries. It has introduced patterns of government-company relations which have been emulated by other resource-rich developing countries (see Chapter 3).

[36] See also Zuhayr Mikdashi, *The Community of Oil Exporting Countries* (London: Allen & Unwin; Ithaca: Cornell University Press, 1972), pp. 165–95.

OPEC's strength does not derive in essence from a political alliance. It derives mostly from the market leadership of its major producers and the characteristics of the oil industry. In particular, Saudi Arabia, given its ample reserves, can set the pace or initiate terms for other members to emulate or closely follow. Alternatively, it can block moves by individual OPEC members in about the same way as a leader in an oligopoly. There have been attempts to turn OPEC into a worldwide oil cartel with price-fixing and export control powers. But production control schemes could not stick, given the multiple divergences among members, the potential threats of defections, and the advent of newcomers. Nevertheless, OPEC has been referred to after 1970, mostly by policy-makers and writers from consumer countries and their companies, as a "cartel," largely owing to OPEC countries' ability to raise significantly their oil export prices.[37] But one should not overlook intra-OPEC price competition.[38] And if one applies the definition of export cartels adopted by developed countries (for example, the 1918 Webb-Pomerene Act of the United States), OPEC does not pass the test. An export cartel not only must include fixed agreements on prices, but also related agreements in such key areas as production control and market sharing. The export cartel must also be responsible for monitoring the activities of its constituent members with a view to policing violations and penalizing violators.[39] The OPEC member governments do not perform any of these cartel functions. Their agreement on oil export prices is strictly voluntary, and does not carry with it sanctions or rewards. Moreover, the agreements leave to the discretion of each member government the setting and changing of prices within a range considered reasonable by OPEC members. A close scrutiny of OPEC's resolutions shows that the organization does not have supranational powers, and its resolutions are merely guideposts for ac-

[37] Although it admitted that OPEC does not fit the strict definition of the term "cartel," one serious treatise used the term "as a shorthand reference to OPEC price-influencing behavior." The study argued that it adopted the word because of its widespread use in the press and in other writings, and because "alternative description terms are cumbersome"! See D. R. Bohi and M. Russell, *U.S. Energy Policy: Alternatives for Security,* Resources for the Future (Baltimore: Johns Hopkins Press, 1975), p. 6n.

[38] See, for example, "Libya Trims Prices," and "Iraq Goes it Alone," *Petroleum Economist,* August 1975, pp. 289–91 and 292–301 respectively.

[39] See OECD, *Export Cartels,* Report of the Committee of Experts on Restrictive Business Practices (Paris, 1974); "Should Export Cartels Be More Closely Controlled," *OECD Observer* (Paris), November 1974, pp. 30–32; and "Cartels: Who Gains," *Economist,* April 12, 1975, pp. 99–100.

tion. Member countries do not delegate to any central body their decision-making powers. Indeed, they jealously guard their sovereignty, and consider their freedom of action to be paramount.

Moreover, OPEC resolutions pertaining to price and related matters are not always followed by all members at the right time. In fact, OPEC members could not abide by cartel discipline. As put by an acknowledged father of OPEC: "It must be borne in mind that the governments are sovereign and can in no way be compelled to fulfil to the letter their obligations toward OPEC which, in any case, are more in the nature of moral obligations." [40]

Whither OPEC?

Prior to 1945, leading industrial countries and their transnational companies could readily impose their will on the resource-rich developing countries by economic or political-military actions. Since the end of World War II, competition among the major powers coupled with their concern to reduce the chances of direct confrontation have led them to exercise greater restraint. The last three decades have accordingly witnessed a dramatic improvement in LDCs' bargaining power. The oil exporting countries, in particular, have taken advantage of the international environment to exploit with greater freedom their natural resources, asking for substantially better terms without undue fear of forceful punitive reaction by the industrial powers. A premier of Japan likened OPEC countries, in their endeavour to raise their benefits, to a "labour union" facing an "employers' league" of Western oil consuming nations. [41]

The economic gains oil exporting countries have been able to derive so far, or could achieve in the foreseeable future, cannot make them comparable in economic strength and stature to the industrially advanced countries. Not only is their economic power smaller (using for example gross national product as a criterion), but the foundation of that power is too narrow and vulnerable, being based on the export of a single depletable resource. Moreover, this economic power does not translate into military power of any international significance, since these countries do not possess the industrial-military technology and the manpower to confront the advanced industrial countries.

[40] "Pérez Alfonso Clarifies Venezuelan Attitude toward OPEC," *MEES Supplement,* October 11, 1963.

[41] *Japan Times,* September 26, 1973, p. 1.

Some oil exporting governments have accumulated sizable monetary reserves, mostly beginning with 1973. Independent observers have noted that "these countries have managed their reserves with great prudence and with due concern for the monetary interests of other countries." [42] Others have argued that oil exporting governments have the capacity to use their monetary reserves—shifting them from one country to another and affecting, among other things, exchange and interest rates—to obtain "unfair" economic or political gain. Assuming that oil exporting governments are able to accumulate large monetary reserves for such purposes, these countries are faced with considerable financial risks in keeping their assets liquid in periods of rising prices and currency depreciation. Moreover, governments of the developed countries can freeze the oil countries' assets or otherwise prevent their free movement. U.S. Treasury Secretary George Shultz proposed the imposition of such restrictions to the International Monetary Fund Committee of 20. [43]

Advanced countries wield other important economic weapons besides their ability to freeze funds. They can raise the price of commodities required by the oil exporting countries, withhold resources critically needed for socioeconomic development, or impose various other discriminatory or punitive restrictions. Advanced countries can in the long run reduce their dependence on oil exporting countries by subsidizing ventures aimed at developing competing sources or forms of energy. In the shorter term, they can build large strategic reserves and storage capacities to weather periods of crisis.

To bring oil prices down, policy-makers and writers in oil importing countries have recommended that governments of major consuming countries act collectively. One distinguished scholar advocated forcing the transnational companies to divest out of producer countries in the interest of the consumer countries. His argument was that resultant pressures for price cutting among oil exporting countries to increase export volumes would be irresistible. He furthermore invited Western governments to provoke intra-OPEC competition "by seeing to it that no OPEC government can count on sales in the United States without shading prices." This assumes that the world leader in commercial oil reserves, Saudi Arabia, is eager to expand its export of oil. Saudi officials have indicated,

[42] See, for example, Reginald Maulding, "A View from the Middle East," *Euromoney* (London), July 1973, p. 63.
[43] See *Financial Times,* July 10 and 11, 1973.

however, that they have reservations about speeding the depletion of their oil resources beyond the needs of their national economy.[44] In a period of inflation and depreciation of major currencies, the government of an oil exporting country may naturally favor oil resources in the ground instead of monetary reserves held in foreign financial institutions.

The majority of the policy-makers in the industrial oil importing countries have favored forming a countervailing organization in their endeavor to reduce OPEC prices. Their instrument of action has been the International Energy Agency (IEA), limited to OECD members. IEA's objectives are to develop a capability to deal with serious supply interruptions by building emergency stocks, sharing supplies, and cutting domestic consumption; and to reduce the group's dependence on imported oil through coordinated efforts in the areas of conservation and new energy supplies. Unlike OPEC, IEA has established a strong executive secretariat and a system of weighted voting. Each member country receives three general weights plus additional weights based on oil consumption. The United States had as of late 1975 the highest combined weights, reaching about 30 percent of the total. Most decisions are to be made by a majority vote of 60 percent. Along with the creation of IEA, the major OECD industrial nations agreed to create a $25 million mutual insurance fund. Its purpose is to furnish loans and guarantees to those IEA member nations hardest hit by balance of payments deficits or by shifts, withdrawals, or cut-offs of funds from OPEC countries.[45]

Another approach to countering OPEC's power is to encourage internal dissension. This is done, with the help of transnational enterprises, by playing off one OPEC nation against another: for example, through cutting back liftings from a single member country which has pressing needs for oil revenues in order to trigger an intra-OPEC competition. Abu Dhabi, one of the member states of the United Arab Emirates (U.A.E.), was faced with such a situation early in 1975, when the liftings of the transnational companies dropped unexpectedly by two-thirds. The president of the U.A.E. claimed that the companies were attempting to break OPEC by destabilizing the oil exports and the revenues of his country. "The companies' objective," he said, "was to split us away from

[44] M. A. Adelman, "The Oil Cartel Will Get Us If We Don't Watch Out," *New York Times,* April 21, 1973; and statements by Ahmad Zaki Yamani in *MEES,* March 16, 1973, pp. 1, 2, and April 20, 1973, p. 2.

[45] See U.S. Secretary of State Henry Kissinger's address to the National Press Club, "International Response to Energy Problem," Washington, February 3, 1975, reprinted in *MEES,* February 7, 1973.

OPEC.'' The U.A.E. minister for petroleum and mineral resources furthermore disclosed that transnational oil companies asked his government in 1975 to nationalize their joint concession in Abu Dhabi (of course with adequate negotiated compensation).[46] Their implied motive was that they could exert their oligopsonistic influence to import crude oil at cheaper prices, once out of that country.

A fourth approach has been the threat of military invasion. U.S. officials insinuated early in 1974 that military action might be a last-resort measure in the case of strangling actions (including price increases or production cutbacks).[47] The sovereigns and heads of OPEC states reacted to this in their first summit meeting in early March 1975: ''[We] denounce any grouping of consumer nations with the aim of confrontation, and condemn any plan or strategy designed for aggression, economic or military, by such grouping or otherwise against any OPEC Member Country.'' They unanimously and collectively agreed ''to take immediate and effective measures in order to counteract such threats with a united response whenever the need arises,'' notably in the case of agression, notwithstanding that the developed countries ''hold most of the instruments of progress, well being and peace, . . . [and] destruction.'' [48]

Some spokesmen of industrial countries at least hope to weaken OPEC and break its so-called ''cartel type'' price-fixing power.[49] To those who believe or wish that OPEC will break up at some point, the Saudi minister of petroleum and mineral resources has responded: ''This is either wishful thinking or a blind attitude.'' [50] It appears that OPEC has enough cohesion to withstand internal or external pressures. Despite their multiple differences and divisions, OPEC leaders have realized that unless they hang together, they will hang separately.

---

[46] Mana' Al Otaiba, in an interview in the Arabic weekly *Al-Hawadess* (Beirut), August 22, 1975, pp. 48–49.

[47] See Zuhayr Mikdashi, ''The OPEC Process,'' in *The Oil Crisis: In Perspective,* Fall 1975 issue of *Daedalus;* and ''Would We Really Kill for Oil,'' *New York,* October 14, 1974, pp. 35–40.

[48] Solemn Declaration of Sovereigns and Heads of State of OPEC Member Countries, Algiers, March 6, 1975, reprinted in *MEES Supplement,* March 7, 1975.

[49] See statement by EEC energy commissioner Henri Simonet, as reported in *The Times* (London), June 8, 1974; and Thomas O. Enders, U.S. assistant secretary of state for economic and business affairs, ''OPEC and the Industrial Countries: The Next Ten Years,'' *Foreign Affairs,* vol. 53, no. 4, July 1975, pp. 625–37.

[50] Interview published by the *Washington Star,* April 19, 1975, reprinted in *MEES Supplement,* April 25, 1975, p. 5.

3. Cooperation in Other Primary Commodities

The "demonstration effect" of OPEC has been remarkable. Encouraged by the relatively successful cooperation of oil exporting governments, and pressured by rising import bills of essential goods such as food, fertilizer, energy, machinery, and equipment which they need for their survival and development, several primary exporting countries have attempted to increase their benefits from trade through concerted action. Their achievements have been less spectacular than oil exporters', not necessarily owing to absence of will as much as to the constraints imposed by their particular commodities and markets, and by socioeconomic disparities among producer countries.

The urge among resource-exporting developing countries to form OPEC-like alliances is widespread. As described by close observers of the commodity markets:

A sense of disappointment at their overall treatment by the industrial countries is almost universal among developing countries. For the producers of minerals, there is moreover (as for oil) the keen sense that their minerals are nonrenewable, an asset that should produce the greatest possible return and if possible have its useful life stretched out. Hence, it is only natural that producers should seek to change a situation in which, by and large, the sellers of non-fuel minerals are competing, diffuse, and unorganized in the face of relatively few and well-organized buyers on behalf of the consuming countries.[1]

Copper Exporters and CIPEC

Concerned about their economic vulnerability, leaders from four major copper exporting countries—Chile, Peru, Zaire, and Zambia—conferred

---

[1] B. Varon and K. Takeuchi, "Developing Countries and Non-Fuel Minerals," *Foreign Affairs*, April 1974, p. 505. An earlier draft of certain sections of this chapter benefited from information and comments offered by M. J. West, editorial director of the *Mining Journal*.

in June 1967 in Lusaka and agreed to form the Conseil Intergouvernemental des Pays Exportateurs de Cuivre (Intergovernmental Council of Copper Exporting Countries), or CIPEC, to defend their mutual interests. CIPEC countries accounted in 1975 for about 35 percent of the total copper mine capacity outside Eastern Europe and China, for 65 percent of world primary copper exports, and 45 percent of world exports of scrap and primary copper combined. They have in common with other LDC mineral producers several characteristics: their mineral industry is export oriented, since their domestic consumption is very limited (1 to 2 percent of output); like many developing countries, they rely heavily on one or two commodities for foreign exchange receipts, fiscal revenues, national income, and socioeconomic development; their mineral resources have been controlled, until recently, by expatriate operators; and all are striving to increase their economic benefits from the exploitation of their resources (for the location of major mineral reserves, see Table 5).

CIPEC Functions

Like OPEC, CIPEC is primarily an economic consultative organization. Its objectives are defined in Article 2 of its charter:

(a) to coordinate measures designed to foster, through the expansion of the industry, dynamic and continuous growth of real earnings from copper exports, and to ensure a real forecast of such earnings;

(b) to promote the harmonization of the decisions and policies of the member countries on problems relating to the production and marketing of copper;

(c) to obtain better and more complete information and appropiate advice on the production and marketing of copper for member countries;

(d) in general, to increase resources for the economic and social development of producer countries bearing in mind the interest of consumers.

The organization explicitly highlights its objectives of fostering "continuous growth of *real* earnings," that is, after adjustment for inflation, but subject to this being consistent with an expanding world consumption of copper. It also seeks to provide "complete information and appropriate advice on the production and marketing of copper," and notably on the ways and means of moderating excessive fluctuations in price.

CIPEC is composed of four organs: the Conference of Ministers, the Governing Board, the Executive Committee, and the Information Secretariat. The Conference of Ministers is the highest authority. It meets in ordinary session once every two years, unlike OPEC's Conference which

Table 5. Locations of the major mineral reserves (1974)

	Percentage of world reserves		Percentage of world reserves
Bauxite		**Manganese**	
Australia	30.3	Gabon	15.0
Guinea	22.6	Republic of South Africa	8.5
United States	0.3	United States	—
Communist countries	3.9	Communist countries	41.5
Others	43.0	Others	35.0
Chromium		**Mercury**	
Republic of South Africa	62.9	Spain	49.1
Southern Rhodesia	32.9	Yugoslavia	8.7
United States	—	United States	7.2
Communist countries	1.3	Communist countries	13.2
Others	2.8	Others	21.9
Cobalt		**Nickel**	
Zaire	27.5	New Caledonia	33.3
New Caledonia and Australia	27.1	Canada	13.6
Zambia	14.0	Cuba	9.1
United States	1.0	United States	0.4
Communist countries	21.9	Communist countries	21.6
Others	8.5	Others	21.9
Copper		**Tin**	
United States	22.4	Thailand	33.5
Chile	15.7	Malaysia	14.4
Canada	8.9	Indonesia	13.2
Communist countries	11.4	United States	0.1
Others	41.6	Communist countries	17.1
Iron ore		Others	21.6
Canada	14.5		
Brazil	10.8	**Tungsten**	
United States	3.6	United States	6.4
Communist countries	46.6	Communist countries	77.5
Others	24.5	Others	16.1
Lead			
United States	38.9	**Zinc**	
Canada	13.2	Canada	26.0
Australia	8.3	United States	22.9
Communist countries	17.4	Communist countries	15.3
Others	22.2	Others	35.9

Note: Reserves are defined as known, identified deposits of mineral-bearing rock from which minerals can be extracted profitably with existing technology and under present economic conditions. Aside from the United States, nations shown are those which individually account for at least 8 percent of total world reserves. "Communist countries" excludes Yugoslavia.

Source: *Morgan Guaranty Survey,* March 1974, p. 11.

meets at least twice a year. The more frequent meetings of OPEC ministers certainly represent an advantage in promoting the habit of consultation and in closer cooperation. However, in order to expedite matters under consideration, CIPEC has its conference classify subjects for discussion into those of major and minor importance. The major subjects require unanimous vote, minor ones need a simple majority only.

Composed of high-ranking officials, two from each country, the Governing Board is responsible to the conference for fostering technical and administrative cooperation among member countries. It meets in ordinary session once a year (twice for the board of OPEC). A quorum is established with at least one representative from each member country. Decisions are, as in the case of the conference, subject to the same classifications of major and minor.

The Executive Committee comprises one representative from each member country. On behalf of the Governing Board, it supervises the Secretariat in administrative and financial matters, prepares the budget for approval by the board, determines studies to be undertaken, and makes various other recommendations to the board.

The highest administrative post in CIPEC is that of Executive Director. The executive director is appointed by the unanimous vote of the Governing Board for an initial period of two years. After the expiration of this period, he holds office on a permanent basis, unless removed at the request of two member countries. The executive director's indeterminate appointment contrasts with the two-year term of OPEC's secretary-general rotated among member countries. A long period of appointment is indeed a beneficial feature to the extent it enables the chief executive to plan and implement an administrative program.

CIPEC's executive director need not be—and in fact was not from 1967 to 1975—a national of any member country. He is selected on merit to supervise and represent the Secretariat, and to act as secretary of the Conference, the Governing Board, and the Executive Committee, with the right to speak but not to vote. Moreover, the Governing Board empowers the executive director to appoint technical and administrative staff, besides those on endorsement by member governments. Neither the executive director nor any member of the staff may have any financial interest in copper or any other metal.

Member governments have had several meetings aimed at devising a support system for the world market price of copper. To remedy price fluctuations, CIPEC countries would probably have to adopt a buffer stock scheme buttressed by a production control scheme. One trade source has claimed that CIPEC countries did once propagate the rumor of a scheme for supporting the copper price by means of a stockpile. The rumor, the source alleged, "netted the CIPEC members a cool £5 million by the psychological uplift it gave to prices." [2] London Metal Exchange (LME) dealers became much more sceptical about CIPEC's ability to introduce a price support scheme once it was known that member nations could not agree on base levels of production or sales from which cutbacks could be assessed.

It was not until late 1974 that CIPEC countries agreed to cut their exports, encouraged by OPEC countries' ability to tolerate cutbacks (admittedly in an uncoordinated manner). CIPEC countries agreed on November 18–19, 1974, for the very first time, to cut the volume of their exports by 10 percent (in comparison with levels achieved in the first half of 1974), and by another 5 percent in April 1975. Their objective was to sustain the open market prices. These measures proved inadequate in 1975. This was largely due to the relatively moderate size of cutbacks, bearing in mind that CIPEC countries control only about 35 percent of world mine production; the large accumulation of commercial inventories following the world recession; the absence of a buffer stock; and most importantly the low demand elasticity for copper. [3]

Besides instituting export controls, CIPEC arranged an agreement with a major copper importing country, Japan, on methods to moderate disposal of excess inventories. Owing to the economic recession which hit the Japanese industry in 1974–1975, CIPEC countries cut their exports to Japan by an amount slated to reach 30 percent by January 1975. Representatives of MITI and the Japanese smelters further agreed to halt Japanese exports of copper to the LME market from accumulated commercial stocks in excess of domestic demand; Japanese copper exports to other markets were cut by 50 percent—both measures were to apply for the balance of 1974. [4]

A major hurdle faced by CIPEC countries in stabilizing copper prices is the cost of financing a stockpile. Unlike the producer countries in the

[2] *Metal Bulletin* (London), May 28, 1971, p. 17.

[3] See CIPEC's *Copper Market,* 3rd quarter 1974, app. I, p. 28; "Copper's bid for 'Producer Power,' " *Financial Times,* November 28, 1974, p. 28; and "Whatever Happened to the Commodity Boom?" *Economist,* June 14, 1975, p. 48. Demand elasticity was estimated to vary between 0 and 0.3. See comments of J. C. Burrows, vice president, Charles River Assoc., in U.S. Congress, *Outlook for Prices and Supplies of Industrial Raw Materials,* Hearings before the Subcommittee on Economic Growth of the Joint Economic Committee, 93rd Cong., 2nd sess., February 1974, p. 79.

[4] *Copper Market,* 4th Quarter 1974, p. 4; and UN, ECOSOC, Committee on Natural Resources, *Permanent Sovereignty over Natural Resources,* Report of the Secretary-General, New York, January 31, 1975, p. 12 (E/C.7/53).

International Tin Agreement, these countries do not have access to the International Monetary Fund (IMF) buffer stock financing facility. The IMF, which provides financing at concessionary rates, limits its assistance to commodity agreements where both importer and exporter countries are represented. Although not eligible for buffer stock financing, CIPEC countries are eligible for the fund's compensatory financing program which applies to countries experiencing a temporary shortfall in export earnings largely attributable to circumstances beyond their control. Chile, Zambia, and Peru used this facility in 1971–1972 to buy the equivalent of $39.5 million, $19 million, and SDR 30.75 million respectively in foreign currencies.[5]

Unable to get buffer stock financing from the IMF, CIPEC countries have turned to the World Bank (more formally known as the International Bank for Reconstruction and Development or IBRD). The Zambian minister of finance, John Mwonakatwe, appealed in November 1971 for financial assistance to build up a stockpile of copper out of surplus supplies in order to remedy prevailing "abnormally low prices," with the understanding that the proposed stockpile would also be used to ease prices whenever they reached abnormally high levels. The bank did not respond to the Zambian plea.

Besides the problem of financing a buffer stock, CIPEC countries are faced, like OPEC countries, with other problems. They have different sociopolitical conditions and goals, and different mining conditions. Such disparities are bound to constrain group action. Even if cooperation is assumed to be beneficial for the whole group, members of the group are not likely to benefit equally. Among differences, one could mention the extent of contribution of the mineral industry to the national economy—for example, in exports earnings—and the relative costs of production. Copper accounted in 1973 for over 80 percent of the export earnings of Chile and Zambia, but only about 50 and 30 percent for Zaire and Peru respectively. Production costs for 1969–1970 were reckoned to be lowest in Peru, followed by Chile, Zambia, and Zaire. Chile's production costs were rising fastest, from 24.3 cents per pound in 1969 to 33.6 cents in 1970, and to an estimated 40 cents in 1971.[6]

[5] See "Chile and Zambia Purchases from Fund," in IMF's *International Financial News Survey* (*IFNS*), December 15, 1971, p. 409; and "Purchases from Fund by Argentina and Peru," *IFNS*, June 21, 1972, p. 185. One SDR (Special Drawing Right—an IMF unit) was equivalent to close to $1.20 in August 1975.

[6] *Mining Journal* (London), November 20, 1971, p. 476.

Given the constraints encountered in the marketplace and within the individual member countries, CIPEC has been most successful in the collection and dissemination of information and the preparation of studies. It has encouraged a greater awareness of a community of interests, and this has led to greater solidarity. For example, CIPEC countries came to the rescue of Chile in 1973 in its confrontation with Kennecott, whose properties were nationalized by Chile in 1971. Kennecott had won court orders in some West European countries imposing liens on Chilean copper exported from the ex-Kennecott mines, on the grounds that no compensation was paid for nationalization. The other CIPEC countries "agreed not to replace copper on the world market where Chilean copper is seized as part of the legal action started by the Kennecott Copper Corporation." CIPEC countries furthermore agreed to set up "a permanent mechanism of protection and solidarity in the event of economic or commercial aggression against any of the Organization's member countries." [7]

Further support for Chile's nationalization acts came through an UNCTAD resolution on permanent sovereignty over natural resources sponsored by Latin American countries (8.XII; October 19, 1972). CIPEC countries also gave moral support to Zambia against Rhodesia, which was accused of economic aggression when it closed its frontiers and disrupted the normal export routes of Zambia copper.[8]

Chile, one should add, compensated the nationalized U.S. companies after the overthrow of the constitutionally elected leftist president, Salvador Allende, by a military junta friendly to transnational companies. For Anaconda, the compensation reached $253 million, and for Cerro $41.8 million. The Chilean government, furthermore, indemnified the U.S. government agency, the Overseas Private Investment Corporation (OPIC), which had insured Kennecott and other U.S. companies' interest in Chile.[9]

---

[7] "Copper Nations Form Pact to Support Chile," *Times* (London), January 16, 1973, p. 15; and *Copper Market,* 4th quarter 1972, pp. 2–3.

[8] See "UNCTAD: Permanent Sovereignty over Natural Resources," *Journal of World Trade Law,* May–June 1973, pp. 376–82; and *Copper Market,* 1st quarter 1973, app. C.

[9] "Pour l'indemnisation de deux mines de cuivre, la société américaine Anaconda reçoit 251 millions de dollars," *Le Monde,* July 26, 1974, p. 4; "Anaconda and Chile in $253M Mines Settlement," *Times* (London), July 25, 1974, p. 22; "Anaconda, Chile Reach Settlement," *International Herald Tribune,* July 25, 1974, p. 3; *Metal Bulletin,* April 30, 1974, p. 20; "Chile Makes First Payment to OPIC," *Topics* (OPIC), vol. 3, no. 2, April 1974,

The CIPEC organization is only the beginning of cooperation among a limited number of copper exporting countries. Beyond institutionalizing the channels of conversation, CIPEC is considering widening its membership to cover other major copper exporters, and has offered assistance to non-CIPEC members.[10] It has also established lines of communication with groups which sell other raw materials, including OPEC and the International Bauxite Association (IBA).

Transnational Efforts at Price Stabilization

Prior to CIPEC, non-U.S. international copper firms attempted individually as early as May 1955, and jointly since then, to stabilize world copper prices outside the United States. Joint pricing was undertaken from October 1961 to April 1966,[11] using concomitantly two instruments: voluntary output restrictions and sale-purchase operations on the LME.

The copper price stabilization experiment was initiated by the transnationals Anglo-American Corporation (AAC) and Roan Selection Trust (RST), and supported by producers in Canada, Chile, and Zaire. Under conditions of "surplus" production, the LME cash price reached a low level of £227 per long ton in September 1963. Zambian producers supported LME prices initially at that level. Subsequently, support was raised to £234 (offer) and £236 (sale), the difference being the dealer's margin. In their support action, Zambian producers bought 150,000 metric tons by November 1963. Purchases by copper firms coupled with production restraints (averaging 10 to 15 percent of capacity) contributed to an effective pegging of the LME price in 1962–1963 at a floor price of £234 per long ton. Adding tariff (1.7 U.S. cents per pound) and transport charges, this balanced with the then current U.S. producers' price of 31 cents per pound, creating in effect a single world price for copper.[12]

---

p. 1; and Charles Fortin, "Compensating the Multinationals: Chile and the United States Copper Companies," *IDS Bulletin* (University of Sussex, Brighton), April 1975, pp. 23–29.

[10] The chief economist for CIPEC assisted the Papua New Guinea (PNG) government in renegotiating its agreement with the Rio-Tinto Zinc group (RTZ). See Stephen Zorn, U.S. adviser to the PNG government, "Renegotiating Mining Agreements: The Case of Bougainville Copper," UN Training Workshop on Negotiation and Regulation of Foreign Investments, New Delhi, 1975, p. 34 (typescript).

[11] See Raymond Vernon, *Manager in the International Economy* (Englewood Cliffs, N.J.: Prentice-Hall, 1972), pp. 169–71.

[12] Charles River Assoc., *Economic Analysis of the Copper Industry*, prepared for the General Services Administration (Cambridge, Mass., 1970), p. 167.

Upward pressures on prices started late in 1963 as demand began to outstrip supply. To counter these pressures, producers restored cutbacks and started selling their stockpiled copper, but they realized by January 1964 their inability to maintain the price at £234 per ton—notwithstanding that production was restored to capacity late in 1963. In mid-January 1964, the two main transnational mining groups operating in Zambia (RST and AAC), followed by most other major transnational copper producing companies, replaced the former practice of pegging LME prices with a "producer" price offering metal at £236 per ton. This price was to remain insensitive to daily fluctuations such as those at the LME, but was supposed to reflect annual or long-term changes in the supply-demand balance.

The major transnational copper companies' adoption of a producer price system in January 1964 came at a time when the market shifted from a "buyers' market" with excess availabilities to a "sellers' market" with tight supplies. This system, lasting until April 1966, applied mostly to the newly mined or primary copper of the major firms. It excluded the "free" or "residual" market which comprised the primary production of the smaller mining concerns (probably with a 10 to 15 percent share of all newly mined output), the stocks of metal dealers, and the supplies largely derived from secondary copper or scrap. Supplies from the latter sources continued to depend for pricing on the open market.

In the 1964–1966 period, three types of prices obtained with wide differences (in U.S. cents per pound):

		U.S. domestic price for majors	Producer price outside U.S.	LME cash price
1964	January	31	29.5	29.7
	March	31	30.5	33.7
	May	32	30.5	37.5
	September	34	32.5	52.5
1965	May	36	36	62.4
	October	36	38	63.5
1966	January	38	42	76.1
	April	38	42	86.4

The above figures show that LME prices more than doubled (from 29.7 to 62.4 cents per pound) between January 1964 and May 1965, while producer prices in the United States and outside the U.S. rose by less than 18 percent, namely by 5 and 6.5 cents a pound respectively. To a supporter of producer pricing, the LME or open market was then a residual market; as such, it could not be fully indicative of all pricing possibilities.[13]

The wide discrepancy between the U.S. domestic price and the non-U.S. producer price on the one hand, and the open market price on the other hand, was detrimental to two groups: the relatively small nonintegrated copper fabricators which had to satisfy their requirements from outside the major producers' channels at the higher, fluctuating prices of the LME; [14] and exporting countries whose fiscal and foreign exchange revenues were largely based on producer prices lower than LME prices.

Of particular significance to copper price control were pressures the U.S. government exerted to keep producer prices of copper metal (but not of fabricated copper products) at artificially low levels. This was done by using direct controls or other measures such as actual or threatened releases of large quantities from the U.S. strategic stockpile. Indeed, the U.S. government, with the acquiescence of the major United States copper groups, followed a policy of holding down prices. They thereby deprived the nonintegrated independent copper companies and host countries selling to the United States of the opportunity to benefit fully from the sizable open market price increase of 1964–1966. Since the major American copper companies are largely vertically integrated, the U.S. government's success in imposing low producer prices has, for all practical purposes, not adversely affected the overall profits of these companies: what matters mostly to them are sales receipts, which are largely derived from the fabricated and semifabricated goods. These goods have not been subjected to price control.[15]

On the role of the U.S. government in holding down copper prices, one U.S. researcher commented:

Over the long run the United States Government has exercised far greater control over the price of copper [than the governments of producer countries, like Chile], partly through tariffs, partly through direct price and production controls or stimuli, and partly through the operation of a strategic stockpile of copper. . . .

[13] Of the 1964 non-Soviet world primary production (that is, excluding the significant volume of scrap), only 10 percent was not sold at producer prices. See statement of RST chairman on October 24, 1964, for the *Annual Report*.
[14] See IBRD, *Documents Listed in Annex to the Report of the Executive Directors on the Stabilization of Primary Products,* sec. 2, *Copper* (Washington, 1969), p. 8.
[15] See Peter Bohm, *Pricing of Copper in International Trade: Case Study of the Price Stabilization Problem* (Stockholm: School of Economics, 1968), p. 10.

When in the past, prices were driven high by collusion, the profits went entirely to producers and not to host governments. Now that countries such as Chile could recapture a large share of those profits, producers are unable or unwilling to force prices up or to take full advantage of periods of scarcity.[16]

On January 3, 1966, the Chilean copper groups raised their copper price to 42 cents, and on April 16 to 62·cents. On April 25, Zambian copper groups, which regarded Chile's 20 cents per pound increase in one single move as making nonsense of the producer price system, decided not to follow and abandoned the producer price in favor of LME three-month-forward quotations. (Three months normally represents the maximum time needed to ship copper from producing centers to major consuming areas.) In the then tight supply conditions, that basis gave Zambia a higher price. Chilean groups reacted on July 15 by again raising their producer price to 70 cents, but on August 12 they abandoned the producer price system altogether in favor of the LME price.[17]

American Producers' Price System

It is important to note that the U.S. market has, for several decades, followed the producer price system for primary or mined copper. This applied not only to domestic production but also to imports, excluding scrap. Canadian producer prices have always moved in harmony with changes in U.S. producer prices, in as much as the United States has represented the major outlet for Canadian copper.

The American price, however, has been a composite price. To the extent U.S. firms were importing metal from mines not under their own management they were normally obliged to pay LME prices. Thus their composite price was made up of domestic production based on a producer price, plus imported Chilean production based on a producer price—as long as the American companies managed Chilean operations—and other imports based on the LME price. So far as the Canadians were concerned, their sales were of three parts. Canadian producers have for some years been required by their government to sell to Canadian fabricators on a comparatively low-priced producer basis. Their sales to the United States have been at U.S. producer prices, while their sales to overseas

[16] Joseph Grunwald and Philip Musgrove, *Natural Resources in Latin American Development* (Baltimore: Johns Hopkins Press, 1970), pp. 232–233n; also IBRD, *Copper*, p. 9.

[17] Chase Manhattan Bank, *World Business*, April 1969, p. 10.

customers have normally been based on the LME or on a complex formula (for example, to the Japanese) which sought to provide a compromise between the LME and the American producer price.

It has been suggested—with no supporting evidence, however—that the U.S. copper producer price has generally been below the open market price as a result of deliberate collective company policy.[18] That policy is said to aim at protecting the long-term competitive position of copper vis-à-vis substitutes, notably aluminum, in the U.S. market. It also purports to discourage other copper producers, mainly the Canadians, from opening up new mines or expanding existing ones.[19]

A U.S. Cabinet committee has also decried "the inequities and economic inefficiencies caused by the two-price market [the producer price and the open market price] and the present system of allocation [by major copper producers to fabricators in the U.S. market]." [20] The chairman of that committee criticized the producer price system, which has been generally below the dealer's price and has been sustained by rationing: "Obviously this is not an equilibrium situation and could not have occurred in a competitive market. For clearly any time the same commodity is sold at significantly different prices no buyer would purchase at the higher price if he had access to the lower price. A two-price market means a market that is not free." [21]

Past experience shows that it is more feasible for operators to jointly contrive an increase in prices, either through purchases in the open market, through production cutbacks, or even through a producer price system—as compared with a price decline. Stocks have to be very large to sustain booming demand at a stable price, or production has to be readily expandable. However, copper is an expensive metal, and few companies and very few countries can afford to stockpile large quantities. More-

[18] About 22 percent less than the average LME cash quotation over the period 1953–1973.

[19] See F. M. Fisher and P. H. Cootner, "An Econometric Model of the World Copper Industry," M.I.T. Department of Economics Working Paper no. 70, April 1971, pp. 6–7; and Charles River Assoc., *Economic Analysis of Copper Industry,* p. 179.

[20] Remarks of the chairman of the Subcommittee on Copper of the Cabinet Committee on Economic Policy, Hendrik S. Houthakker, Washington, May 18, 1970, p. 14.

[21] Hendrik S. Houthakker, "Copper: The Anatomy of a Malfunctioning Market," address at Duke University, March 11, 1970, p. 3 (typescript). See also U.S. House, *Copper Pricing Practices,* Hearings before the Subcommittee on Commerce and Finance of the Committee on Interstate and Foreign Commerce, 91st Cong., 2nd sess., July 20 and 21, 1970.

over, copper production is not price elastic in the short term. It takes
months if not years to develop productive capacity.

Industry Characteristics

To understand the scope and limitations of group action among copper
exporters, one has to analyze the salient characteristics of the industry.
Copper uses are multiple: about 30 percent of the copper sold throughout
the world is in the form of copper alloys, with some 27 percent of all
alloys sold in the form of brass. Major nonalloy copper products include
plumbing and other tubes, followed by sheets, rods, and wire. Almost 50
percent of copper products of various types are used in electrical activities, broadly defined. Other uses are utensils, roofs, coins, and art works.

The nine largest transnational copper groups are: Anaconda (U.S.);
Kennecott (U.S.); Phelps Dodge (U.S.); American Smelting and Refining
or Asarco (U.S.); AAC (South Africa); American Metal Climax (U.S.),
which also owns RST; Union Minière du Haut-Katanga or UMHK
(Belgium); [22] International Nickel or INCO (Canada), with about 58 percent of the shares held in the United States and about 28 percent in
Canada; and Noranda (Canada). In addition, some of these companies are
closely interrelated or linked in interlocking directorships.

One of the major final products of copper is cartelized: this is the group
of electric (especially telephone) cable-makers. The cartel, known as the
International Cable Development Corporation (ICDC), has provided for
market sharing and price fixing since it was incorporated under Liechten-
stein law in 1931. Members of the cartel include practically all West European electric cable manufacturers. The leading U.S. cable-maker, International Telephone and Telegraph (ITT), which was until 1975 a
member of the ICDC cartel, withdrew for fear of antitrust investigation.
The major sufferers from the practices of such a cartel are of course the
developing countries. [23]

In addition, most of the American copper companies have fabricating
subsidiaries. It is difficult to ascertain the extent of vertical integration,
though, since ties can be of varying forms. Ownership of fabricating ven-

[22] Changed its name to Union Minière in February 1968 when it reincorporated in
Belgium.
[23] See "Cartels: Who Gains," *Economist*, April 12, 1975, pp. 99–100. See also OECD,
Export Cartels, Report of the Committee of Experts on Restrictive Business Practices
(Paris, 1974), pp. 33–34.

tures may vary from 100 percent to minority interests. There could also be other ties in the form of reciprocal trading agreements.[24] Vertical integration and reciprocal trading tend, of course, to reduce competitive pressures.

With the partial or total nationalization of copper mines in several host (notably CIPEC) countries, and the advent of other privately owned concerns, a significant rise in the number of suppliers in the world market has occurred during the latter 1960s and early 1970s. Accordingly, there has been a dilution in the concentration of world copper sellers, and a corresponding increase in competition. This was acknowledged by the chairman of the board of Anaconda, who said: "Competitiveness is bound to be a larger factor in the 70's than it was in the 1960's, for in addition to other competitive factors, we must add statism to the competitive equation." [25] In 1974 about two-thirds of world primary copper exports were produced by government-controlled agencies.

While the primary copper industry in its mining and refining segments is still relatively concentrated, scrap dealers—supplying about 25 percent of the total consumption in the United States [26]—are by contrast numerous and highly competitive. Scrap dealers, together with the independent sellers of primary copper, are not easily amenable to concerted action or cooperation (notably in the field of pricing) as compared with the few major copper companies.

As for prices, demand and supply conditions of copper are inelastic in the short run and their response to price changes lags over several years. Indeed, a price increase is not likely to induce an immediate substitution of usage by consumers from copper to, for example, aluminum. This is largely due to the fact that users have invested in equipment and other resources; and they may allow these to wear out before making such a substitution. This seems to be true of other minerals; the difference is one of degree.

One study estimated the short-run elasticity of demand at around (minus) 0.2 and the long-run elasticity of demand as high as (minus) 2.8 or even higher. Equally price-inelastic in the short run is copper supply; around 0.2. In the long run, the elasticity of supply is "at least 0.7 and

---

[24] Charles River Assoc., *Economic Analysis of Copper Industry*, pp. 4, 32.
[25] Keynote address by C. Jay Parkinson at the American Metal Market's Second Annual London Forum, October 26, 1970, p. 14.
[26] Houthakker, "Copper," p. 3.

possibly as high as 2.0 or even higher.'' That study, in its conclusion, warns that ''the CIPEC countries must lose [in export earnings] in the long run if they attempt to jack up the price of copper by cutting back their supply on a long-term basis.'' [27] One should add that this conclusion would be valid only if competing products were able to maintain their relative prices, a very unlikely situation in the inflationary period of the 1970s.

Actual and potential non-CIPEC exporters of copper (Australia, Canada, Ecuador, Indonesia, Iran, Papua New Guinea, the Philippines, South Africa, the USSR) have large deposits. Productive capacity in these countries can be increased in the intermediate run (three-to-seven-year period) and threaten the share of CIPEC countries in world trade—should the latter decide to jack up prices. In fact, non-CIPEC governments along with the transnational copper companies have been interested in pushing copper production and exports to the full remunerative levels. The long-run supply elasticity for copper, along with the cross-elasticity of demand, act therefore as brakes on CIPEC wishes to increase prices.

Also, substantial inroads have been made into copper usages. Competition can be attributed to four main factors: the relatively high price of copper, the wide fluctuations of prices, frequent shortages or the fear of them, and economic and technical progress made by rivals, particularly aluminum. Thus in the middle 1950s, makers of transmission lines switched to aluminum; more recently drop lines and other copper products have been increasingly replaced by aluminum products, the price and availability of copper proving unattractive to users.[28] This explains why most copper groups have diversified into the aluminum industry. Such a move is likely to reduce the desire of these companies to protect the sales of copper.

Adding to the relative instability of copper prices, and also tin prices—as compared with other minerals-metals such as oil and bauxite-aluminum—is the absence of a high degree of vertical integration in the industry. Indeed, a large measure of vertical integration, a comparatively short transit line, and fewer independent decision-making centers between

[27] IBRD, ''An Analysis of the Effects of Possible CIPEC Actions on the Copper Export Earnings of Member Countries,'' prepared by K. Takeuchi, Trade Policies and Export Projections Division, July 1, 1971, pp. 7, 9, 26.

[28] See remarks of Charles M. Brinckerhoff, chairman of Anaconda's board, before the Los Angeles Society of Financial Analysts, March 30, 1967, p. 13; and CIPEC, *Report of the Executive Director to the Governing Board, 1971* (Paris, 1972), pp. 83–85.

producer and consumer would lead to more effective coordination. Consequently, the accumulation of stocks would likely be smaller. The long fragmented line of the copper trade from miner to user is bound to lead to larger variations in stockholding at terminal and intermediate points.

The stockholding decisions of producers, traders, and consumers of copper concentrates, metal, and fabricated products are primarily determined by the availability of the metal and its price in the near term. These operators seldom resort to stocking when prices are low, experience has shown. They will, on the contrary, allow a depletion of their stocks down to the equivalent of a ten-day sales period. By comparison, during periods of shortages and higher prices, these same operators will accumulate stocks extending up to three or four months. Assuming three stockholding sales points in the line of producer to consumer, the accumulation in stocks can reach as much as nine months production.[29] The end results of these swings in stock accumulation are bound to accentuate price fluctuations.

In the long term, probably the competitor of greatest concern to CIPEC countries is the seabed. In fact, large quantities of mineral nodules are found on the ocean floor. These are concentrates the size of potatoes: they contain high percentages of manganese, nickel, copper, and cobalt. An informed source indicated that at the 1972 world consumption level, the 8 billion tons of copper lying on the seabed would suffice for 1,100 years, the 15 billion tons of nickel for 23,500 years, the 358 billion tons of manganese for 34,800 years, and the 5 billion tons of cobalt for 260,000 years. Moreover, nodules are created by the thousands of tons annually. Their remunerative exploitation is now well established, and methods of collection and processing have been successfully developed. Their large scale commercial development only awaits the formulation of the legal status of the deep seas.[30]

Iron-Ore Exporters and AIOEC

In keeping with the UN's 1974 Declaration and Programme of Action on the Establishment of a New International Economic Order, other ex-

---

[29] Michael West, "Copper," draft article for *Optima*, July 3, 1974.

[30] See R. Radetzki, chief economist for CIPEC, "The Last Great Colonization on Earth," *Cooperation Canada*, March–April 1974, pp. 3–8; and "Tapping the Lode on the Ocean Floor," *Business Week*, October 19, 1974, pp. 130, 132, 134.

porter associations have been set up in the mineral and agricultural fields along the OPEC-CIPEC models. These associations aim broadly at ensuring the same benefits as their models.

The post-World War II period has witnessed a relatively rapid growth in the size and number of iron-ore producers, and in the discovery or beneficiation of vast reserves. Technological developments have been instrumental in this process. With "surplus" productive capacities contributing to price weakness, several iron-ore exporter countries have seen their export proceeds decline.

Aware that national measures are ineffective in influencing world market conditions, a number of iron-ore exporting countries have, in the past few years, sought to exchange information—in the hope that this might possibly lead to a coordination of policies or even to collective action.

Venezuela deserves the credit for spearheading this consultation. The Venezuelan minister of mines and hydrocarbons, Pérez Alfonso, attempted in 1958 to call a meeting of iron-ore exporting countries to explore means of cooperation.[31] This proved of no avail. A decade later, having grown stronger with the relative success of OPEC, of which it was a founder, Venezuela tried again. The new minister of mines and hydrocarbons, Antonio Mayobre, again invited representatives of iron-ore exporting countries to convene in Caracas in September 1968. That was the first meeting which aimed at forming an exporters' group.

Exporter Cooperation

The Caracas meeting was attended by Brazil, Chile, India, Liberia, Peru, and Venezuela. Mauritania was unable to send delegates but expressed its support for the objectives of the meeting. These seven countries accounted in 1967 for 34 percent, by value, of world exports of iron ore, and for 84 percent of iron-ore exports from developing countries. A press communiqué issued after the Caracas meeting stated that the meeting had examined different aspects of the iron-ore market and expressed common concern about the continuous erosion of prices. Furthermore, "there was a consensus that parallel to the internal measures that each individual country has taken or could take for the defense of their interests, it was desirable to exchange information and ideas on this matter with a view to promoting a coordinated action in the initiatives to be undertaken in this field."

[31] Interviewed by author in Caracas on August 8, 1969.

At the meeting, most member governments favored institutionalizing cooperation by starting with the iron-ore exporting countries of the developing world, and later hopefully adding the developed exporting countries—Australia, Canada, and Sweden. As an alternative to a producers' association, a commodity agreement between iron-ore exporter and importer countries similar to the International Tin Agreement was suggested. Certain delegations, however, strongly favored an exclusively producers' group in the hope that this arrangement would improve the bargaining position of iron-ore producers in relation to consumers, and would raise their chances of stabilizing prices at the level they considered most attractive. At any rate, the primary concern of all participating countries was to insure, for a start, the exchange of information through the creation of an information bureau.[32]

The participants of the Caracas meeting met again in Geneva in February 1969, with the addition of Gabon. Among the different subjects discussed [33] were means to bring "some order" into the iron-ore markets. The meeting agreed to strengthen the common stand of the participating countries, particularly with respect to the implementation of Resolution 16 adopted at the Second UNCTAD Conference in New Delhi. This resolution urged the holding of intergovernmental consultations between producers and consumers to identify problems faced by the commodity, determine techniques appropriate for dealing with them, and agree on appropriate remedial measures.

An evolution in the position of the participating LDC iron-ore exporters is evident in comparing the Caracas and Geneva meetings. At Caracas, contacts and exchange of information among iron-ore exporting countries were stressed as the main objective. At Geneva, this idea was not abandoned, but the dominant theme had become the proposal for wider deliberations comprising iron-ore importing countries as well. For the UNCTAD Secretariat, the case for an enlarged forum was justified on the grounds that "the participation of a larger number of countries, including the main consuming countries, would make it possible to throw much more light on many of the problems involved and partly on the fact that any international remedial actions which might be considered desira-

---

[32] Venezuela, Ministerio de Minas e Hidrocarburos, "Los Precios Internacionales del Mineral de Hierro," Reuniones Informales Sobre Mineral de Hierro, Caracas, September 1968.

[33] Venezuela, Ministerio de Minas e Hidrocarburos, *Carta Semanal*, March 1969.

ble could be far more effectively implemented by the joint action of a bigger group of exporting and importing countries than by a limited group of exporting countries acting alone.'' [34]

The Geneva meeting agreed, furthermore, to hold the Third Informal Consultative Meeting on Iron Ore in Monrovia, Liberia, in September 1969,[35] but the meeting failed to materialize. The secretary-general of UNCTAD nevertheless succeeded in holding a meeting of exporter and importer countries in Geneva, January 19–23, 1970. This meeting was attended by twenty-five government delegations representing four major groups: developed net-importing market economies—Belgium, France, West Germany, Italy, Japan, Netherlands, United Kingdom, and the United States; developed net-exporting market economies—Australia, Canada, and Sweden; East European socialist economies—Czechoslovakia, Poland, Romania, and the USSR; and developing net-exporting countries—Algeria, Brazil, Chile, Gabon, India, Liberia, Malaysia, Mauritania, Peru, and Venezuela.

The proceedings of the UNCTAD meeting showed a polarization of views between two groups, the developing exporting countries and the developed importing countries. Moreover, the views of the developed net-exporting countries were generally in harmony with those of the developed importers—while the East Europeans sympathized with the developing group.[36]

When representatives of developing countries later proposed linking iron-ore export prices to those of steel, representatives of developed market economy countries questioned the economic soundness and the practicality of this approach. They argued that such a link-up with rising steel prices could eventually lead to still higher prices. But these higher prices could eventually prove impossible to maintain because they would unleash opposite reactions: the curbing of consumption and the stimulation of excessive production of ore.[37]

Linking raw material prices to those of final products has been resorted

[34] UNCTAD Secretariat, *Problem of the World Market for Iron Ore*, Geneva, 1966, p. 25 (TD/B/C.1/66). This report was revised and issued on May 26, 1971 (TD/B/C.1/104).

[35] Press release of the Second Informal Consultative Meeting on Iron Ore, Geneva, February 28, 1969.

[36] See UNCTAD, *International Action on Commodities in the Light of Recent Developments:* Report of the Ad Hoc Meeting on Iron Ore, Geneva, February 1970, 13 pp. (TD/B/C.1/75).

[37] UNCTAD, *Report on the Consultations on Iron Ore Held at the Palais de Nations on 24 and 25 February 1972*, pp. 5, 6 (TD/B/C.1/IRON ORE/CONS/1).

to in a number of mineral industries (for example, bauxite-aluminum) and other commodities. The link, however, should not be too rigidly used. In periods of sellers' markets, raw material producers can raise prices along with increases in end product prices; but during periods of buyers' markets, raw material producers would be well advised to moderate price increases lest they price their commodity above readily available substitutes, or lest they drastically constrain consumption.

At the Third UNCTAD Conference in 1972, the Indian minister for foreign trade, Shri Latit Naraijan Mishra, went even further by advocating a cutback of production by the developed countries in favor of production by the developing ones: "We made a strong plea for arresting erosion in export prices and the need for developed countries to stop further expansion of output so that the competitive position of the developing nations does not get further weakened." [38] It remains to be seen whether developed countries will agree to sacrifice national production as a means of assistance to LDCs, rather than because of lower prices.

In any event, Brazil, a leader of iron-ore exports, was reportedly "quietly looking for partners in a united front to push ore prices up." Venezuela and Australia were cooperating.[39] In fact, Australia's iron-ore exporters, under the strong urging of the Labour government's federal minister for minerals and energy, Rex Connor, obtained in July 1973 a 15 percent increase in prices of Australian iron ore exported to Japan, retroactive to April 1, 1973. The increase was intended to compensate for U.S. dollar depreciation. Brazil and India followed suit.

Agreement to establish the Association of Iron Ore Exporting Countries (AIOEC) was finalized at a meeting of eleven ministers from major iron-ore exporting countries in April 1975. The agreement, with no price-fixing power, was signed by Algeria, Australia, Brazil, Chile, India, Mauritania, Peru, Sierra Leone, Sweden, Tunisia, and Venezuela. The Australian minister for overseas trade, Frank Crean, expressed on July 3 his government's support for AIOEC and its "commitment to seek closer relations with developing countries, and to assist them in their economic and social development." [40]

---

[38] His inaugural address at the Annual Session of the Federation of Indian Mineral Industries at Vigyan Bhavan, New Delhi, June 29, 1972, p. 4 (typescript).

[39] *Business Week,* July 14, 1973, p. 42.

[40] "Iron Ore Agreement Signed," *Weekly Bulletin Review of the Press* (OPEC), April 1, 1975, p. 10; and *Australian Weekly News Roundup* (Australian Information Service, New York), July 9, 1975, p. 3.

Market Conditions

Iron-ore deposits are found in ample quantities in various parts of the world. A marked change has been occurring, however, in the location of surplus deposits for export, and therefore in the pattern of world trade. With the end of World War II, the existing iron-ore mines in major industrial countries were increasingly faced with the competition of new higher-grade ore deposits. The search efforts of large steel companies, ore producers, and traders—especially those of the United States, Europe, and Japan—have paid off as several ore fields have been found and developed in Canada, Africa, and Australia.[41] Canadian ores are largely low grade but can be easily concentrated; the others are high grade.

With the new discoveries, some relatively low-grade ore mines (in Western Europe and the United States), unable to meet the competition of foreign ores, had to close or cut back their output. Other low-grade open-pit mines in these areas—thanks to technological improvements—have become large-scale developments by upgrading and classifying their ores using various beneficiation processes and pelletization.

In their drive to improve the competitiveness of their ores, several iron producers spent large sums on beneficiation and pelletizing plants; alternatively they reduced prices in order to defend their market position against incursions by newcomers. This can be inferred from operating data. For example, the Swedish LKAB's iron-ore production rose from 13.8 to 19.7 million tons between 1957 and 1966 (43 percent); its sales rose from 820 to 920 million kroner ($164 to $184 million or only 12 percent). Most significantly, LKAB's net profit fell by a spectacular 40 percent.[42] In their 1967 annual report, LKAB's board acknowledged their price-cutting policy in order to maintain their competitive advantage in the European market: "LKAB's sales for 1968 indicate that the considerable price reductions for phosphor ore made for 1967 deliveries, together with the further reductions promised for 1968 with a view to establishing a proper price relationship metallurgically with low phosphor ore, has led to a strongly improved demand for phosphor ore."

[41] Steel production, it should be added, does not rely completely on the use of iron ore since about 40 percent of the world steel output comes from scrap—that is to say, from metal recovered from the steel-making plants themselves and from the disposal of obsolete machinery and equipment.

[42] *Journal of Commerce* (New York), International Edition, March 14, 1969.

Generalizations on iron-ore prices are difficult to make because of the wide variety of ores. Terms of iron-ore sales contracts are occasionally made public,[43] except for the considerable amount of ore moving in integrated channels or between associated iron-ore producers and steel companies. Quotations for certain types of ores usually represent reference prices which may differ from realized prices. Great care is therefore needed in interpreting data. Though it is obvious that iron-ore prices generally suffered substantial declines in the 1960s, to measure the extent of the decline or to make comparisons from one exporting country to another could easily be misleading. A country normally does not export a single type of iron ore but a variety with differing composition and degrees of processing. Moreover, some countries enjoy certain freight advantages.

The substantial increase in the size of ore carriers and the consequent decline in ore freight rates, as well as the location of steel plants on seaboards and the opening of water channels, have also contributed to greater competition. They have enabled distant ores to compete in major industrial regions among themselves and with traditional sources of supplies. For example, the U.S. East Coast (Birmingham, Philadelphia, Baltimore) started receiving in the mid-1960s large imports from Venezuela, Brazil, Chile, Peru, and Liberia in competition with U.S. Mesabi ores.

As to types of producers, iron-ore production and trade in the major exporting countries are carried out by private operators, by state-owned enterprises, or by companies of mixed ownership. While iron-ore producers have widely different production capacities, a few are of world-wide importance. Among leading transnational private companies producing iron ore are U.S. Steel, Bethlehem Steel, Kaiser, Hanna Mining, Cleveland-Cliffs Iron, Marcona Mining [44] (all U.S. corporations), and the British-based Rio Tinto-Zinc (RTZ). Among state-owned companies, the largest are the Swedish LKAB, the Brazilian Companhia Vale de Rio Doce, the Indian Minerals and Metals Trading Corporation, and the Chilean Compania de Acero del Pacifico.

About two-thirds of the world trade in iron ore (including exports from the Soviet Union to other East European countries) are "tied": they rep-

---

[43] See, for example, terms of iron-ore import contracts negotiated by Japanese buyers, with details published in Tokyo by the *Tex Report*. Details cover quantities, qualities, prices, schedules, loading ports, shippers, producers, and importers.

[44] Equally owned by Utah International and Cyprus Mines.

resent intracompany transfers or long-term contracts (common among Japanese firms) fixing tonnages and prices.[45] These "ties" contribute to a greater degree of security in the flow of iron ore to its markets, and help mineral ventures raise from the steel companies and from capital markets some of the capital required for their costly projects. Vertically integrated facilities under one ownership and management such as those of U.S. Steel—as compared with arm's length deals or even long-term contracts—offer the advantage of avoiding the problem of the balance between iron-ore production and consumption. Ore production is coordinated closely with the requirements of that company's steel mills.

A few Australian company officials indicated in interviews with the author in 1972 that they were disillusioned with long-term contracts negotiated by Japanese trading groups. They argued that the latter, by offering optimistic forecasts of consumption, built high expectations which caused Australian producers to expand productive capacity. They claimed that raising such expectations in order to stimulate expansion enabled the Japanese firms to push down the terms of purchase. Whether Japanese firms contrived to create conditions of surplus and play one producer against another is difficult to document. Nevertheless, it is interesting to note that Japanese iron-ore buying syndicates asked for ore deliveries below the minimum set in their contracts of 1971–1972—invoking as a reason the recession in their domestic steel industry. The Japanese groups undertook, however, to make up the reductions as soon as possible.[46]

Cutbacks of production notwithstanding, Australian mineral exporters suffered from the substantial devaluations and depreciation of the U.S. dollar in the early 1970s, since their long-term contracts were expressed in that currency. This has been the case with several other primary exporting countries. With the support of their government, Australian iron-ore exporters banded together and obtained relief for the dollar devaluations from the Japanese steel industry; ore export prices were adjusted upward by 20 percent.[47]

[45] UNCTAD Secretariat, *International Action on Commodities in the Light of Recent Developments: Problems of the World Market for Iron Ore*, Geneva, May 26, 1971, pp. 31–32 (TB/C.1/104).
[46] For example, 6 percent below minimum contractual tonnage deliveries of Hamersley's Holdings, as per Chairman's Supplementary Statement of April 11, 1972, Melbourne. See also Colonial Sugar Refining Company, *Annual Report, 1972*, p. 24. CSR, a Sydney-based corporation, has an interest in Mount Newman Iron Ore Venture.
[47] Statements by the minister for minerals and energy, R. F. X. Connor, Canberra, May 29, 1973, and November 17, 1974. Indian and other iron-ore producers obtained similar treatment. See "Iron Ore in October 1973," and "Iron Ore in August 1974," *Mineral In-*

A relatively high concentration in the demand for iron ore is found in major steel producing industrial regions such as the United States, Western Europe, and Japan. In the United States, eight companies account for about 75 percent of both domestic steel production and total ore purchases. In Japan, four companies produce roughly 80 percent of the steel; furthermore, they normally pool their purchases of iron ore from overseas. In Europe, a few major steel producers have emerged in the recent past as a consequence of nationalization or government-supported or sponsored mergers for the purpose of raising efficiency: [48] in Germany (three companies); in France (two companies); and in Italy, Luxembourg, the Netherlands, and the United Kingdom (one each).

As a result of this concentration, European and Japanese steel companies, well aware of their relatively strong bargaining position in the international market, have been acting in a concerted way towards ore suppliers. A clear example of this common approach has been the creation of ore-buying syndicates in the main consuming countries of Western Europe. In fact, the British steel industry used to acquire overseas supplies through a single body even before the nationalization of the industry. The British Iron and Steel Corporation (BISC) has been the only British agency responsible for dealing with foreign suppliers and has likewise been empowered to negotiate freight rates. In Germany, two central purchasing bodies, the Rohstoffhandel GmbH in Dusseldorf and the Erzkontor Ruhr GmbH in Essen, centralize the purchases of all the Ruhr plants as well as of some other German plants, and they negotiate agreements with the iron-ore producers as well as with shipowners. In Belgium, Groupement des Hauts Fourneaux et Aciéries Belges is responsible for the ore purchases of the steel industry. In other European countries, the bulk of ore purchases are effected by the largest national steel company like Usinor in France, the state-owned Finsider in Italy, and Hoogovens Ijmuiden in the Netherlands. [49]

This cooperation among iron and steel companies at the national level is further developed within the framework of consortia or joint ventures (for example, the Iron Ore Company of Canada). These associations rep-

---

dustry Surveys (U.S. Bureau of Mines), December 20, 1973, and October 29, 1974, respectively.

[48] See U.S. Cabinet Committee on Economic Policy, *Reports to the President on the Economic Position of the Steel Industry,* July 6, 1971, pp. 37–38.

[49] See Jean-Claude Caillat, *La Route du fer: Essai de stratégie économique* (Paris, 1967), pp. 221–223.

resent appropriate frameworks for the exchange of views and possibly for working out common attitudes and policies. This oligopsonistic power of iron-ore buyers was acknowledged by the president of Marcona, a leading iron-ore producer: "During this period [1960s] there has been cooperation between the ore buyers of Japan and Europe in driving prices down to the lowest possible level." [50] One should not, however, overlook the fact that nonintegrated iron-ore sellers are large enough (for example, Hanna Mining, Pickands Mather, Cleveland-Cliffs, LKAB, and Marcona) to be capable of exerting countervailing forces. These sellers have yet to make use of their potential collective countervailing power. Iron-ore exporter governments responded to the challenge in the creation of AIOEC in 1975.

Sulfur Exporters and Sulexco

Fluctuation in, or deterioration of, the price level of sulfur has been of serious concern both to governments of exporting countries and to the transnational companies. It has spurred their interest in joint action among their respective groups, which is facilitated by a relatively high concentration of companies.

By the early 1950s, four U.S. enterprises dominated the world market: two major ones, Freeport Sulphur and Texas Gulf Sulphur, and two smaller ones, Duval Texas Sulphur and Jefferson Lake Oil. In 1950 these U.S. firms controlled 94 percent of the world sulfur trade, and Norwegian producers the other 6 percent.

While U.S. legislation prohibits restraints of trade in the domestic market, the Webb-Pomerene Act of 1918 permits cartelization in the export trade—including the setting of production quotas, market allocations, price fixing, and penalties for violations of the cartel agreement. In response to this act, the two major U.S. producers, Freeport Sulphur and Texas Gulf Sulphur, set up the Sulphur Export Corporation (Sulexco) in 1922. Soon after Duval Texas Sulphur started production in 1928 and Jefferson Lake Oil in 1932, Sulexco entered into agreement with the two newcomers. In 1933 it established an export cartel which limited export quantities, assigned markets, and fixed prices.

In 1952 Sulexco owners dissolved their association because export control had been introduced by the U.S. government through the rationing of

---

[50] Charles W. Robinson, *Competition in the Sale of Iron Ore in World Markets,* XI Convencion de Ingenieros de Minas del Peru, December 1969.

what were then scarce supplies; Sulexco's control over exports would be superfluous under these conditions. However, following the discovery of new supplies, the emergence of new suppliers outside the United States, and the ensuing severe price competition starting in 1956, the U.S. producers decided in 1958 to re-establish Sulexco with the following equity participation: Texas Gulf Sulphur (37 percent); Freeport Sulphur (37 percent); Jefferson Lake Oil (18 percent); and Duval Sulphur (8 percent). But the re-establishment of Sulexco proved ineffective in supporting prices, largely because non-U.S. newcomers with large supplies were pressing for market outlets. Prices for U.S. exporters fell from $30 per long ton in 1958 to $21 per long ton in 1963.[51]

Beginning in 1963, though, world consumption started to grow faster than production, since expansion in productive capacity had already been cut in response to the 1956–1963 price fall. This led to a new shortage, and U.S. export prices rose from a low of $22 per long ton in 1964 to $40.14 per long ton in 1968. This price encouraged new production and resulted in another surplus. Thereafter, U.S. export prices started falling again, to reach $17.50 per long ton in May 1972.[52]

Canada was, in 1971, the world's largest exporter of sulfur. Although the quantities it exported rose from 2.11 million metric tons in 1968 to 2.99 million tons in 1970, exports proceeds declined from C$76.4 million to C$42.8 million, representing a price decline from C$36.2 per ton to C$14.3 per ton.[53] The world sulfur market was then faced not only with a larger number of sources of supply using various techniques of production (Frasch, native, recovered, pyrites) but also with a larger number of enterprises. Private and state-owned companies had large new sulfur supplies, most of it recovered sulfur from oil and gas.

Both private and state companies expressed concern in 1971 over the decline in sulfur prices. Officials of state-owned or controlled sulfur producing enterprises had extensive consultations in 1971. A representative of the Société Nationale des Pétroles d'Aquitaine (SNPA) of France, Mr. Charvériat, consulted with counterparts in Iran, Iraq, and Kuwait. Simultaneously, the authorities of the province of Alberta, Can-

---

[51] Information based on the Harvard Business School case, "Foreign Investment in the Mexican Sulphur Industry (A)," prepared by Alberto Sanchez under the direction of Professor Raymond Vernon, 1970 (typescript).

[52] See "Sulfur in 1971," *Mineral Industry Surveys,* October 2, 1972, p. 1.

[53] *Mineral Trade Notes* (U.S. Bureau of Mines), February 1972, p. 21.

ada, announced the introduction of compulsory inventory control regulations, aimed at stabilizing prices, to be implemented January 1, 1972. Poland indicated its willingness to go along with price stabilization guidelines; so did SNPA. Mexico outlined plans for export controls, including price increases. These producers considered desirable for 1972 a minimum price level of about $28 per ton for solid sulfur and $30 per ton for liquid sulfur, using Rotterdam as a basing point.

To further their efforts, delegations from sulfur exporting countries (notably Canada, France, Mexico, and Poland) met in June and November 1971 in Montreal, with the objective of concluding an international agreement. The Alberta government, however, abandoned its control scheme late in November 1971. Nevertheless, Sulexco reportedly succeeded in organizing an international cartel covering all countries except Canada, Cuba, and Mexico.[54]

In the mid-1970s mined sulfur appears to be facing increasing competition from sulfur recovered from coal and oil. With the enforcement of stricter clean air laws in industrial countries, supplies of recovered sulfur will become larger. This situation does not augur well for price stabilization.

Uranium Exporters and the Uranium Institute

The limitations of individual action to prevent price deterioration became obvious to uranium producers early in the 1970s. Among the developed countries, Australia and Canada have realized the advantages of joint action. The two countries agreed in 1971 to establish a continuous dialogue among their government officials as an initial step to policy cooperation in minerals, including uranium. The Canadian minister for energy, mines, and resources, R. F. F. Greene, advocated in Canberra in 1971 the establishment of a "world supplier-price for uranium around $6/lb." Australian uranium happens to be extremely rich. It could in 1971 be profitably mined at $3 per pound of uranium oxide, and according to one source could break even at $1 per pound.[55] This situation

---

[54] See "Sulfur Procedures Envisage Price Stabilization Measures," *MEES Supplement,* October 8, 1971; *Mineral Trade Notes,* November 1971, pp. 35–36; Mining Journal, *1972 Mining Annual Review* (London, 1972), p. 265; R. W. Merwin and T. C. Briggs, "Sulfur and Pyrites," in U.S. Bureau of Mines, *Minerals Yearbook, 1971* (Washington, 1972), vol. 1; and OECD, *Export Cartels,* pp. 41–42.

[55] *Mining Journal,* August 6, 1971, p. 113; and *Metal Bulletin,* August 3, 1971, p. 17.

explains the strong desire of Canada and other uranium exporting countries to cooperate with Australia.

For Australia, uranium export contracts should "have what the Government considers to be a reasonable base price with provision for escalation and probably renegotiation later." The contracts approved on August 24, 1972, were worth A$44 million, giving a value of roughly A$6.57 per pound of oxide. An official statement acknowledged that "the Australian government has decided, in common with the governments of practically all other uranium exporting countries, to maintain a system of export control." The statement adds: "For the present this will not involve any quantitative restriction upon exporters," since control will be limited to price for the time being.[56]

As a result, state and private uranium enterprises producing in Australia, Canada, France, South Africa, and the United Kingdom agreed to coordinate their pricing policies at a meeting in Johannesburg May 29–30, 1972. Their first decision was to set a minimum export price of A$6.57 a pound for uranium oxide, valid until 1980. In April 1975 they set up a permanent framework for price coordination known as the Uranium Institute; sixteen enterprises participated. Although the U.S. government and its uranium producers did not participate directly in the Johannesburg meeting, a U.S. administration spokesman in 1972 reportedly favored price increases for uranium produced outside the United States to the extent they would improve the prospects of U.S. exports.[57]

The U.S. government has also favored producers' cooperation through other means. Ostensibly to prevent the spread of nuclear weapons and promote world peace, the U.S. president gathered in London in July 1975 representatives of the major nuclear exporting countries: the United States, Britain, France, West Germany, Canada, the Soviet Union, and a Japanese observer. But to an independent source, the U.S. government was also aiming at reinforcing "the group's near monopoly of the commercial enrichment and reprocessing market," and the "dominant [U.S.]

---

[56] See "$44M in Uranium Exports Approved," *Australian Financial Review* (Sydney), August 25, 1972, p. 1; "Japan Stockpiles Uranium," *ibid.;* and statement by R. V. Swartz, Australian minister of national development, February 18, 1971. See also Australian Senate, Standing Committee on Foreign Affairs and Defense, Submission by Department of National Development, presented by J. B. R. Livermore, Canberra, March 1972, pp. 77–79.

[57] *Australian Financial Review,* August 25, 1972, p. 1, and August 28, 1972, p. 10; and *Business Week,* August 18, 1975, p. 32.

position in that market." Nevertheless, the "participating countries," that source added, "are frightened of appearing to be another energy cartel—the OPEC of the nuclear age." [58] Those countries remaining outside the Johannesburg and London groups were few: Brazil, China, and India.

The uranium industry appears to have a low elasticity of demand: a moderate increase, say of 10 percent, in the price of uranium oxide would have an insignificant effect on the cost of power generation from nuclear plants. This is because the crucial element of cost is not fuel but capital investments.

Bauxite Exporters and IBA

The international aluminum industry has been known for its high concentration, vertical integration, and joint schemes, including cartels. One of the reported cartels was that of aluminum semimanufactures, grouping West European and North American enterprises producing in Europe and selling to Scandinavian countries. The cartel restrictions covered export limitations from member countries, allotment of quotas to member firms, and price regulation. The cartel was incorporated in Zurich on January 19, 1964, under the name of Assocalex.[59]

It is also common for aluminum enterprises to cooperate in their negotiations with host governments. A U.S. State Department official, T. O. Enders, acknowledged that in the 1973–1974 negotiations with the Jamaican government, the U.S. companies "worked in union—as they were discussing questions of taxes." The U.S. government, according to that official, was not only "very closely informed of the course of negotiations, but we did express to the Jamaican Government in as clear terms as we could what we thought would be the consequences of certain actions proposed by them." [60]

A few of the bauxite-alumina exporting countries of the developing

---

[58] P. Lewis, "Uranium Enrichment: Bid for a Big Market," *Financial Times,* July 17, 1975, p. 4.

[59] See OECD, *Export Cartels,* pp. 36–38. For details on the structure of the world aluminum industry, see Zuhayr Mikdashi, "Aluminum," in Raymond Vernon, ed., *Big Business and the State: Changing Relations in Western Europe* (Cambridge: Harvard University Press, 1974), pp. 170–94.

[60] U.S. Congress, *Outlook for Prices and Supplies of Industrial Raw Materials,* Hearings before the Subcommittee on Economic Growth of the Joint Economic Committee, 93rd Cong., 2nd sess., July 1974, p. 185.

world expressed interest late in the 1960s in forming a strictly producers' association. Since August 1968, the Jamaican government in particular has endeavored to establish such a group (initially to comprise the Caribbean–South American countries of Jamaica, Surinam, Guyana, and the Dominican Republic). The initial purpose, as with other such groups, would be to promote a continuous exchange of information and ideas— and possibly the coordination of policies—in the hope of extracting better terms from transnational operators.[61]

Late in 1971, the Jamaican minister of trade and industry expressed his belief that the bauxite exporting countries were ready to cooperate. He had informal talks with his counterparts in Central and South American bauxite exporting countries. Late in 1972, Jamaica, Surinam, and Guyana agreed to exchange information and views on the bauxite industry. Jamaica and Surinam seemed even to be moving towards the adoption of a common bauxite policy.[62]

But industry sources discounted at the time the practicality of forming an Organization of Bauxite Exporting Countries on the grounds that politico-economic differences and rivalries were in the way. Moreover, Australia—with very roughly one-third of the world reserves—was unlikely to join, they contended.[63] Not only does Australia have low-cost production, but its bauxite and alumina are increasingly accessible to Western markets, thanks to the development of bulk cargo handling and large ocean ore carriers. Finally, in the technological and market conditions of the 1970s, the competitive edge of bauxite as a raw material for aluminum metal in relation to other raw materials which could produce aluminum was smaller than that of petroleum vis-à-vis coal, nuclear power, shale oil, or tar sands. This reduces the leverage that the governments of the bauxite exporting countries can apply against the transnational aluminum companies and the major consumer countries.

It was not until March 1974 that government representatives of seven major bauxite exporting countries met in Conakry, Guinea (following an earlier meeting in 1973 in Belgrade, Yugoslavia) to create a permanent

---

[61] *Daily Gleaner* (Kingston, Jamaica), August 24 and 28, 1968.

[62] See "Caribbean Club Move," *Metal Bulletin,* November 21, 1972.

[63] Dennis Topping, "Aluminium Production with Nationalism in the Air: Alcan Plays It Cool," *Times* (London), October 28, 1971, p. 21; and *Mining Journal,* November 12, 1971, p. 429. Another third of the reserves is in Guinea, West Africa. See Ian Coghill, *Australia's Mineral Wealth* (Melbourne: Sorett Publishing, 1972), p. 37.

organization. Its purpose was "to promote the orderly and rational development of the bauxite." Founding members of the International Bauxite Association (IBA) were Australia, Guinea, Guyana, Jamaica, Sierra Leone, Surinam, and Yugoslavia—the first two with the world's largest bauxite reserves. They were joined later by the Dominican Republic, Ghana, and Haiti. In addition, Greece, India, and Trinidad and Tobago were accepted as official observer nations. In 1974, IBA members produced about 63 percent of the world's 65 million tons of bauxite. IBA's Secretariat was set in Kingston, Jamaica.

The formation of IBA represents the accord of its members to: reduce internal rivalry, "secure" for member states "maximum national ownership of their natural resources," promote the exchange of information, raise national benefits, and provide common services, for example, shipping. Benefits could accrue from furthering the processing of bauxite and the fabrication of aluminum products in the resource countries, harmonizing price changes, and preventing transnational firms from adopting predatory measures against any of the member states.[64]

It is remarkable that Australia, thanks to its Labour Government, joined the developing countries in this endeavor, which was primarily aimed at the developed industrial countries and their transnational enterprises. Indeed, the Australian Labour Government has been vocally independent in seeking greater national control over its natural resources and larger socioeconomic benefits. In these dual objectives, the Australian government has shared the aspirations of most developing countries.

More specifically, the Australian government was concerned about the transnational aluminum companies' control of the industry in Australia, and their ability, thanks to their vertically integrated structure, to minimize tax payments. As the Australian minister for minerals and energy explained: "In bauxite, and its derivative alumina, there is the same tale [as in other resources] of economic exploitation by mainly multinationals in what is termed a vertically integrated operation typical of multinational sophistication." Among the examples he offered was that of the Queensland Alumina Refinery at Gladstone,

a classical example of multinational sophistication, and managerial expertise at its fiscal best and worst. It is a highly capital intensive operation on a "take and pay

---

[64] "Bauxite Moderates," *Metal Bulletin*, April 26, 1974, p. 24: "Les Pays producteurs de bauxite s'associent," *Le Figaro*, March 8, 1974, p. 10; and "7 Producers of Bauxite Form Group," *International Herald Tribune*, March 11, 1974.

basis." Each of the Consortium Members takes a proportion of its output equivalent to their financial interest. The actual Company capital of this project is only $2.7M. Its overseas borrowings are seventy times as great, so that it can secure the maximum deduction by way of interest as an offset against possible profits. The large capital outlays also entitle it to claim the largest depreciation charges as a processor against its taxable profit. In addition, until we last year abolished incentives for plant installation in industry, it was claiming the plant investment allowances which were worth 9% of its outlay. As the various interested partners each takes its proportion, at cost, their only liability, by way of company tax, is for the difference between that cost, and what they claim to be the world going price, under the theory of imputed profits. Conversely they can claim imputed losses when trading with themselves, and, for tax minimising purposes, they are completely equipped in financial expertise to do so.[65]

The minister viewed IBA as one means of checking on transnational companies worldwide, and of improving host countries' gains.

Fortified by the formation of IBA, Jamaica assumed the leadership in raising its taxes on bauxite production and alumina processing from $25 million to $200 million in 1974. The position of Jamaica in relation to the transnational companies was strengthened further by the fact that the latter's capital investments in Jamaica reached a gross total of $800 million, and that Jamaican bauxite contributed to 40 percent of the U.S. aluminum production.[66]

The impact of the increase in Jamaica's bauxite levy on the cost of producing aluminum metal was equivalent to about 2.5 cents per pound or 6 to 7 percent of the open market value of aluminum in 1974. The ability of the companies to pass on this cost to the customer was well established, and such a price increase would not by itself damage the competitive position of aluminum vis-à-vis other materials.[67]

After imposing its tax hike on the transnational companies, the Jamaican government outlined as other objectives recovering unexploited bauxite land and establishing partnerships between national companies and foreign companies. This was successfully done with several foreign concessionaires. In order to avoid extranational constraints on its fiscal and control measures, Jamaica had the foresight to withdraw from the World

[65] "The Role of the Multinationals in the Australian Mining Industry," address given by R. F. X. Connor at Teachers' Federation House, Sydney, April 24, 1974.

[66] "Aluminum Producers Buy Time on Bauxite," *Business Week,* June 22, 1974, p. 29.

[67] Stewart Spector's memos in *Aluminum Industry;* and *Bauxite and a Possible OPEC-like Price Agreement,* Oppenheimer & Company, New York, July 18, 1974, and January 11, 1974, respectively. Also Andrew Staines, "Digesting the Raw Materials Threat," *New Scientist,* March 7, 1974, p. 610.

Bank's International Center for the Settlement of Investment Disputes. This action prevented the transnational companies from resorting to the center for arbitration.[68]

Jamaican export levies in particular, and to a lesser extent the recovery of unexploited land from foreign concessions, offered a basis for emulation by other IBA members, notably Australia, the Dominican Republic, Guinea, Guyana, Haiti, and Surinam. This additional income will assist the developing countries of IBA to meet some of the recent increases in foreign exchange costs of basic commodities such as fuel, food, fertilizer, and machinery.[69]

Banana Exporters and UPEB

OPEC-type producer associations are not limited to minerals. Agricultural producers have also attempted to follow that model in order to remedy the deterioration of their export proceeds.

One example is UPEB, the Unión de Paises Exportadores del Banano (Union of Banana Exporting Countries), which was established in March 1974 in Panama by seven Latin American countries: Colombia, Costa Rica, Ecuador, Guatemala, Honduras, Nicaragua, and Panama. UPEB founding members accounted in 1973 for about two-thirds of the world's banana exports, valued at $400 million.

Their production is controlled by three big U.S. firms, the two largest being United Brands (previously United Fruit) and Standard Fruit (owned by Castle and Cooke), followed by Del Monte. These transnational corporations accounted in 1973 for about 70 percent (35, 25, and 10 respectively) of the total world banana trade in terms of value. Their conduct was considered during various periods as acting in restraint of trade.[70]

All banana exporting countries are developing countries, and several of them are heavily dependent on that commodity for employment, national income, and foreign exchange. An UNCTAD study has shown that the fall of banana retail prices in real terms since 1950 "benefited consumers in the developed countries, and deprived the exporting countries of

[68] "Bauxite Levy Protest to World Bank," *Financial Times,* June 26, 1974, p. 29.

[69] UN, ECOSOC, Committee on Natural Resources, *Permanent Sovereignty over Natural Resources,* Report of the Secretary-General, January 31, 1975, pp. 6–10 (E/C.7/53).

[70] UNCTAD Secretariat, *The Marketing and Distribution System for Bananas,* Geneva, December 24, 1974, pp. 13, 26–28 (TD/B/C.1/162). United Brands was accused by the European Economic Community of antitrust violations, in "United Brands Accused by Europeans," *New York Times,* May 7, 1975, p. 63.

the benefits of the cost-reducing innovations.'' Some banana exporting countries had to grant subsidies to growers in order to cope with rising costs and sustain their exports. UNCTAD's secretariat concluded: "Over the past decade, there has been a net transfer of real resources to developed countries from the banana-producing developing countries.'' [71] UNCTAD estimated on a world basis that the share of local growers in the final retail price was 11.5 percent in 1971, as compared with gross margins for foreign enterprises of 88.5 percent (ripening 19, retailing 31.9, freight and insurance 11.5, and others 26.1). The export tax of the producing-exporting countries represented 0.8 percent of the retail unit value, whereas import duties imposed by importing developed countries averaged 6.9 percent or eight times the export tax. [72]

Early in 1974, UPEB members agreed to impose an export tax of up to 2.5 cents per pound ($1 per box of 40 pounds) effective April 15, 1974. The increase came after a long period of twenty years of a "far too low" price, as was admitted by one company official. Notwithstanding this situation, the U.S. companies fought the price increase at the producer end but not at the consumer end. More specifically, Standard Fruit boycotted Honduras and United Brands boycotted Panama. One unnamed "large transnational corporation resorted to the weekly destruction of 145,000 boxes of fruit in a certain Central American republic because of its opposition to the export tax in May–June 1974.'' [73]

The tough stand by Standard Fruit and United Brands originally contributed to welding solidarity among UPEB members, who "still remember the earlier days of this century when the banana companies employed harsh economic and political pressure to establish or topple Central American governments." [74] Ultimately, though, the companies proved stronger. By playing off one country against another, and by cutting back or stopping banana shipments from countries attempting agrarian reform or adhering to UPEB's pricing policy, transnational companies managed to weaken the UPEB front.

[71] UNCTAD, *Pricing Policy in Relation to Marketing and Distribution of Bananas,* May 7, 1974, p. 5 (TD/B/C.1/CONS.10/L.5). See also UN Food and Agriculture Organization (FAO), Intergovernmental Group on Bananas, *Possible International Approaches to Problems of Market Access and Pricing,* Rome, February 1974 (CCP:BA/CONS 74/3).

[72] UNCTAD Secretariat, *Marketing and Distribution for Bananas,* pp. 16, 74.

[73] "Multinationals: A Banana Brouhaha over Higher Prices," *Business Week,* June 22, 1974, p. 42; and UNCTAD Secretariat, *Marketing and Distribution for Bananas,* p. 26.

[74] "Multinationals: a banana brouhaha"; also "Other Nations to Meet on Other Resources," *New York Times,* April 7, 1974, p. 5.

Indeed, addressing an UPEB meeting in July 1974, Panama's minister of commerce and industry, Fernando Manfredo, stated: "The vice president of Standard Fruit . . . announced that his company refused to accept any tax on exportation. And if Honduras and Costa Rica insisted on imposing it, they would stop shipments from their own plantations and from those of the national producers." The minister declared that the company carried out its threat. By the end of 1974, Costa Rica reduced its tax to 25 cents per box of 40 pounds, Honduras to 30 cents, and Panama to 35 cents. In fact, Panama had already disbursed $1 million to Honduras and Costa Rica, which had been seriously hit by company actions. But Ecuador, with 30 percent of Latin America's banana exports, declined to go along with the tax proposal and eventually withdrew from UPEB; so did Nicaragua.[75]

United Brands also resorted to some shady practices. It reportedly paid a bribe of $1.25 million in 1974 to the chief of state of an UPEB member (President Oswaldo López Arellano of Honduras). The bribe was offered for a reduction of the export tax on every 40-pound box of bananas produced and exported by United Brands from Honduras. Honduras supplied about 16 percent of the company's sales. To "relieve" the company, its export tax was reduced to 30 cents, as compared with the 100 cents per box sought originally by UPEB. Arellano was removed from office late in April 1975.[76]

U.S. transnational companies had fought back with noted "ferocity" against UPEB's price increase, mainly by cutting back purchases while raising prices at the consumers' end through the shortage they had helped create. They were therefore charged with profiteering, especially with their profit margin more than tripling from 20 cents a box prior to UPEB's establishment to 70 cents a box shortly thereafter.[77]

The factors responsible for the weak impact of UPEB are multiple. Notable among them are the oligopsonistic influence of the three giant U.S.-based transnational firms, the vertical integration of these firms which control most world marketing outlets, the "dispensable" nature of ba-

---

[75] D. J. Casey, "Banana Exporting Nations Confront Major Crisis," *Action* (UN Development Program), pp. 1, 2; and "Cartels: Just Bananas," *Newsweek,* August 26, 1974, pp. 36–38.

[76] See "Business Corruption: Banana Bribes," *Economist,* April 19, 1975, p. 74; "Honduran Bribery," *Time,* April 21, 1975, p. 46; and "Honduras-Coupe," *Economist,* April 26, 1975, p. 68.

[77] See "Cartels: Just Bananas."

nanas as compared with other commodities such as oil, the absence of effective support or participation from banana exporters both within and outside Latin America, the absence of adequate information on cost-price structures and on legislative and administrative measures affecting banana production and exports, the absence of training and research facilities, the economic and political dependence or weakness of some of UPEB's members, the limited extent of effective coordination and solidarity, and the practical problems of implementing uniform tax rates on exports regardless of the location of banana shipping terminals vis-à-vis major consumer markets. With reference to the latter, it is worth pointing out that a tax of one cent per pound (in relation to 1972 prices) would yield price increases varying between 21 percent for Panama and 40 percent for Nicaragua. The reason for this wide difference is the variation of the export unit value.[78] Harmonization in tax rates to make shippers indifferent as to point of origin is therefore needed.

Other Exporter Associations

The producer association model has also been viewed by other raw materials producers as their opportunity for a new economic order. Producers of phosphate have been most successful in capitalizing on the energy crisis, OPEC's price increases, and the concomitant rise in petrochemical prices. In fact, under the leadership of the major phosphate-rock exporter Morocco, and following on several meetings in its capital Rabat, producers of phosphate rock in Morocco, Tunisia, Senegal, the Spanish Sahara, Algeria, and in South America acted in concert to treble their prices. They also sought national control of their industries. Acting on this policy, Togo early in 1974 engineered a 100 percent takeover of the country's major phosphate-rock mining venture, which had been operated by the W. R. Grace Company of the United States.

Under the leadership of the world's largest mercury producer, Spain (see Table 5), the major producers of that metal (Spain, Italy, Mexico, Algeria, Yugoslavia, Turkey, and Canada) have also formed a club. They met on several occasions, and they agreed in 1973–1974 on a producers' association and a general price policy. The producers have been concerned about a dwindling demand for mercury's main use (chlorine production) owing to environmental decisions in favor of the pollution-free

[78] UNCTAD, *Pricing Policy of Bananas,* p. 15.

diaphragm process. Producer countries generally are seeking to maximize their returns while mercury is still an acceptable product.[79]

Other exporters' associations have been established in the agricultural field. The Association of Natural Rubber Producing Countries (ANRPC) is one example. It includes Indonesia, Malaysia, Thailand, Singapore, Sri Lanka, and South Vietnam. To iron out price fluctuations, ANRPC members (with South Vietnam not represented) agreed early in May 1975 to reduce exports for 1975 to 2.813 million tons—a reduction of 380,000 tons. The reduction will be effected by setting up an international rubber stockpile with an initial size of 100,000 tons, while member countries will absorb the remaining 280,000 tons through national stockpiles and through production cutbacks.[80]

Other primary producers have also attempted the OPEC approach, for example, the group of coffee producers comprising 38 Latin American and African nations that produce nearly all of the world's coffee. This group met in September 1974 and again in February 1975. Their objective was to halt the decline in green coffee prices, and one of their strategies is a collective cutback in production.[81]

Exporter-Importer Cooperation: The International Tin Agreements

In some cases, group action among exporters is ineffective in the absence of the importers' cooperation. The International Tin Agreements offer an example of a reasonably successful cooperative venture between exporter and importer countries.[82]

The objectives of the tin agreements are manifold. The fourth and fifth agreements, especially, center on the problems of maintaining a balance between world production and consumption, preventing excessive price fluctuation, promoting export earnings, and insuring an adequate supply at prices that are "fair" to consumers and remunerative to producers. Ex-

[79] Staines, "Digesting the Raw Materials Threat," p. 116; and Burrows, in U.S. Congress, *Outlook for Prices and Supplies,* p. 81.

[80] *IMF Survey,* February 3, 1975, p. 43; *Times* (London), May 10, 1975, p. 17; "Rubber Cut Agreed," *Financial Times,* May 10, 1975, p. 9; and "Rubber Producers to Limit Output," *New York Times,* May 10, 1975, p. 41.

[81] "Cartels: Trying to Get Together," *Time,* March 3, 1975, p. 38.

[82] For succinct description see H. W. Allen, executive chairman of ITC, "The International Tin Agreements in Operation, 1956–1975," UNCTAD, April 2, 1975, 30 pp. (TD/TIN.5/4). The author benefited from comments on an earlier draft by P. J. Newman, editor of *Tin International.*

cept for speculators, all parties concerned are interested in reasonable price stability and the security of trade flows: governments of tin exporting and tin importing countries, transnational enterprises, tin miners, smelters, dealers, investors and creditors, industrial users, and consumers.

The International Tin Agreements have covered the periods 1956–1961, 1961–1966, 1966–1971, 1971–1976, and 1976–1981. Membership is open to all exporter and importer countries.[83] Each group has an equal voting power of 1,000 votes in the International Tin Council (ITC), whose functions are the administration and supervision of the agreements. Each tin producing country has five initial votes and an additional number in relation to its share of world production or exports based on a formula set out in the agreement. Similarly, each tin consuming country has five initial votes and an additional number in relation to its share of world consumption or imports. However, under no circumstances can a single country have more than 450 votes. Decisions in the ITC are made in principle by majority vote (a majority of votes cast by producing countries and a majority of votes cast by consuming countries, counted separately), although in practice unanimity is sought. The allocation of votes is revised from time to time to take account of changes in production or consumption, and the accession of new members. The ITC holds regular meetings, at least once every three months, in order to assess the probable demand and supply conditions, and to decide on the activities of its buffer stock, on the desirable price range, and on export controls (see below).

Membership of the Fourth Tin Agreement comprised the tin consuming countries of Austria, Belgium-Luxembourg, Bulgaria, Canada, Czechoslovakia, Denmark, Federal Republic of Germany, France, Hungary, India, Ireland, Italy, Japan, the Netherlands, Poland, Republic of Korea, Romania, Spain, Turkey, the United Kingdom, the USSR, and Yugoslavia; and the tin producing and exporting countries of Australia, Bolivia, Indonesia, Malaysia, Nigeria, Thailand, and Zaire.

The United States, the world's leading industrial country, has continually declined membership in mineral-metal commodity agreements. A

[83] For texts of the agreements, see UNCTAD documents TD/TIN.4/7 of May 1970 and TD/TIN.5/8 of June 1975. The guidelines for such commodity agreements were first set forth in a draft charter for international trade organizations, written under UN auspices in 1946–1947 and recommended to governments in UN resolutions.

principal reason for this policy is its wish to maintain its national independence in matters pertaining to stockpiling and disposal of "strategic" commodities. The U.S. policy of stockpiling was instituted in
1940, and purchases or disposals by the U.S. authorities are not prompted
by considerations of price stability, but by "strategic" considerations of
national security. For example, during the Korean War, large tin purchases by the U.S. authorities for military operations, as well as for the
purposes of adding to their strategic stockpile, pushed prices to high levels. By 1953, U.S. purchases tapered off, leading to a substantial deterioration in the price level, given the "surplus" productive capacity already stimulated by the Korean War and U.S. stockpiling. It was in 1953
that the First International Tin Agreement was negotiated with a view to
remedying the deterioration in prices and its adverse effects; the agreement became operative on July 1, 1956.

Following a downward revision of the stockpile objective, the surplus
of U.S. government tin amounted in September 1962 to 148,310 long
tons, over and above a stockpile objective of 200,000 tons. This surplus
was almost equivalent to one year's world production. A surplus of such
magnitude, if released indiscriminately, could well have wrecked the tin
agreement and slashed tin prices. This would have had disastrous effects
on the tin exporting countries, all of which are developing countries (except Australia) dependent to a significant extent on tin for their export
earnings and employment.

Because of this surplus, the ITC cannot operate successfully without
explicit or at least tacit U.S. cooperation. But in fact, in response to the
anxious demands of the ITC, the U.S. government in October 1966 gave
assurance that its policy was to sell only those surplus amounts which
could be absorbed by regular market channels without avoidable loss to
the U.S. government, without creating serious disruptions in the domestic
economy or in friendly foreign economies, and without affecting adversely investment prospects in tin exploration and production. The government agreed "in principle to moderate its tin sales program if it should
be inconsistent with the contingent operations authorized under the International Tin Agreement." Accordingly, sales by U.S. authorities through
the General Services Administration (GSA) from September 12, 1962,
until mid-1971 totaled 96,987 tons valued at $336 million, with 1964 the
peak year of disposals at 31,150 tons.[84]

[84] See Defense Mobilization Order 8600.1A, "General Policies for Strategic and Critical
Materials Stockpiling," *Federal Register*, December 21, 1968; ITC, *Annual Report for*

Besides the pledge to moderate tin sales, another measure of apparent help—proving later to be short-lived—came on March 28, 1969, when the U.S. Office of Emergency Preparedness (OEP) raised the stockpile objective for tin from 200,000 tons to 232,000 tons, thereby cutting the U.S. surplus from about 57,000 tons to 25,000 tons. However, the surplus was "raised" to a massive figure of 191,500 tons when the OEP revised the stockpile objective downward to 40,500 tons on April 12, 1973. Sales in 1973–1975 reduced the surplus to about 160,000 tons by April 1975. Consequently, it has been argued among officials of tin producing countries that the mere existence of the U.S. strategic stockpile or the threat of disposals was conducive to the creation of a market sentiment favoring lower prices. Indeed, U.S. industrial users can always entertain the possibility of resorting to the stockpile in time of price increases or shortages, a fact which makes them less likely to be eager bidders when prices are high.[85]

The ITC had also reached an understanding in 1958 with the USSR (then not a member) regarding its sizable and irregular shipments, mainly the re-export of output from China. The agreement, valid until the early 1960s, led to a moderation of Soviet sales aimed at protecting tin prices from further deterioration.[86]

Methods of Control

As for the instruments to achieve its objectives, the ITC has three main tools: a price-supporting buffer stock of up to 20,000 metric tons, required solely from exporting countries in cash or metal as determined by the council; export controls to be applied initially for one quarter only, subject to quarterly extensions; and the setting and changing of "optimal" price ranges supported by ITC. The last two instruments are for ultimate recourse, should the buffer stock prove ineffective.

The success of the tin agreements hinges on the judicious operation of the above three instruments. In particular, the effectiveness of the buffer stock "rests mainly on the skill with which it is managed and the amount of flexibility and resources which it can command to deal with sudden

---

1966–1967 (London, 1967), p. 35; U.S. Office of Emergency Preparedness (OEP), *Stockpile Report to the Congress, January–June 1971*, p. 21; and *Report by the International Tin Council* (London, 1968).

[85] "Tin in March 1973," *Mineral Industry Surveys,* May 16, 1973, p. 1.

[86] See IMF-IBRD, *The Problem of Stabilization of Prices of Primary Products* [Washington, 1968], pt. 1, p. 88.

changes in the market situation.'' [87] The buffer stock instrument is preferred because its market impact can be felt directly and rapidly. It also spares producing countries the problems of allocating and enforcing fair quotas.

The use of buffer stock is decided in the following manner. Usually following hard bargaining between the consuming and producing countries, agreement is reached on the floor price at which the buffer stock manager must buy, on a ceiling price at which he must sell, on a middle sector in which he does not usually operate, on a lower sector in which he may buy or sell (provided he is a net buyer), and on an upper sector in which he may sell or buy (provided he is a net seller). If he is a net buyer or a net seller in the upper and lower regions, the manager is not limited to any finite period, thus affording much greater flexibility in his operating terms than were provided under the first three agreements, and providing him with the advantage of hiding his movements more thoroughly from the market.[88]

The council can change the floor and ceiling prices in the light of changing market conditions and consistent with the objectives of the agreement. By special dispensation it can also allow the buffer stock manager to operate—on a cash or forward basis—in the middle sector as well. This undoubtedly gives greater freedom to the manager in stemming fluctuations in prices at an early stage, curbing speculative activity, and phasing out tin sales accumulated in the buffer stock if the tin agreement were not to be renewed at its expiration date.

The LME and the Penang markets (see below) are the forums of action for ITC and the buffer stock manager. On July 4, 1972, the tin council decided to express the floor and ceiling prices which dictate the actions of the buffer stock manager in Malaysian currency per picul, instead of sterling per pound. This conversion followed on the British government's decision of June 23, 1972, to float the pound sterling.[89]

The Fourth Tin Agreement (covering 1971–1976) stipulated that the initial contribution of producer members to the buffer stock of 20,000 tons be the cash equivalent of 7,500 tons (Art. 21), and the remainder as

[87] "The Third International Tin Agreement, 1966–1971: Evaluation of its Effectiveness with Special Reference to Malaysia and Other Producing Countries," *Quarterly Economic Bulletin* (Bank Negara Malaysia), September 1971, p. 137.

[88] See "How the Tin Agreement Works," *Tin International,* November 1971.

[89] See *Tin International,* July 1972, p. 195. One picul is equal to 133⅓ pounds, or 1/16.8 long ton.

and when determined by the council. This came out to £10,135,000 shared in accordance with their respective voting powers. Malaysia's share in the buffer stock was set at 45.02 percent, Bolivia 18.36, Thailand 13.29, Indonesia 11.65, Nigeria 4.86, Zaire 3.93, and Australia 2.89.[90] In the Fifth Agreement (1976–1981), an important change was introduced: it required that cash contributions made after the beginning of the agreement be valued at the prevailing floor price rather than, as under the Fourth Agreement, at the original floor price. Under conditions of general inflation, this change will tend to avoid any shrinkage in the ultimate size of the buffer stock contributions which might otherwise result from likely increases in the floor price during the life of the agreement. ITC can furthermore seek additional financing from banking sources.

The government of the Netherlands, a consumer member, offered in July 1972 to make a voluntary contribution of £670,000, followed by France's contribution of £1,215,000 in January 1973.[91] These are small contributions in comparison to those of such producer countries as Malaysia; nevertheless, they represent a significant move insofar as it is the first time financial support has ever been offered to the buffer stock by consumer countries. The Fifth Agreement provided that voluntary contributions by consuming member countries could reach the equivalent of 20,000 tons (thereby matching the contributions by producing countries); this could be interpreted as a desirable target. The performance of this feature of the agreement will be reviewed after two and a half years by the council, which may decide to call a conference to renegotiate the agreement.

Nevertheless, the fact that the buffer stock has been largely financed by producing LDCs has been a source of dissatisfaction to them. They have argued that "its operations are designed to benefit both producing and consuming countries, by assuring for the former a minimum support price for tin ('floor' price) and the latter a maximum price ('ceiling' price) above which prices will not be allowed to rise so long as the Tin Buffer Stock is able to operate."[92]

Another form of assistance has been provided by the IMF. It agreed in June 1969 to extend assistance to member countries with balance of

[90] For Australia, the percentage is based on exports, not on production, as is the case with the other producing members.
[91] *Tin International,* January 1973.
[92] "Third International Tin Agreement," p. 137.

payments needs in connection with the financing of buffer stocks of primary products established under international commodity agreements. All producer members of ITC (except Australia) are developing countries, and several have already resorted to the IMF financing facility.[93] With this facility, a producing member country may under certain conditions draw up to 50 percent of its quota in the fund for its approved buffer stock contributions. However, its total drawings under both the buffer stock facility and the compensatory financing facility, aimed at protecting against export fluctuations, must not exceed 75 percent of its quota in the fund. Repayment of drawings from the IMF must be made within three to five years, or earlier if the buffer stock distributes cash to its members.

To qualify for drawing on the IMF compensatory and buffer stock financing facilities, a country has to demonstrate a balance of payments need, as defined by the fund. Malaysia has complained that a country "may not have a balance of payments problem, but the need to stabilize its export earnings and export prices may still exist. The country may even be pursuing sound domestic policies and may be adopting measures to prevent the possibility of a balance of payments problem. It is ironic that such a country, which has exercised domestic monetary discipline and has done what the Fund required, is penalized in that it cannot make use of these facilities." [94] Malaysia was later authorized to draw on the fund's buffer financing facility.

The buffer stock manager can be faced with serious limitations on his capacity to intervene, and on occasion be completely powerless. One such occasion could be when he is short of funds—including borrowed funds authorized by the council—to buy tin metal during periods of depressed prices, or when he is short of tin metal to sell during periods of high prices. In fact, the size of the buffer stock required from producer countries (25,400 metric tons in the First Agreement, and 20,000 tons in the others) has declined in relation to world tin trade: from about 20 percent in 1956 to about 13 percent in 1973–1974. From the standpoint of tin producing countries, a larger buffer stock can avoid or moderate the

[93] See, for example, "Malaysia Uses Buffer Stock Financing Facility," in IMF's *International Financial News Survey (IFNS)*, August 18, 1971, p. 269; "Purchases from Fund by Bolivia, Indonesia, and Thailand," *IFNS*, March 1, 1972, p. 60; "Purchase by Nigeria for Buffer Stock Financing," *IFNS*, March 8, 1972, p. 65; and William Fox, "The IMF and the Fourth Tin Agreement," *Tin International*, December 1971, pp. 345–46.

[94] Tan Siew Sin, "Statement by the Governor of the Bank for Malaysia," in IMF, *Summary Proceedings: Annual Meeting, 1971* (Washington, 1971), p. 50.

producers' costs associated with the imposition of export controls when prices are depressed (see below), and can iron out price fluctuations more effectively, thereby stabilizing export earnings and improving the commercial attractiveness of tin vis-à-vis substitutes. From the standpoint of tin importing countries, a larger buffer stock can check speculative price increases and defend the ceiling price more effectively, thereby providing importers with greater supply security and predictable prices. It would also serve importers by inducing them to cut down on private commercial stocks and the cost of keeping them.[95]

Available evidence suggests that the management of ITC's buffer stock has generally been run properly. There was, however, one publicly known occasion in May 1975 when the executive chairman of ITC (H. W. Allen of Australia) had to remove the buffer stock manager (R. T. Adnan of Indonesia) and his deputy (J. M. Bueno of Bolivia); the two were later to "resign." Allen's reported reason was to avert a situation nearing "chaos." [96]

If the buffer stock proves ineffective in countering price weaknesses, ITC can then resort to export control. Export control cannot, however, be instituted unless the buffer stock holdings have already exceeded the 5,000-ton mark. During control periods the maximum level of national stocks each producing country may hold in accordance with the Fourth Agreement is roughly equivalent to three months export supply.

The formula devised by the ITC for the allocation of export quotas—and consequently production quotas since permissible stocks cannot exceed 25 percent of productive capacity—does not command the unreserved approval of all parties concerned. Formulas, no matter how sophisticated they are, are bound to contain rigidities. In the case of the ITC formula, the total permissible amount allocated to each member country for a control period is based on the percentage of votes held by that country for that period: that percentage is itself based on average production over the most recent period, usually the year preceding an export control period. This system completely overlooks, among several other

---

[95] UNCTAD, *Discussion of International Measures—Preparation of an International Tin Agreement: Some Policy Issues,* Note by the Secretary-General of UNCTAD, Geneva, April 11, 1975, p. 3 (TD/TIN.5/3).

[96] See, for example, "Resignations of 2 Int'l Tin Council Executives Accepted," *Japan Times,* July 6, 1975, p. 10; see also "Tin Trade Galvanized by Shock Suspension," *Guardian,* May 10, 1975, p. 13; and "Tin Council Suspends Buffer Stock Chiefs," *Times* (London), May 10, 1975, p. 17.

important economic factors, existent and potential reserves and the relative costs of working tin deposits in each member country. Thus a country with a relatively low recent production level but potentially large low-cost reserves and a current rapid growth rate would suffer under this production control system, in comparison with a low-reserve and high-cost producing country whose exports are falling off. Brazil, an example of the first type, refused to join the ITC because it did not want to be restricted by export quotas. Bolivia, by comparison, belongs to the second category. Table 6 shows that the Corporacion Minera de Bolivia (Comibol), the Bolivian state-owned tin mining company, has had substantial net losses, mainly in 1961–1964.[97]

Table 6. The economics of Bolivian tin (Comibol, 1961–1971)

Year	Cost of production ($ per pound)	London cash price ($ per pound)	$ Profit
1961	1.44	1.11	−12,720,867
1962	1.46	1.12	−14,977,811
1963	1.49	1.14	−12,987,079
1964	1.64	1.55	−5,996,108
1965	1.69	1.77	160,342
1966	1.42	1.62	8,197,222
1967	1.47	1.50	1,424,974
1968	1.34	1.42	4,780,071
1969	1.34	1.55	9,340,267
1970	1.47	1.67	8,097,121
1971 *	1.58	1.58	−46,005

* January–March only.
Source: U.S. Bureau of Mines, *Mineral Trade Notes*, November 1971, pp. 37–38.

The ITC formula for allocating export quotas has, however, the merit of being simple and workable (since it is confined to a single objectively definable factor, namely recent past production), although it overlooks a number of other economic variables such as the cost of producing tin and the size of commercially producible reserves. The ITC formula has also the pragmatic advantage of avoiding the elusive concepts of "ability to bear sacrifices," "fairness," or "potentialities." With respect to the cost

[97] Some sources felt that Brazil's tin reserves were about equal to those of all ITC producer countries put together. See *The Guardian,* October 14, 1971; and *Mining Journal,* March 17, 1972. See also "Comibol Back in Deficit," *Tin International,* January 1972, pp. 13–14.

of instituting price-production controls in the tin industry, the burden is normally shared by producing countries, to the extent that contributions to buffer stocks are required solely from them, and by consumer countries, to the extent that they tolerate higher prices than would otherwise obtain in a free market.

Though simple and workable, the ITC control system has had negative results when exports and consequently production have been cut back severely. The impact "might take the form of abandoned, half-mined tin deposits due to the production cutback, leading to waste; the spoilation of fixed capital equipment in the tin mining industry which might involve irreparable damage if the restriction was severe and carried on for a sufficiently long period; and a decline in employment and income." [98] The costly process of rehabilitation of laid-off mines, once demand picks up and production controls are removed, is borne by operators in one group of countries—the producers—unless such costs are shifted onto tin using industries in consuming countries as well.

The challenge of the administrators of the tin agreement is to apply production control with knowledge and skill as a last resort, and to use moderation and appropriate timing. A much larger buffer stock could considerably reduce the need for tin export control, and avoid the latter's costs connected with the shutdown and rehabilitation of mines. Resorting to export controls could be further reduced by long-range planning of imports and the related commitments of importers. This would help producers make appropriate and timely adjustments in their production capacity.

An innovation was added to the Fifth Agreement with respect to export controls in periods of shortages. Whereas under previous agreements, member consumer countries did not have purchasing preference over nonmember consumer countries, the Fifth Agreement provided that "preference as regards the supply of tin available shall be given to consuming countries which participate in this Agreement" (Art. 40).

The third method is the use of price ranges, which were already mentioned. The ITC has to show much wisdom in appraising economic and other trends in order to set the supporting price ranges, changing them in response to fundamental shifts in supply and demand conditions and not in response to seasonal or cyclical fluctuations. Realistic price ranges can

---

[98] "Third International Tin Agreement," p. 139.

avoid draining the tin resources of the buffer stock by selling tin at the ceiling price when this is too low, or exhausting the cash resources of the buffer stock by buying tin at a floor price fixed too high.

The tin buffer stock has been able to alleviate short-term fluctuations in demand and supply, but its resources have been too limited to enable it to counter cyclical fluctuations of demand. This situation called for changing the price ranges more frequently than would have been otherwise the case in the presence of a larger buffer stock. Moreover, the tin agreement is more effective in dealing with a "surplus" situation than with a deficit one largely because production cuts are more readily enforceable than production increases, which require a gestation period of several months or even several years (up to three), depending on the method of production used.

It further appears that tin producing countries are more biased toward higher price ranges than consuming countries. As one Malaysian source said: "As far as the producing countries are concerned, it would be difficult for them to accept any downward revision in the supporting price ranges even if these were unrealistically high at a particular moment of time because it would be difficult to obtain the consent of consuming countries to raise them again if market prices should increase subsequently." [99]

Industry Characteristics

Tin is primarily used in tin plating (about 45 percent), most of which goes into steel cans. The other uses are alloys (such as solder, babbitt, and bronze) and chemicals. Intense research is going on in industrial countries to produce cheaper and long-term substitutes for tin. Already there has been a notable reduction in the use of tin in alloys, and of tin in the per unit area of tinplate. Moreover, significant inroads have been made by more economical substitutes such as aluminum, plastics, and tin-free steel. This explains the moderate size of the rise in the world consumption of primary tin metal: it averaged 200,000 tons in 1972–1973 against 160,000 tons in 1927–1931.

With respect to supply, the world's known commercial deposits of tin ore are limited. They are largely concentrated in eight countries. Over 85 percent of the world production of processed tin ore, known as tin-in-concentrates, has come from the developing producer members of ITC.

[99] *Ibid.,* p. 140.

The more promising areas of production are in the Far East and Central Latin America. Commercial reserves are believed to be large in Brazil, Malaysia, Thailand, Indonesia, and China. Production costs are highest in Bolivia, followed by Nigeria.

There is also secondary recovery of tin metal from scrap in several tin consuming countries. The amount of secondary tin metal is not always a small percentage of the production of primary metal. In the United States, for example, secondary consumption has represented about 28 to 30 percent of total tin consumption; [100] and in a few countries such as Austria and Norway, secondary tin metal assumes even larger proportions.

The production and consumption of tin have been known to diverge frequently, with significant surpluses and shortages. These imbalances can be partly explained by the fact that changes in world consumption have not been uniform over the years, and by the fact that certain miners overrespond to price changes. This situation can be seen in the increases in tin mining units or in investment expenditures—particularly in leading producing countries such as Malaysia, Bolivia, and Thailand—once demand and prices increase. Such an overresponse in productive capacity and actual production leads to surpluses and sharp price falls, that is, under open, unregulated market conditions. And sustained price weakness eventually causes the abandonment of marginal mines and the cancellation or deferment of expansion programs.

Not only is there an overresponse of tin producers to developments in the market situation and in particular to price changes, but that response has a protracted impact. Such a situation was acknowledged by an unpublished report of the Department of Mineral Resources in Thailand:

A sharp increase is to be noted for the year 1965 in which the production rose to 19,047 long tons metal content, 22% greater than that of the preceding year. Apart from growing practice in general, the increase is due to the abrupt [*sic*] increase in the number of operating mines which, in turn, is affected by high and stable price of tin in that particular year. In spite of declining price level in 1966, production of tin in Thailand still rose to make a new record at 22,565 long tons metal content. The increase reveals, partly, that the effect of the high [*sic*] price of tin remains upon the level of tin production.

Indeed, owing to the physical conditions of extractive ventures, the pressure to produce once investments have been incurred, the need to pay

[100] V. Anthony Cammarota, Jr., "Tin," in U.S. Bureau of Mines, *Minerals Yearbook, 1971* (Washington, 1972), vol. 1.

creditors, the fear of abandoning the mine lest restarting costs turn out to be excessive due to flooding in rainy countries—all these factors make tin miners continue operating their economically marginal mines as long as they are covering their variable costs. Some may even increase production, at least for a period, in a price-declining market, in the hope of maintaining their sales proceeds by making the increased production compensate for the loss in receipts per unit, and in the hope that prices might soon recover.

As with other metals, mining of tin ore is conducted by both private and state enterprises. In the leading tin producing country of the world, Malaysia, production is controlled by the private sector, since the Malaysian state corporation Pernas is a newcomer. In the first half of the 1970s, there were over one thousand mines in operation, including a few large units (about sixty) using dredges, and the balance, smaller units mostly using gravel pumps. The share of production of dredges was close to a third.[101] The majority of the dredging units were owned or controlled by European concerns, whereas the gravel-pumping units were owned and run by Malaysians (largely from the Chinese community).

In Bolivia, the second largest tin producer, close to two-thirds of the tin mining production is controlled by the state enterprise Comibol. The balance is produced by two foreign concerns and several hundred small native miners who, by reason of their small production volumes, export their tin concentrates through Banco Minero de Bolivia.

In Thailand, the third largest producer, the industry is largely in the hands of the private sector. The country's sole smelter in 1974, the Thailand Smelting and Refining Company (Thaisarco), was a 40,000-ton plant jointly owned by three partners: two transnational concerns, Union Carbide (U.S.) and N. V. Billiton (a subsidiary of Shell), and the Thai government. The two foreign partners had extensive joint mining interests in Thailand and a joint sales company based in Switzerland.[102]

In Indonesia, the tin industry prior to 1967 was completely state-owned

---

[101] A dredge floats on an artificial pond and digs up the tin-bearing material with steel buckets, then processes the tin ore into tin-in-concentrates, discarding unwanted materials. The gravel pumps operate in open-cast mines which use powerful jets of water to break down tin-bearing gravel which is then lifted by the pumps. Production figures are from *Tin News* (Malayan Tin Bureau, Washington), 1970–1974 issues.

[102] "Thailand Looks for Growth," *Tin International,* August 1971, pp. 219–20; and "Billiton Moves In: International Giant Enters Thai Tin Industry," *Investor* (Bangkok), October 10, 1971, p. 845.

and run. Three foreign firms, N. V. Billiton, Broken Hill Proprietary of Australia, and P. T. Koba Tin of Malaysia, were awarded prospecting contracts on July 6, 1968, May 29, 1971, and October 17, 1971, respectively.[103] In Zaire, the major tin mining venture is Zairetain which is 50 percent owned by the government.

The international tin mining industry is largely dominated by a few companies controlling certain strategic sectors of the industry, notably mining, smelting, or distribution. Tin plating itself is controlled by "a few producers and exporters of tinplate [that] are regulated by a 'tinplate export club', which include arrangements for market sharing between tinplate exporters in their export markets." [104]

Leading tin mining and smelting companies are: London Tin Corporation which controls through Anglo-Oriental large segments of private tin mining in Malaysia, Thailand, Nigeria, and Australia; the Patino Mining Corporation, majority owner (70.3 percent) of Consolidated Tin Smelters, which controls (50.5 percent) Eastern Smelting in Malaysia and has mining interests in various producing countries; Anglo-American Corporation (AAC) of South Africa, and Billiton of the Netherlands.

Regarding the feature of vertical integration, it is estimated that tin operators are less vertically integrated than the transnational oil or aluminum companies. Indeed, a large portion of the operators produce concentrates only. Nevertheless, one sees a trend towards vertical integration or other link-up between industrial tin users and producers. A strategy of vertical integration has appealed to several major users of tin which have acquired tin production rights (for example, W. R. Grace, U.S. Steel, and Lockheed in Bolivia) with a view to meeting their requirements directly.

The fact that there are large numbers of independent and unorganized operators at the mining stage has significant price implications. This permits a quasi–free competition market on the tin supplying side whether supplies are disposed of in Penang, Malaysia, in London, in New York, or elsewhere. Such market structure on the supply side offers greater scope for oligopsonistic bargaining on the part of the few large buyers (mostly the smelters and the steel companies). In fact, the president of the States of Malaya Chamber of Mines publicly stated that the traditional

---

[103] *Tin International,* April 1973, p. 123.
[104] IBRD, *Documents Listed in Annex to the Report of the Executive Directors on the Stabilization of Prices of Primary Products,* sec. 1, *Tin* (Washington, 1969), p. 4.

few (not exceeding fifteen) large U.S. buyers of Malaysian tin metal had attempted to exploit their market position, and had resorted to "a concerted effort to hold down tin prices" in the latter part of 1970.[105] The tin agreement does not cope with the restrictive market practices buyers or sellers may use.

Price Systems

Prices are of crucial importance to the developing tin exporting countries to the extent that export earnings, tax revenues, and the prospects of production and employment are dependent on them. Accordingly, exporting countries are greatly concerned with the mechanisms of setting prices and with the scope they may have in influencing them. There are two main so-called free markets for tin, one in Penang and the other in London. The Penang market is used by ITC's buffer stock manager and its prices serve to determine the taxable income of Malaysian and Thai tin mines. Indonesia depends mostly on negotiated prices for its tin exports.[106] Bolivia, Nigeria, and Zaire rely for large portions of their exports on LME prices.

Penang has long been the major tin exporting port of the world. Sales of the Malacca Straits–quality tin metal (approximately 99.9 percent purity) are effected daily by two smelting companies: the Straits Trading Company and Sharikat Eastern Smelting. The quantity sold by each company is in the neighborhood of 3,000 tons per month and comes from their purchases of tin ore (with tin content ranging from 48 to 77.5 percent) from over one thousand mining units, mostly in Malaysia.

Represented by their agents in Penang, international buyers of tin submit written bids to the two smelters at about 10 A.M. every working day, specifying tonnage and the price per picul. On the basis of these bids the managers of the two companies, working "very closely together" according to one Malaysian official interviewed by the author, determine by noon the price at which the daily tonnage available for sale can be completely cleared. Bids submitted by noon at and above this price are accepted by the two smelters up to the limit of tonnage available; bids

[105] Address by O. L. Gray before the States of Malaya Chamber of Mines, May 27, 1971, reprinted in *Mining Journal,* June 4, 1971, pp. 460–62.

[106] Negotiated prices for Indonesian tin were, in 1969, higher than world market prices on sales reaching some 5,000 tons of tin metal exported to the U.S. Other buyers were German, Dutch, and Soviet concerns. See *Notes on Tin* (ITC), March 1969, p. 2216.

below this price are rejected. The following is an example of a day's bidding:

M$ per picul	Eastern Smelting	Straits Trading
At Market	5 tons	—
625	—	50 tons
623	45 tons	—
621	—	25 tons
619	100 tons	—
618	100 tons	—

Total orders come to 325 tons. But assume that there are only 235 tons offered for sale on that date. Therefore all orders down to and including the M$619 bid would be filled in full, and 10 tons only of the 100-ton bid at the M$618 price would be filled. The price announced for that day would be M$618, and sales to all successful bidders would be made at this one price.[107]

The metal is guaranteed to be physically available to buyers "within two months" of the transaction. In practice, it takes about 15 to 25 days to deliver the metal, which is equivalent to the period required to smelt the tin ore delivered by miners on the day of sale. Payment by buyers is made on the day of delivery of metal at the smelter. Extra charges cover weighing, marking, and moving tin outside of the smelter plus other charges for port, lighterage, and wharfage. This, for the ultimate buyer, excludes the cost of local representation which covers services of handling bids and purchases, arranging for shipments for customs clearance, exchange control documentation, negotiation of bank drafts, and so forth.

In discussions with certain government officials, the author learned that the few big buyers of tin metal can exert a downward pressure on the so-called free market of Penang by operating in concert (formally through a buying syndicate) or informally (for example, through patronizing a single agent in Penang) and pooling bids to offer lower prices.

Across the ocean, the LME is the leading open exchange available for some metals: copper, lead, silver, tin, and zinc. Yet less than 10 percent of its transactions represent physical movements of metal. The balance consists largely of arbitrage and hedging operations by dealers and fabricators, and of speculation.[108] One should add that speculation at the LME

---

[107] See *Notes on Tin,* January 1965, p. 1456, reprinted from *American Metal Market,* November 9, 1964.

[108] Information from Pechiney given to the author in 1972.

increases along with the growing availability of short-term money, which can be manipulated to gain from price variations on the commodity markets, and from inflation or possible changes in the parities of leading currencies. In June 1971 it was recognized that the LME and New York markets had for some time been much under the influence of speculators. The relative diminution of "physical" business in copper and tin in favor of speculation was attributed to the economic recession in the United States in 1970–1971. The LME board has as a result deplored "irresponsible speculation" with its long-term adverse impact on the image and prestige of the exchange. Nevertheless, the LME price level for traded metals reflects on average more than any other price the competitive forces of supply and demand.[109]

Criticism of LME centers around the fact that prices have daily fluctuations and weekly or monthly cycles, thus creating inconveniences and added costs to consumers and producers, who are alike concerned with reducing uncertainty in their future plans. Many of these fluctuations, and especially the daily ones, are not justifiable in terms of underlying changes in supply and demand conditions. These fluctuations happen because the market's turnover is low and the users of the market have overreacted to false reports, to rumors, or to currency speculation. Tin has been used by speculators hedging against currency uncertainties largely because of its high value among the openly traded base metals, its inelastic supply, and the price supporting operations of the International Tin Agreements. Other important factors of price instability are changes in the level of industrial activity in major consuming countries, releases (actual or intimated) of stockpile tin by the U.S. authorities, transport problems, labor unrest, and political instability in producing countries.[110] It is claimed that the LME price level is over the long term broadly related to that of Penang, with due allowance for freight, time lags, financing charges, insurance, and the action of speculators.

The New York tin market is an over-the-counter market. It is the outcome of telephone calls made by the tin editor of the daily *American Metal Market* (*AMM*) to dealers asking them about their willingness to sell or buy, and at what price. Prices represent offering levels at which

[109] See *Copper Market,* 4th quarter 1971, p. 4; and *Mining Journal,* June 25, 1971, p. 518.
[110] The Economist, Intelligence Unit Ltd., *The London Metal Exchange* (London, 1958), pp. 167, 169; and "Third International Tin Agreement," p. 136.

dealers are willing to sell to other dealers. Some dealers have different prices for regular industrial users, often at discounts from listed prices.[111]

Parallel to the "free" markets, there are "managed" markets for tin—as is the case with crude oil, bauxite-alumina, iron ore, and other primary commodities. In the latter markets, producers list prices at which they are willing to sell, and change them in response to their judgement of market forces. The practice of producer price listing has offered a certain measure of stability. This has most probably been at the expense of sensitivity and quick response to changing balances of supply and demand.

Statistical evidence shows that the International Tin Agreements have had a noted effect on moderating price fluctuations as compared with other nonferrous base metals—copper, lead, and zinc—which are not governed by international commodity agreements. A study to this effect was conducted by the ITC, and the coefficient of variation between the monthly average price was calculated for each metal for the years 1950–1970. Results show that before the introduction of the First International Tin Agreement in mid-1956, there was a much wider variation of tin prices than later. Copper, lead, and zinc have all shown greater variation than tin.[112]

But is the success of ITC to be measured solely with respect to stabilizing prices in real terms at a given rising level, regardless of adverse impact on growth of tin consumption? Those who consider growth of consumption at lower prices more desirable than higher price levels with lower consumption feel the ITC pricing policy has stultified the development of tin, and has enabled substitutes (synthetics and aluminum, among others) to capture larger shares of the packaging business.[113]

[111] *Notes on Tin,* January 1965, pp. 1457–59, reprinted from *American Metal Market,* November 16, 1964.

[112] Lead and zinc have an International Study Group which includes all major consumer and producer countries of market and socialist economies, and government delegates work very closely with industry advisers. Production and consumption figures, including forecasts, are prepared by the Secretariat on the basis of reports by member countries. Plans for closing mines and smelters and for exporting are readily made available, and solutions to specific problems are suggested. Although the study group does not have a mechanism for direct market interventions as provided for in the International Tin Agreements, the non-American private zinc producers are organized into a cartel. They have successfully maintained a producer-nominated price system since 1964. See also Burrows, in U.S. Congress, *Outlook for Prices and Supplies,* p. 87; and *Notes on Tin,* April 1971, pp. 3735–36.

[113] See, for example, IBRD, *Tin,* pp. 17–19.

The International Tin Agreements have yet to address themselves to developmental aspects affecting tin exporting countries. These countries need the cooperation of major tin importing countries to permit the establishment of processing, smelting, and fabricating facilities for tin products. Such cooperation could come through the elimination or reduction of tariff barriers in the developed countries, and through the transfer of appropriate know-how and technology at reasonable terms. The developed tin importing countries have so far even declined to contribute funds to the International Tin Research Council, whose aim is to promote the consumption of tin.[114]

This chapter has shown that cooperation among exporters of primary commodities (to the exclusion of importers) has had its serious limitations. This is largely due to the presence of competing sources and substitutes, and the noncooperation of major industrial countries. Under the circumstances which the LDCs face, the support of the major importer countries is crucial. Such support exists in the case of tin. Viewing it from the angle of international cooperation, the International Tin Agreements can therefore be considered reasonably successful over their twenty years of operation. During that period sovereign governments of producing and consuming countries have learned to work together towards the task of harmonizing their interests in a basic commodity. Obstacles to cooperation in the tin industry have existed and will continue to exist, but these governments have developed the talent of getting along and have achieved their minimum objective, the ironing out of short-term price fluctuations.

Industrially developed countries which import raw materials will continue to counter the unbridled collective actions of primary producing countries aimed at maximizing gain. One approach developed countries will continue to use is to join producers in commodity groups (like ITC) to moderate producers' demands for larger gains. Another approach is to counter exporter groups (such as OPEC) with importer groups (such as the OECD International Energy Agency). A third approach is to devise a stockpiling or reserve capacity system aimed at cushioning supply shortages. Commending the last approach and chiding developing mineral-exporting countries, a U.S. Interior Department planner said: ''What the

[114] See UNCTAD, *Discussion of International Measures,* pp. 9–10.

stockpile has provided is tremendous bargaining power for this country in the international sphere. With it, you don't let these bandits hold you up."[115] But even though LDC primary producers are wary of the industrial countries' countervailing power which could frustrate their endeavors, many LDCs are encouraged by the achievements of their commodity groups, and will continue in these efforts.

[115] Richard J. Levine, "America's Dependence on Imported Metal Seen Leading to New Crisis," *Wall Street Journal,* December 26, 1973, p. 7.

4. Policy Issues and Suggestions

The disputes between businesses and governments generally focus on a few policy issues of significance. These include development financing and foreign investments insurance, and the problems of, and opportunities for, accommodating foreign investments with a host country's perception of its sovereignty and developmental priorities. They also include the problems of interruptions in resource flows, and the mobilization and effective transfer of key information to LDCs.

Development Funds and Investment Insurance

As explained by one senior U.S. official: "The World Bank and the regional banks are important, but they are the chosen instruments of the rich nations, not of the poor." And according to a scholar and Canadian diplomat who served the World Bank as a senior official for several years: "The World Group is now a very unequal partnership between the rich and the low-income countries." He noted that in April 1973, nationals of rich countries held 68 of the top 80 positions in the management and staff of the bank and its affiliate, the International Development Association (IDA). Only 10 came from the low-income member countries, and 2 from middle-income members. He acknowledged that the advice of the bank group would be sounder and more effective if the governments and nationals of low-income countries had more influence in shaping the bank's policies and programs.[1]

---

[1] Charles W. Yost, chief U.S. delegate to the United Nations (1968–1971), "Growing Sentiment for Isolationism," *Washington Post,* November 7, 1971, p. B6; Escott Reid, "McNamara's World Bank," *Foreign Affairs,* July 1973, pp. 794–810; and Reid, "The World Bank Group: An Unequal Partnership," *Cooperation Canada,* November–December 1973, pp. 15–21. Parts of this chapter are taken from Zuhayr Mikdashi, "Policy Issues in Primary Industries," *Vanderbilt Journal of Transnational Law,* vol. 7, 1974, p. 281. Reprinted by permission.

And the support of rich nations to the World Bank Group has not been unswerving. For example, early in 1974 the U.S. House of Representatives rejected a 9 percent increase, in real terms, of its contribution to IDA. The president of the World Bank called this action "an unmitigated disaster for hundreds of millions of people in the poorest nations of the world." [2]

Even among the few developing countries with financial resources larger than the opportunities for domestic investment, some private citizens, enterprises, and government agencies have channeled substantial amounts of their surplus resources into the developed countries. It is difficult to estimate the size of financial resources held by LDC nationals and agents in the developed money and capital markets, but estimates for oil exporting countries in 1975 reached several billion dollars.

On the other hand, one leading example of long-term credit offered by a developing country to other developing countries is that of the state-owned Kuwait Fund for Arab Economic Development (KFAED), established at the time of Kuwait's independence in 1961.[3] KFAED's capital resources were raised to $3.45 billion in 1974, and were made available to *all* developing countries. Another developing country, Abu Dhabi, created a similar fund in July 1971; its capital amounted in 1974 to $500 million. In 1974 Saudi Arabia and Iraq created their own development funds, with authorized capital of $2.8 billion and $170 million respectively.

In addition, regional developmental funds or banks conceived and owned by several developing countries have increased in number and in resource with the growth of surplus funds available to a number of LDCs. These include the Arab Fund for Economic and Social Development (capital $1.3 billion), the Arab International Bank for External Trade and Development £30 million), the Arab Investment Company ($200 million), the Arab Company for Petroleum Investments (capital $1.035 billion), the Arab Bank for Economic Development in Africa ($231 million), and the Arab Support Fund for African Countries ($200 million), aimed at reducing the burden of the 1973–1974 oil price increases.[4]

[2] "Statement by Robert S. McNamara," IDA press release, January 24, 1974.

[3] See Abdelatif Y. Al-Hamad, *Financing Arab Economic Development: The Experience of the Kuwait Fund,* KFAED, May 1972; and Ibrahim Shihata, *The Kuwait Fund for Arab Economic Development: A Legal Analysis,* KFAED, 1973, pp. 7, 8.

[4] Ibrahim Shihata, "Arab Institutions for Developmental Financing," paper (in Arabic) offered at National Institute for Administration and Development, Beirut, June 1975, 32 pp. (typescript).

Several developing countries, notably the leading oil exporting countries, have offered aid to existing international organizations, mainly the World Bank, the IMF, and to a lesser extent to other specialized UN agencies. Several of the oil exporting countries have also offered substantial financial assistance through bilateral arrangements. In fact, estimates of their effectively disbursed aid in 1974 show that it exceeded 10 percent of their Gross National Product (GNP) on the average. Commitments were three times as much. Aid given by the developed countries of the OECD group was, by comparison, about 0.3 percent of their GNP. The discrepancy would appear larger in favor of oil exporting countries if oil revenues were treated as part income and part capital. Indeed, there are computational problems in measuring the GNP of mineral-producing countries. Some writers consider that current GNP estimates are inflated, to the extent that the production of mineral deposits represents for a large part the monetization of a capital asset. In his September 1974 address to the World Bank Board of Governors, President McNamara suggested a 30 percent depletion factor—a figure considered too low by the Kuwait Fund, which likened the current GNP accounting of oil revenues to the situation of "a man who, forced to sell his house on instalments, is being persuaded that his receipts are a sort of income." [5]

Notwithstanding these assessment problems, oil exporting countries' aid in the 1970s was substantial and varied. Venezuela was especially innovative in its aid to other developing countries. On December 14, 1974, at the closing of a conference among the president of Venezuela and the presidents of five Central American countries (Guatemala, Nicaragua, El Salvador, Costa Rica, and Panama), Venezuela agreed to underwrite coffee sales by the Central American republics. A special fund of up to $80 million was created to finance the stockpiling of Central American coffee beans. In the 1974–1975 harvest, 590,000 bags (of 132 pounds each) were to be retained in the stockpile, the equivalent of 10 percent of the 1973–1974 harvest. The fund was to operate through certificates of deposit equaling 27 cents for each pound of coffee held back, until the "equitable" price of 60 cents a pound is reached in the world market.

Another innovative aspect of Venezuelan aid concerns the financing of

[5] See Abdelatif Y. Al-Hamad, Director-General of KFAED, "Towards a Reassessment of the Recycling Problem," address to the Royal Institute of International Affairs, Chatham House, London, April 1975, reprinted in *Arab Oil and Gas* (Beirut), August 1975, pp. 22–30; also "Petro-Aid Takes Off," *Economist,* February 15, 1975, pp. 72–73.

Venezuelan oil sales. The Central American countries will pay only $6 per barrel for Venezuelan oil, about half the market price. The difference between the purchase price and the market price will be deposited, in the form of a loan by Venezuela, in the central bank of each country and in that country's national currency, to be used for development programs.

In addition, Venezuela offered a fifteen-year $40 million line of credit to the Central American Bank for Economic Integration, half in dollars and half in bolivares, to be paid back in the same currencies. The interest charge was 8 percent.[6]

Distribution of aid among developing countries has not necessarily followed the criteria of need or development opportunities. Indian Prime Minister Indira Gandhi complained that not enough was done by oil exporting countries to rescue countries like hers, which as a result of oil price increases suffered serious reverses in its balance of payments and development programs. Since the Indian government supported oil price increases by LDC host governments as a method of remedying exploitation and recuperating concessionaires' excess profits, Gandhi expected in exchange to receive aid and the investment of petro-dollars in mutually beneficial projects. OPEC countries did not generally consider a two-tier price system in favor of developing countries an acceptable alternative to financial aid, since such dual pricing would leave loopholes and lead to black marketing.[7]

Another source of aid is the Revolving Fund for Natural Resources Exploration, recommended by the UN Economic and Social Council (ECOSOC) and established on December 17, 1973. The fund is supported by voluntary contributions, and its financial resources will be replenished from the proceeds of successful exploration projects at a uniform rate of 2

[6] See Norman Gall, "The Challenge of Venezuelan Oil," *Foreign Policy,* Spring 1975, p. 51; "Coffee Price Stability Also Is Aim: Venezuela Offers Cheap Oil as Aid to Central Americans," *International Herald Tribune,* December 17, 1974, p. 4; and "Venezuela, Central American Countries Boost Cooperation at Historic Meeting," *Japan Times,* July 5, 1975, p. B2. For the advisability of setting up international stocks of commodities, see UNCTAD, *The Role of International Commodity Stocks,* and *A Common Fund for the Financing of Commodity Stocks,* Report by the Secretary-General of UNCTAD, Geneva (TD/B/C.1/166/Supp. 1, and TD/B/C.1/166/Supp. 2).

[7] Interview of Indira Gandhi by *Al-Nahar* (Beirut Arabic daily), April 29, 1975, pp. 11, 13. A small quantity of Saudi oil was reportedly sold at about $1 per barrel below the price paid by the majors. See *Business Week,* December 7, 1974, p. 44. Libya also sold oil to Malta at below market prices as part of its aid program. See *Alam An-Naft* ("World Oil"— Beirut *Arabic weekly*), August 23, 1975, p. 9.

percent of the gross sale value at the mine, for a period of fifteen years from the start of commercial production.[8]

Developing countries were generally in favor of the fund, and within one month of its establishment twelve LDCs indicated potential projects. The fund, however, started in February 1975 with only modest resources of $5.4 million. Several developed countries, including the USSR (with large potential natural resources itself), were quite reserved about helping establish the fund.[9]

Aid and development credits, whether provided by developed or developing countries, are not always prompted by pure altruism. For example, Kuwait has used loans to neighboring Arab countries partly as a means of winning friends and of averting territorial ambitions. Iraq, which laid claim to all of Kuwait in 1961, reluctantly relinquished its claim in 1964 and became (along with other Arab countries) a major beneficiary of Kuwaiti credits.

Obviously the challenge of development calls for novel approaches and new financial institutions to meet the growing and evolving problems of poverty. One such institution may well be an interregional Third World Bank (TWB), largely owned and financed by nationals and governments of LDCs which have surplus financial resources. Its function would be to service eligible LDCs worldwide.

In order to encourage the flow of financial resources and venture capital among developing nations, institutional frameworks aimed at resolving disputes, or at insuring risks not normally covered by commercial underwriters, are needed. With respect to insuring expatriate firms for their investments, bilateral or multilateral arrangements could be set up. In fact, most developed market economy countries have bilateral insurance arrangements against so-called political risk losses sustained by their firms: such losses may arise from currency inconvertibility, expropriation, or damages from war, revolution, or insurrection. Multinational investment insurance is currently under revived consideration, including an

---

[8] *United Nations Revolving Fund For Natural Resources Exploration,* Report by the Secretary-General, New York, April 8, 1974, art. 20, p. 6 (DP/53).

[9] See *The United Nations Revolving Fund For Natural Resources Exploration,* Report of the Secretary-General, New York, February 13, 1975, pp. 2–3 (E/C.7/54); and UN, ECOSOC, Committee on Natural Resources, *Report on the Third Session,* New Delhi, February 6–17, 1973, Supplement no. 4, p. 16.

international attempt spearheaded by the IBRD and based on an earlier project.[10]

The U.S. government has been a leader in insuring private U.S. investments in LDCs since 1948. It institutionalized this insurance function with the creation of a specialized corporation called Overseas Private Investment Corporation (OPIC) on January 19, 1971. According to its legislative charter, OPIC's insurance is available to new investments by private U.S. enterprises in friendly LDCs. The latter was interpreted to include East European countries (for example, Romania and Yugoslavia). The investment project should be commercially sound, be beneficial to the host country, and earn the approval of the U.S. government and host country authorities.[11]

With a view to broadening its insurance basis, OPIC successfully negotiated with Lloyd's of London to reinsure its insurance liabilities. These amounted early in 1974 to $920 million for inconvertibility, $2.5 billion for expropriation, and $2.1 billion for war risks, and covered U.S. investments in some 90 developing countries. Lloyd's agreed in 1974 to pay 45 percent of any valid claim of first losses, up to a maximum of $18,225,000 per country and $54,765,000 annually worldwide.[12]

Not only did the state-owned OPIC reinsure with Lloyd's of London, it placed another large part of its expropriation insurance liability with a group of transnational underwriters. In that group was the Soviet Union's majority-owned Black Sea and Baltic Insurance Company, registered in the United Kingdom as a subsidiary of Ingosstrakh, the Soviet state insurance agency. OPIC's president noted that "it is the first time that an arm of the USSR government has supported the United States government in insuring U.S. private investment overseas. We hope this is the beginning of similar mutually satisfactory arrangements between our two countries." This was an important shift in the policy of Moscow and a departure from its Marxist economic philosophy. In the words of an Indian trade journal, "The meaning of the Russian decision to underwrite American investment is this: Whenever a developing country nationalizes a

---

[10] IBRD, *Multinational Investment Insurance: A Staff Report* (Washington, 1962).

[11] *Topics* (OPIC), vol. 2, no. 2, May 1973, pp. 1, 2, 4; and *Foreign Assistance Act of 1969,* Public Law 91–175, 91st Cong., H.R. 14580, December 30, 1969.

[12] OPIC press releases TS/258 and TS/268, January 24 and March 21, 1974, respectively.

firm without paying adequate compensation it is not only the western firm but the Soviet Union, as an insurer, who would also be a loser." [13] The Soviet move should be viewed as one element in the nexus of detente between the U.S. and the USSR.

U.S. and European transnational companies, which are eligible for their own national insurance programs, favor multilateral insurance schemes. The president of Anaconda has argued that these would "help stimulate and encourage such needed investments [in less stable areas]." It could make "unfair and discriminatory" expropriation against one investing country "an offense" against all investing countries, according to Sir Ronald Prain. He reportedly was not against nationalization so long as terms (including compensation) were laid down clearly in investment codes prior to foreign investment commitments. Multilateral insurance has also been supported by a U.S. presidential commission of business leaders and scholars. It recommended "the creation of a multilateral insurance agency which would include the less developed countries among its membership, and in which the costs would be equitably shared among the members." It further recommended "that the United States encourage developing countries to adhere to the Convention on the Settlement of Investment Disputes, and to use the facilities provided by the Convention." [14]

But the establishment of such insurance schemes (by governments of developed countries for the investment of their enterprises in developing countries) could well be a source of disincentive for transnational corporations to respond to changing circumstances, and to allow the host countries in due course an effective role in the management of their resources, and an increase in their benefits. Commenting on OPIC's role, one U.S. scholar with extensive knowledge of developing countries, notably Latin America, argued: "In view of the successful experimentation

[13] "More Reinsurance, Russians Included," *Topics*, vol. 1, no. 2, June 1972, p. 7; "USSR Company Participates in United States Government Venture," *Survey of International Development* (Society for International Development, Washington), May 1972, p. 3; and "Soviet Union Underwrites US Investments," *Commerce* (Bombay), May 6, 1972, p. 1158.

[14] Jay Parkinson, keynote address at American Metal Market's Second Annual London Forum, October 26, 1970, p. 16; Sir Ronald Prain, Chairman of RST, reported in *Metal Bulletin* (London), October 22, 1970, p. 29; and *United States International Economic Policy in an Interdependent World*, papers submitted to the Commission on International Trade and Investment Policy and published in conjunction with the Commission's Report to the President (Washington, 1971), pp. 250, 252–53.

that American companies have begun to spread their financial risk, it seems reasonable to predict that they would be equally imaginative in working out new arrangements to avoid the tensions of direct ownership if they did not have the large disincentive provided by the United States guarantee program." [15]

Indeed, "Latin American governments view U.S.-inspired guarantee and insurance schemes for DFI [Direct Foreign Investment] with skepticism and suspicion, and have flatly rejected the World Bank's convention on the settlement of investment disputes as an infringement on national sovereignty and contrary to national constitutions. Guarantees and arbitration procedures offered multilaterally by Latin American nations, and administered jointly by them, perhaps with the help of regional or subregional institutions, may prove to be workable and acceptable arrangements." This position is similar to that held by other developing countries which fear that a worldwide multilateral scheme of insurance and settlement of disputes would be dominated by the rich and powerful. [16]

The first known example of insurance against investment risks on a regional basis among LDCs is that of the West African countries. It was established on June 9, 1966, by Dahomey, Ivory Coast, Niger, Togo, and Upper Volta, and joined later by four other countries. The joint loan guarantee fund, known as the Fonds d'entraide et de garantie des emprunts du Conseil de l'Entente, had an initial pool of resources of $5.3 million subscribed by members. [17]

Other developing countries have recently recognized the advantages of a regional scheme for reducing the noneconomic uncertainties faced by current and potential investors. One notable merit of such a scheme is that it makes financial and investment resources of capital-surplus developing countries more readily available to capital-deficit developing coun-

---

[15] T. H. Moran, "The Evolution of Concession Agreements in Underdeveloped Countries and the United States National Interest," *Vanderbilt Journal of Transnational Law,* vol. 7, Spring 1974, p. 331.

[16] C. F. Diaz Alejandro, "Direct Foreign Investment in Latin America," in C. P. Kindleberger, ed., *The International Corporation: A Symposium* (Cambridge: MIT Press, 1970), pp. 338–39; and UNCTAD Secretariat, *Private Foreign Investment in Its Relationship to Development,* Report by the UNCTAD Secretariat, Geneva, November 17, 1971, p. 23 (TD/134).

[17] UN Department of Economic and Social Affairs, *Foreign Investment in Developing Countries,* New York, 1968, p. 26 (E/4446).

tries—instead of these resources being siphoned to the developed market economy countries, as has been usually the case.

By 1975, fourteen Arab countries agreed to set up the Inter-Arab Investment Guarantee Corporation (IAIG), headquartered in Kuwait with an open-end share capital amounting initially to 10 million Kuwaiti dinars.[18] Unlike its West African predecessor, IAIG's main function is not limited to guaranteeing losses sustained by lenders. It covers both lenders and investors in Arab member countries. Protection against losses covers noncommercial risks such as expropriation, nationalization or confiscation of property; inability to transfer income or principal out of the host country as a result of unforeseen restrictions; and losses due to acts of war, military operations, or civil disturbances.[19] The corporation started its activities late in 1974.

The amount of compensation remains a *critical* problem. The principles for determining compensation differ dramatically between buyers and sellers. Each can be internally logical. Accordingly, it may prove wise to agree on the method for assessing compensation at the time the decision to invest is made.

In the view of several scholars and practitioners of development, an assured flow of financial resources is not the major bottleneck to development: it is primarily the absence of managerial capacity. An experienced manager of a development organization concluded: "Finance can normally be obtained from outside a developing country, given a certain minimum level of stability, to supplement local resources provided the right kind of projects are there. In fact, it is in most cases the scarcity of the right sort of people in the right organization mobilized to identify, investigate, promote and finally to manage commercial projects that constitutes the effective limiting factor on development."[20]

Among the capital importing LDCs, Egypt's experience in the 1970s is worth noting, bearing in mind that this country has had a single ruling

[18] *Middle East Journal* (Washington), Autumn 1971, p. 507. See also Ibrahim Shihata, "Arab Investment Guarantee Corporation: A Regional Investment Insurance Project," *Journal of World Trade Law* (Geneva), vol. 6, no. 2, 1972.

[19] See KFAED, *Eighth Annual Report, 1969–1970*, pp. 10–11; Z. A. Nasr, *The Kuwait Fund Scheme for the Guarantee of Inter-Arab Investments,* KFAED, May 1972; and Shihata, *Arab Institutions for Developmental Financing,* pp. 27–29.

[20] Sir William Rendell, "Commonwealth Development Corporation Experience with Joint Ventures," in Peter Ady, ed., *Private Foreign Investment and the Developing World* (New York: Praeger, 1971), p. 248.

party, ostensibly socialist. In order to attract large investors from neighboring capital-surplus countries, a foreign investment law was issued in 1974 providing for a five-year tax holiday, freedom to repatriate principal and profits, and guarantees against nationalization or expropriation. Such investments can be made in industries within delineated custom-free zones, that is, areas not subject to several of the restrictions or constraints normally applying to domestic enterprises.[21]

"Naturalizing" Foreign Ventures

Students of international economic relations generally agree that conflicts between host governments and transnational firms usually center on the issues of the division of benefits and extraterritoriality. Related sources of conflict may arise from the transnationals patronizing suppliers and contractors outside the host country, dominating the domestic credit market to the detriment of the smaller, less resourceful local firms, refraining from plowing back earnings into nationally desirable new activities, and refusing the joint participation of national capital and management.[22] Various resolutions of UN and LDC groups have solemnly upheld the inalienable right of permanent national sovereignty over natural resources. The Council of Ministers of the Organization of African Unity (OAU) in a resolution passed at its Seventh Ordinary Session in Addis Ababa on June 15, 1971, went further. Besides denouncing "the economic and political pressures which certain developed countries are attempting to bear on African countries with a view to threatening their development and to obstructing them in the exercise of their sovereignty over their natural resources, [it] recommends the formation of an African Union of Mineral Exporting Countries" [CM/Res. 245 (XVII)]. The

[21] *Law No. 43 of 1974 concerning the Investment of Arab and Foreign Funds and the Free Zones* (Cairo: C.B.E. Printing Press, 1974); major features summarized in *Topics Spotlites,* December 1974, pp. 5a–7a.

[22] See, for example, H. G. Johnson, "The Multinational Corporation as a Development Agent," *Columbia Journal of World Business,* May–June 1970, p. 30; I. A. Litvak and C. J. Maule, *Foreign Investment: The Experience of Host Countries* (New York: Praeger, 1970), pp. 23–27; P. N. Rosenstein-Rodan, "Multinational Investment in the Framework of Latin American Integration," in Inter-American Development Bank, *Multinational Investment, Public and Private, in the Economic Development and Integration of Latin America,* Round Table (Bogota, Colombia, 1968), pp. 80–87; United Nations, *Multinational Corporations in World Development,* New York, 1973, p. 46 (ST/ECA/190); and John Diebold, "The Multinational Company: Doing Business in Developing Countries," *Financial Executive* (New York), December 1973, pp. 25–30. See also Chapter 1 of this book.

implementation of such an ambitious scheme has not begun, however (see also Chapter 5).

Several host countries—whether developed or developing—have attempted to challenge the intrusion of foreign laws, regulations, and policies coming through the channels of diplomats, transnational enterprises, or governmental agencies of the major industrial powers.[23] Most prominent in this respect have been Canada, Japan, and the West European countries, whose actions have contained such intrusion while still providing opportunities for foreign investments under effective national control. On the other hand, LDCs' response to foreign intervention may vary from inaction or mild action to drastic measures such as nationalization.

Nationalization need not be prompted solely by economic conflict, but may arise out of a political conflict as well. This was the case when Iraq nationalized the interests of two American firms, Exxon and Mobil, in the Basrah Petroleum Company on October 7, 1973. The Iraqi government's nationalization move was triggered by the Israeli-Arab military hostilities of October 1973. It was reportedly prompted by the unremitting and massive political, military, and financial backing offered by the United States to Israel.[24]

Of course, reasons for nationalization, whether political-ideological or economic-developmental, have not existed in isolation. Moreover, the division between the two classes of reasons is theoretical. Depending on the country and the time, there was at work a combination of complex and interrelated forces—some fundamental or long standing, and others circumstantial.

For example, President Ahmad Hassan al-Bakr of Iraq, in prefacing his decision to nationalize the Western oil concessionaire, the Iraq Petroleum Company (IPC), on June 1, 1972, linked the political to the economic. He alleged that both his country's independence and its economic development were in jeopardy because of foreign exploitation of Iraq's natural resources. He argued "that the oil companies are the dangerous tools

---

[23] See, for example, the episode regarding the U.S. ambassador's agreement with Jamaica's prime minister not to interfere in Jamaica's 1971 elections if the prime minister refrained from making a campaign issue of the nationalization of American bauxite ventures in Jamaica, in "Jamaica, Upset over U.S. Envoy, Requests Ouster," and "U.S. Recalls Envoy at Jamaica's Request," *International Herald Tribune,* July 23 and 26, 1973, pp. 3 and 5 respectively; and U.S. Senate, *The International Telephone and Telegraph Company and Chile, 1970–71,* Report to the Committee on Foreign Relations by the Subcommittee on Multinational Corporations, 83rd Cong., 1st sess., 1973, pp. 16–20.

[24] See *Weekly Bulletin* (Iraq National Oil Company), October 20, 1973, pp. 1–6.

which represent imperialist logic, the logic of plunder and monopolistic exploitation and the impoverishment of the masses.'' [25]

The fundamental cause of this confrontation was the Iraqi government's refusal to concede the right of IPC to compensation for areas taken over by the government under Law No. 80 of 1961. The immediate cause which propelled the Iraqis into total nationalization was IPC's severe cutback in production in 1972, reaching 44 percent in April 1972 as compared with February 1972. On an annual basis, this meant a loss of oil revenues exceeding £110 million, or over 50 percent of Iraq's foreign exchange receipts. [26]

In the concessionaire's view, the reduction in the off-take of crude from the northern oil fields of Iraq was a direct and necessary result of the agreements covering short-haul crude which followed the Tehran Agreement of February 1971. These officials argued that Iraq and other governments involved must have been aware of the dangers of pricing crude oil at a level which would appear commercially unattractive in relation to the longer-haul crudes (in the Arabian Persian Gulf) once tanker freight rates fell.

For the vertically integrated owners of IPC, though, the competitiveness of Iraqi oil was not affected solely by changes in freight rates. More importantly, even the new rates could not justify such large reductions of Iraqi crude exports. The transnational oil companies owned more than one-third of the world tanker fleet and chartered over half of it on a long-term basis. Moreover, other short-haul crude—namely Nigerian oil and Saudi oil from Tapline at the East Mediterranean—had not experienced reductions in exports despite their similar price structure and geographical locations. It appeared that the owners of IPC wanted to provoke the Iraqi government into a settlement agreeable to the companies. [27] On this point *The Guardian* commented on May 31, 1972: "Iraq cannot be expected to run its economy subject to IPC's commercial whims. It is entitled to expect a steady and predictable income from its own resources, and this points to the need for more constructive discussions by both sides."

[25] *MEES Supplement,* June 2, 1972, p. 7. IPC was owned by five transnational companies: BP (23.75%), CFP (23.75%), Shell (23.75%), Exxon (11.875%), and Mobil (11.875%), with the balance belonging to an "independent" party (the Gulbenkian estate).

[26] Iraq's Ministry of Oil and Minerals, *The Nationalization of Iraq Petroleum Company's Operations in Iraq: The Facts and the Causes* (Baghdad: INOC Publications, 1973), pp. 17–20.

[27] See "Background to the Iraq Oil Nationalization," *MEES Supplement,* June 16, 1972.

In order to ease tension and reduce the chances of confrontation between expatriate firms and their parent countries on one hand, and host countries sensitive about their "sovereignty" on the other hand, a variety of approaches are possible. The following analysis considers three: renegotiating the economic terms of foreign ventures, forming partnerships of foreign enterprises and host government enterprises, and gradually divesting foreign affiliates. Each approach should be assessed in the light of the individual host country's social, political, and economic circumstances. The decision should be based on the objectives of the host government in terms of both economic and noneconomic costs and benefits.[28]

Renegotiation of Terms

From the standpoint of the host government, new terms offered to a foreign enterprise obviously cannot fall below a range which would still make it worthwhile for the enterprise to locate in the country concerned. To estimate this optimal range, a government should ascertain the competitive economic advantage its territory can offer, and should aim at gaining most of that advantage for itself. Ignorance often causes host governments to forego benefits by offering incentives beyond those needed to induce foreign operators to establish or expand their activities: "The trouble is that governments do not know what their bargaining position is, and they *do not know how to find out*. How profitable are the company's operations in the country concerned compared to others the company has elsewhere? How important to it, geographically and politically, is this particular source of production? How keen are its rivals to come in? How expensive would it be for the company to pull out? How much profits (and also length of lease, etc.) the company would need, to choose this particular country?" [29]

Some developing countries with limited sophistication have encountered company negotiators who have exploited their superior knowledge and skills to advantage.[30] Moreover, according to a well-informed author

---

[28] See C. P. Kindleberger, "U.S. Policy toward Direct Investment with Special Reference to the Less Developed Countries," in *United States International Economic Policy in an Interdependent World,* vol. 2, p. 338; also Raoul Prebisch, "Issues to Be Brought before the Commission on International Trade and Investment Policy Concerning Relations with Developing Countries," in *ibid.,* p. 302.

[29] Dudley Seers, "Big Companies and Small Countries: A Practical Proposal," *Kyklos* (Basel), vol. 16, fasc. 4, 1963, p. 601 (his italics).

[30] See C. J. Lipton, *Government Negotiating Techniques and Strategies,* UN Interregional Workshop on Negotiation and Drafting of Mining Development Agreements,

and consultant, "many cases could be described in which the U.S. company representative bargained determinedly for relief from local taxes even though the savings would be almost exactly offset by the higher United States taxes that result from the loss of foreign tax credits." [31]

A leading transnational enterprise acknowledged that "competition among developing countries in providing incentives can become so great that overly generous incentives are offered." [32] But these incentives may prove meaningless if the enterprise's home country applies the full home tax rate to all income from foreign investments. This situation obviously calls for a change. The host country should be able to recuperate from the foreign enterprise's affiliate tax proceeds which are payable on that affiliate's profits in the host country, but which are in fact paid abroad because of the host country's overly generous incentives.

Another reason for a host country's intervention in a transnational enterprise is price discrimination. Investigations have shown that for key imports the majority of developing countries have had to pay transnational firms prices that were "higher than competitive prices" available to the developed countries. This is especially the case for imports of energy [33] and technology. [34] France, for example, through its *monopole délégué* ("delegated monopoly") system, can insist on "most favored treatment" in supply prices of crude oil. The French government made

---

Buenos Aires, November 1973, 17 pp. (EAS/RT/AC.7/11); and Stephen Zorn, *Renegotiating Mining Agreements* (see Chapter 3, note 10).

[31] Louis T. Wells, "The Multinational Business Enterprise: What Kind of International Organization?" *International Organization,* vol. 25, no. 3, 1971, p. 460. Nevertheless, Professor Wells' report for the renegotiation of the 1967 Bougainville Agreement of 1967 in Papua New Guinea (PNG) proved, according to the PNG government's adviser, to be quite mild in the changes it requested, and generally easy on the company compared with the eventual settlement. See Zorn, p. 32. The Wells report is summarized in *Bougainville Copper Ltd.,* a case prepared by Gerald Allan, under the supervision of John S. Hammond and Louis T. Wells, Harvard Business School, October 1974, 25 pp.

[32] Statement of Emilio G. Collado, executive vice president, Exxon Corporation, in UN, ECOSOC, *The Impact of Multinational Corporations on the Development Process and on International Relations,* New York, September 11, 1973, p. 20.

[33] See UN, ECOSOC, *Report of the Secretary-General to the Committee on Natural Resources,* January 3, 1972, p. 2 (E/C.7/20/Add. 2). See also Michael Tanzer, "Investment Requirements and Financing of Petroleum Refineries in Developing Countries," and P. H. Frankel and W. L. Newton, "Delivered Cost of Crude Oil to Petroleum Refineries in Developing Countries," both in *The Proceedings of The United Nations Interregional Seminar on Petroleum Refining in Developing Countries,* January 22–February 3, 1973, published by the Indian Oil Corporation, New Delhi, vol. 1, pp. 223–37 and 102 respectively.

[34] See UN, ECOSOC, *Impact of Multinational Corporations,* May 24, 1974, pp. 55–57 (E/5500/Add.1/Part.I); and "Licensing: A Revolt against 'Exorbitant' Fees," *Business Week,* July 14, 1975, p. 69.

the extension of marketing licenses of affiliates of foreign companies conditional on the written understanding that France be given supply terms equal to those given to the country of the head office.[35]

A third reason for changing the economic terms under which business enterprises operate is that of windfall profits. A number of countries have enacted legislation to permit the renegotiation of certain terms of contracts entered into by governments and private businesses. This can be set at specified intervals or be linked to certain significant changes in circumstances. Such changes in circumstances can be assessed using both measurable and nonmeasurable criteria. Measurable criteria would include effects of inflation, windfall profits, and changes in terms of exploitation in similarly placed countries. The nonmeasurable criteria of policymakers are normally expressed in such terms as "fair," "politically judicious," and "national control."

Using the measurable criterion of profitability, the U.S. Renegotiation Act of 1951, for example, aims at profit limitation on contracts (and their subcontracts) entered into by federal agencies, notably those concerned with defense, space, aviation, atomic energy, procurement, and maritime transport. The act empowers its board, by agreement with private companies or by order, to recoup excessive profits as defined by the act from contractors and related parties (such as banks, insurance companies, lessor companies, manufacturers' agents, and brokers). The board's determinations of excessive profits and voluntary refunds and price reductions exceeded $2.5 billion by mid-1973.[36]

The U.S. fiscal authorities have had a challenging and complex task in ascertaining "excess profits." The U.S. Renegotiation Act, in determining "excess profits," gives favorable recognition to the efficiency of the contractor "with particular regard to attainment of quantity and quality production, reduction of costs, and economy in the use of materials, facilities, and manpower." Other factors considered are reasonableness of costs and profits, net worth, extent of risk assumed, nature and extent of contribution to the defense effort, including inventive and developmental

---

[35] *Europ-Oil Prices* (London), July 9, 1973, p. 5; and *Petroleum Press Service* (London), August 1973, pp. 291–93.

[36] Renegotiation Board, *Sixteenth Annual Report, 1971* (Washington, 1971), pp. 1–2; *Seventeenth Annual Report, 1972* (Washington, 1972), p. 12; and *Eighteenth Annual Report, 1973* (Washington, 1973), p. 13.

contribution, complexity of manufacturing, extent of subcontracting, and rate of turnover.[37]

U.S. government decisions on normal return and excess profits are not confined to procurement contracts; they also pertain to public utilities. Moreover, U.S. authorities have stretched their regulations to include companies operating beyond their national boundaries. Thus the U.S. Federal Power Commission (FPC) recommended that return on equity investment by a U.S. company (El Paso) from the export of Algerian natural gas to the United States be *limited* to 16 percent of equity investment in this project.[38]

By comparison, a developing country, Papua New Guinea (PNG), agreed late in 1974 with its concessionaire Conzinc Riotinto (owned 80.65 percent by the transnational Rio-Tinto Zinc or RTZ, and 19.35 percent by the Australian public) to define "reasonable" profit as 15 percent of total investment, after payment of a company profit tax of 33⅓ percent. Because of the two-to-one debt equity ratio in the project, and an average interest rate of 9 percent, the return on equity becomes about 27 percent. Since some of the equity was obtained through sale of public shares at a premium by the concessionaire, the latter's return on its par-value equity investment would work out to about 34 percent. The excess profits thus defined are subject to a flat 70 percent tax.[39]

In comparing U.S. and PNG definitions of "reasonable" profit, it is difficult to ascertain whether the much higher PNG figure is due to higher risk or lower bargaining power. The latter interpretation would appear more tenable if one were to compare PNG's effective normal return (34 percent) with that agreed to by a developed country for capital investments in a developing area at an early stage of exploration. The French government, for example, has considered 10 percent a normal return on CFP's capital investments in the Near East. Excess profits were then shared by the government at a highly progressive rate.[40]

Another developed country apparently did not fare as well as France in

[37] Sec. 103(e), as amended through July 1, 1971.

[38] FPC, *Initial Brief of Commission Staff* (*on Algerian Gas Imports by El Paso*), August 16, 1971, p. 25; and FPC, *Opinion No. 622,* June 28, 1972, p. 13.

[39] Zorn, *Renegotiating Mining Agreements,* pp. 40–41. See also Bougainville Copper, Ltd., letter to shareholders, November 29, 1974.

[40] See Zuhayr Mikdashi, *A Financial Analysis of Middle Eastern Oil Concessions, 1901–65* (New York: Praeger, 1966), pp. 102–3, 325.

taxing transnationals: Australia, negotiating with the same transnational as its protected territory Papua New Guinea (PNG became independent in September 1975). The Australian minister of minerals and energy talked in April 1974 about the transnationals' "economic exploitation" of Australia, especially with respect to tax payments. One of several examples the minister referred to was the small 1971–1972 royalty payments by Comalco (72 percent owned by RTZ and Kaiser Aluminum): only $1.5 million on a $300 million yearly turnover.[41]

Renegotiation clearly provides a measure of flexibility for adapting to changed circumstances and reduces the chances of confrontation and deadlock. It can help the firm by lightening its fiscal burden and easing its other terms should mineral discoveries prove disappointing. Renegotiation could also provide the host government with the opportunity to benefit from windfall gains or from tax credits in the firm's home country. The desirability of renegotiation was underlined by one U.S. economist who said: "Renegotiations of contracts with long life when the underlying conditions change is familiar in the Anglo-Saxon tradition. We have renegotiation of U.S. government procurement when subsequent information reveals that profits would be exorbitant at the costs the contractor is able to achieve." [42]

Some LDCs have attempted to emulate the U.S. experience. They have, on several occasions, asked for the renegotiation of contracts affecting the exploitation of their natural resources. Several host governments, as owners and lessors of these resources, have claimed the right of recouping excess profits. Others have asked for equity and management participation in mineral ventures. Of course, there are many conceptual and computational problems in ascertaining what are "normal" and what are "excessive" profits. The present state of accounting techniques does not permit an accurate measurement of the economic concepts of costs and profits for a business enterprise in a given period of time, and are far from uniform worldwide.[43] For example, on a "first-in first-out" accounting basis, material withdrawn from stocks for processing or sale is

---

[41] Connor, "Role of Multinationals in Australian Mining Industry."

[42] C. P. Kindleberger, *American Business Abroad* (New Haven: Yale University Press, 1969), p. 151.

[43] For details, see Mikdashi, *Financial Analysis of Oil Concessions,* pp. 244–45, and app. 2; also Mikdashi, *The Community of Oil Exporting Countries* (London: Allen & Unwin; Ithaca: Cornell University Press, 1972), pp. 138–142.

assumed to be that which has been in store the longest. In a situation of rising prices, that material will be the cheapest, and abnormal stock profits would appear on the books of the company following that method. No such profits will appear for a company on the "last-in first-out" basis. Most U.S. firms follow the latter approach, while a number of European firms follow the previous one. Also, conventional accounting principles and tax laws permit deductions for depreciation on the original cost of the plant and equipment concerned. No account is taken of the increased replacement cost resulting from inflation.

The problem for the government of a developing country is not confined to determining the largest share of economic rent consistent with development. There is also the problem of defining and ascertaining the size of a venture's income in a host country in a period of inflation. The problem becomes more complicated in the case of an international oligopoly characterized by vertical integration. In such a case, market forces do not have full play to allow for the free valuation of raw materials or intermediate products. Accordingly, profits generated by a given function or activity in a host country for a vertically integrated petroleum firm have to be imputed.

Different approaches have been followed by tax authorities in assessing business profits for vertically integrated and transnationally spread enterprises. Notable approaches include prorating the consolidated profits of the transnational firm in accordance with the geographical location of invested capital (for example, a refinery plant or a section of a pipeline); [44] attributing a "normal" or "reasonable" return on the firm's investments in the processing, manufacturing, or servicing functions, and leaving the residual as profits on exploration and extraction of minerals; attributing a "normal" or "reasonable" return on invested capital in the exploration for, and production of, minerals; valuing sales receipts, and consequently profits, on the basis of whatever price evidence exists on arms' length prices in the open market; and negotiating "acceptable" taxable profits margins by the interested parties (the parent country, the host country, and the transnational firm), and agreeing on methods for changing them.

[44] See, for example, Zuhayr Mikdashi, "Towards Maximizing Oil Revenues: With Special Reference to Transit Countries of the Middle East," *Middle East Economic Papers, 1961*, American University of Beirut, pp. 64–68; and Mikdashi, "Some Economic Aspects of Pipeline Transport in the Arab World," Third Arab Petroleum Congress, Alexandria, October 1961, pp. 1–26.

The latter approach offers greater scope for the exercise of bargaining powers and skills. With the availability of more information and the increased expertise of their officials, some LDC governments have been able to raise their returns from their primary exports. According to the government of Jamaica, "due to the bauxite industry's control over information, the terms of the contracts agreed upon in several instances proved later to be unfavorable to the Government, causing substantial loss of revenue." The government, in reply to a questionnaire from the U.N. secretary-general, stated that

agreements with the bauxite and alumina companies were renegotiated in 1957, and again in 1962/63 [and again in 1970/75] [45] when it was apparent that the older valuations placed on the mineral were inadequate. In every instance the effects of renegotiations were unequivocally favorable. Neither reinvestment nor capital inflow declined, but in fact has continued to increase apace. Foreign investors pay mineral royalties, and income tax on profits earned in the operative basis of assessment is on notional profits which are negotiated between the companies involved and the Government. [46]

From the host government's point of view, whether economic rents are reaped by taxes, royalties, or governmental participation is a matter of legal formality; the rent collection is the only thing of economic consequence. In selecting one method of payment over another, a transnational enterprise, by comparison, is concerned with selecting the one which will reduce its global tax payments. The enterprise, for example, will be affected by the tax treatment in its own home country of its payments to host countries.

Tax-subsidy opportunities offered by developed countries have not been always fully used by developing countries. For one example, the minimum tax bill on U.S. transnational corporations whose subsidiaries in developing countries promptly repatriate profits is achieved by not setting the developing countries' rate at zero, but at one-half the U.S. corporate profits tax. [47] The state of ignorance on the part of several developing countries concerning tax matters calls for the creation of a technically

[45] See *Mineral Trade Notes* (U.S. Bureau of Mines), September 1971, pp. 3–4; and *Business Week,* June 22, 1974, p. 29.

[46] UN General Assembly, *The Exercise of Permanent Sovereignty over Natural Resources and the Use of Foreign Capital and Technology for Their Exploitation,* Report of the Secretary-General, New York, September 14, 1970, pp. 107–8 (A/80581).

[47] Carl S. Shoup, "Taxation of Multinational Corporations," in UN Department of Economic and Social Affairs, *The Impact of Multinational Corporations on Development and on International Relations,* New York, 1974, p. 33 (E.74.II.A.6).

qualified worldwide body to diffuse information and advice on tax and related matters (see below).

Joint Ventures

In response to changes in the world economic and political environment—particularly the rise of economic nationalism—transnational firms agreed in the 1970s to speed the process of host country participation in their affiliates, albeit reluctantly. Some host governments have even obtained majority ownership, but foreign partners have extracted assurances that they will share in decision-making in such major business areas as budgeting and planning, production and control, pricing and marketing, and organizing and staffing.

Countries at an early stage of development are wise not to jump into the race of seeking control over their foreign-owned and operated enterprises. An inexperienced host government, by gaining control of a complex operation, could encounter net costs. These would include, notably, absence of easy and regular access to markets and to technical skills and managerial abilities. Commenting on the subject of national control, the minister of petroleum and mineral resources of a young and small developing country, the United Arab Emirates, said: "We are now at the 60 percent stage of participation and before we proceed any further, we ought to ask ourselves whether we are in a position to run the oil industry? The answer is clearly no, because if it is effective control we are after—control in the legal, fiscal, economic as well as the technical fields—then this is not the same as nominal participation. . . . We must be honest with our people. Running the oil industry is no mean task. We lack the trained people to run the industry." [48]

The minister explained that the national company could not even arrange to sell independently its 60 percent share of production. It lacked the marketing organization, and it had to compete with transnationals selling the same oil at a loss to preclude the entry of the national company into world markets. In 1975 the national company managed to sell to independent buyers only 5 percent of its 60 percent share of oil in the joint venture; the balance was channeled to the transnational corporations. [49]

[48] Mana Said Otaiba in *MEES*, April 18, 1975, p. 1.
[49] M. S. Otaiba, in *Akhbar al-Petrol wal-Sina'a* ("Petroleum and Industry News"—Abu Dhabi Arabic magazine), May 1975, p. 16; and *Al-Hawadess* (Beirut Arabic weekly), p. 48.

Through joint ventures, some host governments hope to influence their foreign partners more effectively than they would be able to influence the 100 percent foreign-owned affiliates. Such influence might include inducing the joint venture to carry out other business activities ranking high in national priorities. For the president of Zambia, Kenneth Kaunda, joint ventures between foreign companies and the national group (called ZIMCO) are more conducive to growth than total national ownership: "In order that this growth may continue unfettered ZIMCO is going to need money and technical expertise and this is where our philosophy of permanent partnership as against transient partnership is in our opinion particularly suitable to our situation. We need to augment our domestic sources of investment with foreign sources of investment. We need to augment our domestic skills with the sophisticated technical know-how of other countries. We need partners in progress." [50]

A number of foreign enterprises have offered host governments participation in their ventures at a distant date, after they reap the attractive initial profits. One example in mining is the iron-ore concession granted by Peru to Marcona Mining Company in 1952. The Peruvian state-owned steel company, Corporacion Peruana del Santa, holds an option to acquire 50 percent ownership in 1982 (thirty years after the original award date) without cash investment.[51] To one well-informed researcher, the concessionaire Marcona had exploited to advantage the fact that it had among its shareholders the politically influential Prado family. In 1960 the president of Peru was Manuel Prado, while the president of Marcona was Max Pena Prado. Such associations have apparently helped the company to obtain more attractive terms, to the detriment of Peru's better interest.[52]

Another leading exponent of participation in 1973 was Saudi Arabia. Its minister of petroleum and mineral resources defended participation on the following grounds:

[50] Zambia Industrial and Mining Corporation (ZIMCO), *Chairman's Statement, 1971.*

[51] Charles W. Robinson, president of Marcona, "Competition in the Sale of Iron Ore in World Markets," XI Convencion de Ingenieros de Minas del Peru, December 1969, p. 2 (typescript). The principal shareholders of Marcona are Utah International and Cyprus Mines, both from the United States.

[52] W. F. C. Purser, *Metal-Mining in Peru: Past and Present* (New York: Praeger, 1971), pp. 156–59. The Prado family, in a joint fifty-fifty venture with Standard Oil of California, also won a refinery concession in 1960. See Anibal Quijano, *Nationalism and Capitalism in Peru: A Study in Neo-Imperialism* (New York: Monthly Review Press, 1971).

Nationalization does not guarantee the state concerned the means to market its crude, particularly if the quantities involved are substantial. . . . The real problem is how can any state, Arab or otherwise, continue to search for new oil resources once it embarks on nationalization. The question is not one of finance but a question of the technology which is required for drilling operations. . . . There is however an alternative method of gaining control, while at the same time maintaining the continued flow of foreign capital and expertise as well as marketing outlets for our output, and this alternative is participation. On the other hand, if we nationalize our crude and try to sell it on the international market, the prices will crash resulting in a drastic drop in our revenue. Thus what is said about nationalization is just a way of inflaming the demagogic sentiments of the public and is against national interests of the Arab nation.[53]

In order to get a balanced and enlightened view of the role of foreign investment in LDCs, it is again helpful to look at Egypt's position in the 1970s. This is especially so because Egypt wields influence among several Asian and African countries, and because the country officially has a socialist political system achieved through a series of nationalization measures. The chairman of the government-sponsored Arab (previously called Egyptian) International Bank, in a fundamental departure from the nationalization approach, stated unequivocally in 1971 that his country sought a "healthy partnership" with foreign investors. He outlined the respective opportunities and responsibilities of foreign investor and host government as follows:

It has become clear to foreign investors that there are certain fields of activities that should be left to local capital and initiative, that they should bring with them a positive contribution to the economy of the country (not only in the form of a participation in capital) but also in technical skill and technological advancement, and that they should give the local citizens adequate opportunities to assume responsibility on a gradual basis. It has also become clear to developing countries that if they want the co-operation of foreign capital they must start by indicating the fields in which they would welcome such co-operation and then when foreign capital is invested in agreed ventures and activities they must give it a fair chance to make adequate profits, they must give the necessary guarantees for its safety, for the transfer of its profits, and they must not construe every movement as an attack on their sovereignty.[54]

[53] *MEES Supplement,* January 5, 1973, p. 3.

[54] Abdel Mon'em Kaissouni, chairman, the Arab International Bank, speech delivered at a meeting of the American-Arab Association for Commerce and Industry, New York, November 3, 1971; see also "Egypt Seeks New Investments," *Bulletin of the American-Arab Association for Commerce and Industry* (New York), November 1971, pp. 1–2. On the interests of local partners, see also L. G. Franko, "International Joint Ventures," *Law and Policy in International Business,* vol. 6, no. 2, Summer 1974, pp. 315–36.

In fact, Egypt has long welcomed U.S. petroleum companies (Exxon, Mobil, Standard Oil of Indiana, Continental, Phillips) in joint ventures with the state-owned Egyptian General Petroleum Company. Despite the turmoil between the U.S. and Egyptian governments since the mid-1950s, U.S. enterprise in Egypt has been spared the fall-out in political relations.

In general, host governments have been able to enter into partnerships with transnational enterprises when they could offer comparatively attractive terms for domestic inputs, fiscal incentives, and assured domestic export markets, or when they could play on the rivalry of several firms. The resistance of a transnational enterprise to any threat to its centralized control or to its full ownership of ventures in host countries has been broken only when strategic inputs—which could be technology, raw materials, capital, managerial know-how, or others—or market outlets are available outside the oligopolists. In support of majority ownership by host governments in joint ventures, one investigation dealing with Canada concludes that "the alleged redistribution of oligopoly profits from foreigners to Canadians may be an illusion" if minority ownership of foreign enterprises is promoted. That author argues that "the ultimate impact of promoting minority ownership may be to erode the political basis of other, more effective policies seeking to control foreign investment behavior." [55]

To increase national ownership of key industries, several developed countries have offered financial aid to nationals. The Australian government, following on a precedent set by the Canadian government (see Chapter 1), established on June 10, 1970, an Australian Industry Development Corporation to financially assist Australians interested in acquiring ownership of, and eventually control over, industries and resources hitherto dominated by foreign interest. Unfortunately, LDCs are far less equipped to protect their interests with minority ownership. There are many examples of "straw men" domestic partners, private or state-owned, that do not play an active role in an enterprise labeled "joint."

Host governments, developed or developing, have over various periods and in different circumstances supported the model of joint ventures be-

[55] See L. T. Wells, "Multinational Business Enterprise," p. 458; L. G. Franko, "Do Joint Ventures Still Make Sense in Europe," *Worldwide P&I Planning* (Stamford, Conn.), January–February 1972, pp. 22, 25–30; and Thomas Horst, *On the Benefits of Domestic Minority Ownership of Foreign-Controlled Firms,* Harvard Institute of Economic Research, February 1971, no. 176, pp. 2–3.

tween local partners and transnational firms—although in several instances local partners were interested in maximizing their private gain. But host governments are increasingly interested in acquiring for the domestic economy the necessary managerial and technological skills. The transnational enterprise is naturally reluctant to acquiesce in such a transfer lest it lose its comparative advantages and monopolistic privileges.[56]

Service Contracts and Divestment

In their search for self-reliance and development, several host countries have sought to assume the principal role in the management of their resources, making use of expatriates' skills for certain functions, such as international marketing and financial and technical management, until local capabilities are developed.[57] These countries have generally favored the service contract or limited tenure approach. Under one type of service contract currently popular, the foreign firm assumes the managerial-technical responsibility and underwrites over a prearranged period the financial-operational risks of building or operating a domestic venture. In return, the foreign firm is rewarded—short of a share in ownership—by a "fee." This can be a payment in kind or in money; it can be fixed or graduated in relation to the size of discoveries of natural resources, the size of production, profits, foreign exchange savings, ventured resources, or other variables of inputs or performance.

Service contracts are extremely flexible devices which meet the needs of host countries for filling gaps in managerial know-how, technology, and other inputs. They can be adapted to widely diverse circumstances, and offer the best hope of balancing the objective of greater local control with

[56] See, for example, Lawrence G. Franko, *Joint International Business Ventures in Developing Countries: Mystique and Reality,* Centre d'études industrielles, Geneva, May 1973, pp. 15–17.
. [57] Even long-established national companies have not been immune from bad management, for example, Pertamina, the national petroleum company of Indonesia. In 1975 the Indonesian government had to call on Western financial advisers (S. G. Warburg of London, Lazard Frères of Paris, and Kuhn, Loeb of New York) to remedy Pertamina's financial mismanagement and to rescue its extravagant projects. See "The OPEC Member That Spent Too Much," *Business Week,* March 31, 1975, pp. 25–26; "Indonesia: An All-Out Effort to Rescue Pertamina," *Business Week,* July 21, 1975, p. 30; and Zuhayr Mikdashi, "Influencing the Environment for Primary Commodities," *Journal of World Trade Law* (Geneva), vol. 8, March–April, 1974, pp. 166–68.

that of maximum national economic gain.[58] They are also more likely to survive changed political conditions or revolutionary upheavals than traditional types of investments and control. The likely stability of a service contract can be explained in terms of its characteristics, notably: the ownership-managerial control it offers the host country, the provision for renegotiating terms, and the relatively limited period of foreign involvement.

As for divestment, few major transnational firms with direct foreign investments have, as a matter of policy, voluntarily offered purchase options or the phasing out of their ownership and control of affiliates in LDCs. Their opposition to divestment usually stems from the desire to maintain their dominant position or their monopolistic advantages in a given market, and the absence of other profitable opportunities or lines of business.

Nonetheless, with the growth of economic nationalism, foreign-owned ventures may have to accept a gradual divestment (also known as fadeout or attenuation) of their ventures in host countries, starting at a reasonably early date, say within fifteen years from the beginning of commercial operations. The expatriate companies would then cease being direct owners in host countries and become service contractors, suppliers of know-how, and buyers of materials. Optimal divestment calls for devising a framework for the orderly, gradual, and appropriate timing of transfer of ownership and management, so as to permit proper training of the nationals over a period of partnership with the transnational firm.

Scholars and policy-makers have advocated such transfers of ownership and control of foreign ventures to local interests as a means of speeding up their economic development.[59] It is possible, though, that total local ownership can reduce the availability of foreign capital and know-how, and slow down development. For each country there is an optimal mix of what is politically desirable and what is economically feasible. In

---

[58] See Gerald Meier, *Leading Issues in Economic Development* (New York: Oxford University Press, 1970), pp. 306–8; and Peter P. Gabriel, "MNCs in the Third World: Is Conflict Unavoidable," *Harvard Business Review,* July–August 1972, pp. 98–99.

[59] See, for example, A. O. Hirschman, *How to Divest in Latin America, and Why,* Essays in International Finance, Princeton University, November 1969; Paul Streeten, "Obstacles to Private Foreign Investment in the LDCs," *Columbia Journal of World Business,* May–June 1970, pp. 37–39; Grunwald and Musgrove, *National Resources in Latin American Development* (Baltimore: Johns Hopkins Press, 1970), p. 241; and Alejandro, "Direct Foreign Investment," p. 340.

a number of cases, divesting foreign firms have continued to contribute to host economies through a broadening and deepening of their involvement. Accordingly, "a program of divestiture that cuts off this process could be hurtful to the governments that were demanding it." [60] Foreign firms could also be induced to pass on new technology on a royalty basis.

For development purposes, foreign investment could therefore serve "as a rotating fund that temporarily, over periods of varying lengths, depending on the kind of investment, offsets the shortage of technical and financial resources on the part of local enterprise." According to this view, "the foreign investor should be prepared at all times to transfer majority interest in the firm to local investors and be ready to seek other investment opportunities in those activities where technological contributions continue to be of fundamental importance." [61] The host country may take the initiative in pointing to those activities or sectors of the economy where a transient role for foreign enterprise is welcome.

In order to smooth the transfer of foreign interests in developing countries, while not undercutting the availability and flow of foreign capital and know-how, a novel international financial institution, with regional or national affiliates, may be needed. This could be called the International Divestment-Investment Corporation (IDIC), and it could supervise the progressive liquidation of foreign investments and the transfer of their ownership and management to national interests. It could also act as a bridging financier or trustee for a period of transition if national interests did not have adequate financial resources or the managerial capacity and technical know-how. IDIC could furthermore guarantee debtor obligations and act as a neutral arbiter in settling disputes over the valuation of assets. Finally, IDIC could act as an investment catalyst channeling divested resources into new productive ventures in various developing countries.

The above-mentioned functions of financial intermediary would of course require IDIC to have resources of its own. Whether these resources should be raised from the international money and capital markets, or whether they should be raised from existing international finan-

[60] See, for example, Raymond Vernon, "Problems and Policies regarding Multinational Enterprises," in *United States International Economic Policy in an Interdependent World*, p. 999; also, Vernon, *Sovereignty at Bay* (New York: Basic Books, 1971), p. 20.

[61] Inter-American Development Bank, *Multinational Investment, Public and Private, in the Development and Integration of Latin America*, Round Table (Bogota, Colombia, 1968), p. 15.

cial institutions, deserves a special investigation. Such an investigation will also have to assess the basis of contributions to be made by divesting-investing firms, host countries, and parent countries. On this point, Raoul Prebisch commented: "It may perhaps be difficult to understand how an advanced country could contribute financial resources in order to enable Latin American [and other LDCs', one should add] private initiative to obtain control of undertakings which would otherwise remain in the hands of the developed country's private enterprise. But this would be too shortsighted a view. . . . The continuing process of technological improvement will leave foreign enterprise ample scope for action, since as soon as domestic initiative has acquired a controlling interest in certain enterprises, new opportunities for association on a basis of reciprocal benefits will supervene." [62] Although these "new opportunities" could very well fail to materialize in a specific country, they would probably at least occur in that region or in the developing world at large.

Already the Commonwealth Development Corporation (CDC)— formed in 1948 by the British Treasury—contributes to the development of LDCs (until 1969 confined to the Commonwealth) through equity capital, soft-term loans, and managerial know-how. It has agreed to arrange for a gradual transfer to local ownership and mangement of the productive enterprises it has helped set up. This transfer is done selectively. As the general manager of CDC, Sir William Rendell, explained:

We tend to be inveterate "ad-hocers" on this, formulas that give options for purchasing X per cent of the shares of such-and-such a company at such-and-such a price over a given period of years. In our experience it never really works out. But the answer is that it is our policy to dispose of our projects when we can get a reasonable price for them and when we can afford to do so, and particularly—I have stressed this—to local investors, not just to sell them to somebody in London who may wish to make an African investment—if there are such people. That is part of our policy. [63]

Other countries also have specialized investment institutions aimed at floating developmental projects with divestment features in favor of host countries—notably West Germany (German Development Company),

[62] *Change and Development: Latin America's Great Task,* report submitted to the Inter-American Development Bank, July 1970, p. 159.

[63] Ady, ed., *Private Foreign Investment,* pp. 235–6.

and Denmark (Danish Industrialization Fund for Developing Countries).[64]

A broadly similar function is performed by the International Finance Corporation (IFC), a member of the World Bank Group. One major difference in the nature of functions between the two institutions is that IFC is committed to assisting only private enterprises—to the explicit exclusion of government-owned or controlled institutions—while no such limitation is found with CDC. In support of divestment by foreign private investors in favor of local interests, an executive of IFC commented that "absentee landlordism in industry has had its day." He stated that in IFC's experience it had not been difficult to find and work with local partners.[65]

Such divestment should come after the foreign investor has been able to recuperate both capital and adequate profits, given the risks attendant to his investment. This period would thus be longer for a company exploring for a resource in a virgin territory as compared with an already proven territory. Flexibility should be exercised in the sale of investments, and the host government and its nationals should be able to exercise the purchase option over reasonably long periods. Equally, the expatriate company should be given the opportunity to run the venture for a longer period alone, or in partnership with local interests, if the two parties find it in their mutual interest to do so.[66]

It is probable, however, that the leading developed countries and their transnational firms would be reluctant to support an institution such as IDIC.[67] In view of the likely political difficulties, it would be more practical to have each country set its own legal framework for foreign enterprises, with divestment, reinvestment, or other guidelines preagreed on in individual contracts. There are, in fact, a number of transnational companies which have accepted on a voluntary basis the conversion of their

[64] John K. Freeman, "Channelling Funds for Development," *Columbia Journal of World Business,* Spring 1973, pp. 66–71.

[65] William S. Gaud, executive vice president of IFC, *Private Foreign Investment in the '70s,* speech at the annual meeting of the Association Internationale pour la Promotion et la Protection des Investissements Privés en Territoires Etrangers, Munich, October 31, 1972, p. 9.

[66] See also Vernon, "Problems regarding Multinational Enterprises," p. 1000.

[67] See Inter-American Development Bank, *The IBD's First Decade and Perspectives for the Future,* Round Table (Punta del Este, Uruguay, 1970), pp. 38, 157, 233, 234, 235.

investments into joint ventures with domestic enterprises, whether these are state-owned or privately owned. There have also been cases where a functionally diversified enterprise voluntarily divested or sold one affiliate in order to develop other activities.

A notable example is that of Mexico. Mineral deposits in that country are owned by the state, and until 1961 mining concessions were given for perpetuity, assuming normal conditions. But in 1961 the Mexican government introduced tax laws which reduced to twenty-five years the life of mining concessions, with renewals subject to majority (51 percent and above) equity interest by Mexican nationals. To induce such "mexicanization," the government granted a 50 percent reduction in production and export taxes. Several transnational enterprises have found the Mexican offer enticing. Anaconda, traditionally the largest producer of Mexican copper, took advantage of the mexicanization law in 1971. The principal obstacle to its divestment was "a shortage of liquid investment capital in Mexico available to purchase a majority interest." [68] As it turned out, the largest group of Mexican investors with available resources were the government agencies.

In another example, the International Telephone and Telegraph Company (U.S.) in 1969 sold its telephone system in Peru to the government for $17.9 million. It also agreed to use $8.2 million from the proceeds to expand locally in the hotel business and to set up a joint venture with the government for the construction of a telephone equipment factory. Probably the most elaborate agreement for divestment-investment, however, has been that between a Canadian holding company, Brazilian Light and Power Company, and the federal government of Brazil. The company, which is controlled by North American and West European capital, agreed in 1966 to sell its telephone assets for $93.3 million. It concurrently agreed to reinvest $65 million in Brazilian ventures and to observe important guidelines: the enterprises invested in should contribute to Brazil's development, investment should be used to add to productive capacity not to buy out existing owners, and investment should be as a minority shareholder only. The Brazilian precedent could well offer a pattern worthy of emulation by other developing countries. [69]

Some transnational corporations have responded individually or collec-

---

[68] Anaconda Company, *Annual Report,* 1971, p. 9.

[69] W. G. Friedmann and J. P. Béguin, *Joint International Business Ventures in Developing Countries: Case Studies and Analysis of Recent Trends* (New York: Columbia University Press, 1971), pp. 397–99, 294–95.

tively to the wishes of developing countries to promote and strengthen their small-business enterprises using the divestment approach. The leading example is the Atlantic Community Development Group for Latin America (ADELA), an investment company supported by 235 transnational corporations and banks, mostly from the United States, Canada, Western Europe, and Japan. ADELA's function is to engage in joint ventures with private or public enterprise in Latin America as a minority shareholder. Its purpose is to start new industries which it gradually relinquishes once the projects are well established, and to reinvest released resources in new projects. As described by its president: "ADELA is not simply an 'investment company.' More than a mere provider of capital, it stimulates private initiative and provides development services and financing to economically viable new projects and for the growth of existing enterprises. *It shares the high initial risk inherent in new ventures in developing countries and divests when enterprises mature.*" [70]

ADELA's remarkable contribution lies in the initiative and capability it has in identifying, studying, structuring, promoting, and implementing projects with maximum economic impact. These are defined as labor-intensive projects (construction, tourism, and agribusiness excluding natural resources) and projects producing and exporting nontraditional goods. Late in 1973, ADELA's cumulative loans and investments exceeded $1 billion servicing some four hundred small enterprises in over twenty Latin American countries. [71]

The concept of ADELA is extremely popular with developing countries. Many policy-makers and scholars feel that its advantages could be even more substantial if it were not restricted to small enterprises, since some medium- or large-sized national enterprises in developing countries could benefit from ADELA's expertise and resources.

With adequate incentives, a divestment-investment mechanism can clearly yield valuable benefits in the transfer of technology and know-how and the development of managerial ability and new processes of production. This would hopefully lead to a self-sustained momentum of development. The orderly transfer of management and ownership to national interests need not, furthermore, lead to a divorce between the transnational firm and its erstwhile affiliate. The new domestic venture can and may well be advised to maintain business relations with its former parent, especially to arrange for managerial and technical cooperation and

[70] ADELA, *The ADELA Group* (Switzerland, 1972—italics supplied).
[71] *Ibid.;* and statement of Collado, pp. 10–11.

the use of trademarks to take advantage of the transnational company's continually evolving technology.[72] This author feels that it is also in the interest of the divested domestic venture to arrange to maintain normal trading relations with the former transnational parent and its clients. This strategy is especially beneficial in the case when the domestic venture is producing specialized items which specifically fit the production system of the transnational enterprise. It is also useful when the domestic venture does not have ready access to international markets, or to the requisite technology. This cooperation builds economic interdependence of buyers and sellers, and promotes the security of trade flows.

Divestment can also be profitable for the transnational enterprise. Not only will divestment enable the parent company to maintain lucrative service contracts for technical know-how, marketing arrangements, and other matters. It could also improve the divesting firm's return on equity—especially if host countries offer tax incentives which are not nullified by home countries. A 2 percent annual divestment rate would result in a 50-year-life company, and a 3.6525 percent rate in a 27-year-life company. It has been demonstrated that in countries with a 50 percent income tax rate, reductions of the tax rate to 45 percent for a 2 percent annual divestment, and to 40 percent for a 3.65 percent annual divestment, are more profitable to stockholders of the divesting firms than conventional corporate ventures with a perpetual life.[73] Divesting with profit has the advantage of attracting other foreign investments and providing a mechanism to convert established foreign ventures into national ones. Ownership for transnational enterprises need not necessarily be cause for a drive to efficiency and a commitment to profit-making. Efficiency and profit-making could be sought through appropriately designed management contracts.

If a private foreign enterprise is offered a divestiture plan with a net incremental profit to its stockholders, one should expect the enterprise, prompted by the profit motive, to accept. If the foreign enterprise declines the offer a host country might well be justified in introducing a tax penalty on the recalcitrant company.[74] Furthermore, governments of

---

[72] Prebisch, *Change and Development,* pp. 157–58.

[73] Shann Turnbull, "Multinationals: Fading Out with a Profit," *Development Forum* (Geneva), vol. 2, no. 5, June 1974, p. 3; also Turnbull, "Eliminating Foreign Ownership," *Growth 26* (Committee for Economic Development of Australia), December 1973, pp. 1–13.

[74] *Ibid.*

some developing countries believe that compensation to transnational firms for take-overs could be negligible, or even negative. They have argued that these firms' "excessive profits" and their inadequate payments of taxes to host countries justify this.[75]

Under some circumstances, though, divestment could hurt the interests of transnational enterprises and their parent countries, to the extent divestment cuts them off from secure cheap sources of supplies and lucrative returns. Under other circumstances, divestment of transnational firms from their ventures in LDC mineral exporters may very well prove to be in the interest of the advanced consumers to the extent it promotes harmony and amity between producer and consumer. One Western economist even surmised that if transnational companies pulled out completely from oil exporting countries, the latter, especially the ones with large reserves, would then be tempted to compete against each other and bring prices down. He accordingly recommended, in the interest of the developed industrial countries and their consumers, that the transnational companies voluntarily divest their producing ventures in the host countries.[76]

In contrast, a U.S. presidential commission came out bluntly in 1971 against programs aimed at facilitating the sale and transfer of U.S. foreign affiliates to host countries: "In some countries, an important new deterrent to investment from abroad is developing—the 'Fade-out' arrangement, which requires that established as well as new foreign investors sell their ownership interests to local owners, either government or private, over a period of years. We believe the United States should actively discourage host countries from instituting fade-out requirements and from prescribing the form and extent of local equity participation." [77] And in 1972 President Nixon came out sharply against LDCs' nationalization of U.S. property. As he put it, his new approach to the developing nations "includes strong penalties designed to discourage the expropriation of American property abroad." [78]

In addition, case studies have shown that leading U.S. concerns have had significant success in influencing the U.S. Congress and administration to prevent divestiture or nationalization of their ventures abroad,

[75] See, for example, UNCTAD Secretariat, *Private Foreign Investment in Its Relationship to Development*, p. 18.

[76] M. A. Adelman, "Is the Oil Shortage Real? Oil Companies as OPEC Tax-Collectors," *Foreign Policy*, Winter 1972–1973, pp. 87–88.

[77] *United States International Economic Policy in an Interdependent World*, p. 251.

[78] Nixon, "The Real Road to Peace," *U.S. News & World Report*, June 26, 1972, p. 39.

even at times where U.S. public interest was not necessarily or unequivocally being adversely affected.[79]

In fact, it is clear that divestment or nationalization has to be done with at least the tacit approval or neutrality of the major industrial countries, lest these countries use their potent trade, aid, and other instruments against the LDC. For example, if "prompt, adequate, and effective" compensation acceptable to nationalized U.S. interests is not paid, the U.S. president can cut bilateral aid (the so-called Hickenlooper Amendment of the Foreign Assistance Act), and can instruct U.S. executive directors in the World Bank Group, the Asian Bank, and the Inter-American Development Bank to vote against any loan for that country.[80]

A good example of the policy of requiring foreign private enterprises to divest gradually major portions of their ownership and control is the Andean Pact.[81] This group includes Colombia, Ecuador, Bolivia, Peru, and Chile. The pact requires an obligatory divestment on the part of all wholly foreign-owned enterprises, up to a minimum of 15 percent of the capital within a period not exceeding three years from the date of enforcement of the Cartagena agreement, or the date of production of said enterprise. Divestment is graduated to 51 percent in favor of nationals, with slower schedules (over twenty years) for Bolivia and Ecuador as compared with Chile, Colombia, and Peru (over fifteen years). As a *quid pro quo* for gradual divestment, the divesting firms benefit from the incentive of duty-free movement of goods within the five countries. One writer believes that the foreign investor in raw materials can rationally be expected to exercise control for a period of "15 years and maybe much shorter," recover its investment plus its opportunity cost, and accept surrender of its concession at the end of that period.[82]

---

[79] See, for example, the excellent study of U.S. diplomat and economist Richard J. Bloomfield, "Who Makes American Foreign Policy? Some Latin American Case Studies," Harvard University Center for International Affairs, March 1972 (typescript); Mason Gaffney, "Benefits of Military Spending," paper presented at 10th Annual Conference, Committee on Taxation, Resources, and Economic Development, Madison, Wisconsin, October 25, 1971 (typescript); also, "U.S. Reportedly Withheld Ecuador Aid on I.T.T. Plea," *New York Times,* August 10, 1973, pp. 37, 40.

[80] Public laws 92–245, 92–246, and 92–247 of the 92nd Congress, March 10, 1972.

[81] See "Common Treatment of Foreign Capital, Trademarks, Patents, Licensing Agreements, and Royalties in the Andean Common Market," *Journal of Common Market Studies,* June 1972, pp. 229–359.

[82] Vernon, *Some Notes on Concessions Policy.*

Security of Resource Flows

Interruptions in trade flows may result from war, natural disasters, civil disturbances, political actions (embargoes, blockades, trade barriers, expropriations), or company actions (lockouts of labor, boycotts of supplies).

Since basic minerals and several other commodities are vital to modern economies, there is wide international concern for "security of supply" and "security of demand." The term security may convey different meanings to different parties: it may mean the continued and regular physical availability of commodities regardless of the economic or non-economic terms, or it may mean physical availability at economically and politically acceptable terms. For the world's leading industrial power, national security with respect to oil has four major objectives as defined by the director of the U.S. Office of Emergency Preparedness (OEP), George A. Lincoln:

(1) Maintain a satisfactory level of domestic reserves of crude oil, supplemented from secure sources of origin supply;
(2) Maintain spare capacity to produce and deliver crude oil when international factors disrupt supplies from other sources;
(3) Maintain refinery capacity in the United States adequate to meet both defense and essential civilian needs in periods of disruption of normal world oil trade; and
(4) Provide a petroleum industry in the United States with the capacity to meet the nation's defense and essential civilian needs at all times.[83]

In the United States, restrictions on oil imports were in force from 1958 to 1973 to protect the domestic petroleum industry. This precluded undue dependence on foreign sources—admittedly at a cost to consumers. Estimates of the cost of the U.S. imports program vary considerably. Evidence submitted to a congressional joint economic subcommittee suggests, however, that net cost for the U.S. public has increased by "a rock-bottom minimum of $7.4 billion more in the six-year period ended in 1970 than in the previous half-dozen years." It was running at an estimated $5–7 billion per year in the early 1960s.[84]

---

[83] U.S. Senate, Committee on Interior and Insular Affairs, *Hearings on National Goals Symposium,* pt. 2, 92nd Cong., 1st sess., October 20, 1971, pp. 489–90.
[84] *Washington Post,* January 9, 1972, p. A5; and U.S. House, *Oil Import Controls,* Hearings before the Subcommittee on Mines and Mining of the Committee on Interior and Insular Affairs, 91st Cong. March–April 1970; and Mikdashi, "Influencing Primary Commodities," p. 147n.

Though observers are generally familiar with aspects of supply security,[85] the concept of demand security has not until recently received equal attention, at least by academicians and analysts.[86] "Demand interruption" may be defined as the decision of one or more of the industrially developed countries and their transnational enterprises to interrupt, curtail, or boycott directly or indirectly the demand for the regular exports of one country or a group of countries. As on the supply side, such interruptions may be prompted by mixed politico-economic motives, such as a change in the political regimes of certain countries or the nationalization of foreign assets. The LDCs faced by demand interruption may not have the resource flexibility and administrative ability to change their pattern of exports in the short or intermediate run. In addition, the absence of a diversified economic base precludes them from making up for a loss of exports in one commodity by increased exports in other commodities. Faced with demand interruption, these countries could have their socio-economic programs and their internal stability greatly impaired.

One historical example of demand interruption was that connected with the nationalization of the Iranian oil industry in 1951. For over three years, Iran was faced with a total boycott of oil exports instituted by major transnational companies which supported the Anglo-Iranian Oil Company (later BP) in questioning the legitimacy of Iran's nationalization. Moreover, Anglo-Iranian and the British government threatened companies which might break the boycott with confiscation of Iranian oil on the high seas and with legal pursuits. Also the World Bank and the IMF denied financial assistance to Iran for a time. The industry boycott was maintained until the October 1954 settlement, which was made on the grounds that compensation originally offered by the Iranian government to BP was inadequate. The impact of the suspension of oil flows on the Iranian economy, dependent for some 80 percent of export earnings on oil, was shattering.

Another example of demand interruption was the French decision around mid-1971 to boycott Algerian oil, which had enjoyed a traditional

[85] See, for example, Sam H. Schurr and Paul T. Homan, *Middle Eastern Oil and the Western World* (New York: American Elsevier Publishing Co., 1971), pp. 14–16; and Resources for the Future, *Energy Research Needs*, staff report prepared for the National Science Foundation, October 1971 (National Technical Information Service PB 207–516).

[86] See M. Tanzer, "The Naked Politics of Oil: Oil Boycotts," in *The Political Economy of International Oil and the Underdeveloped Countries* (Boston: Beacon Press, 1969), pp. 319–48.

market in France (about two-thirds of total exports). In this action, the French were prompted by their dislike of Algeria's partial nationalization (up to 51 percent) of French-controlled companies in Algeria, and by their disapproval of compensation terms offered originally by Algeria in June 1971. Moreover, the French government was reported to have pressured the U.S. government to ban Algerian gas imports into the United States; the World Bank and other financial institutions to block any loans to Algeria until France received terms it deemed satisfactory; and other trading partners of Algeria, notably West European countries, Japan, and the USSR.[87] The dispute between Algeria and France was resolved by the end of 1971.

Supply problems which had their apparent source in LDCs have been widely publicized. Yet there are several cases of supply interruptions or curtailment which had their sources in individual developed countries (for example, the United States) or groups of countries (for example, the European Economic Community or EEC).

Among Western countries, the United States is well known for its official policy of denying so-called strategic exports to given countries on political grounds. And the definition of strategic commodities has been so widely interpreted as to include consumer goods. The Trading with the Enemy Act was enforced against the Soviet Union and its allies in 1947, against China in 1949, against Cuba in 1960, and against Chile in 1970. The U.S. government has also exerted pressure on nonsocialist nations to participate in its embargoes. For example, the neutral Swedish government was reportedly forced to constrain its trade with communist nations in the 1950s or lose essential raw materials. Also, in the 1960s the United States succeeded in preventing the Swedish steel industry from producing nickel from Cuba by threatening to stop large Swedish exports of special steel to the United States.[88] Cuba was even denied oil for thirteen years, not only from U.S. enterprises but also from other sources, due to U.S. influence over the international oil oligopoly. Similarly, Canadian affili-

---

[87] *MEES*, June 18, 1971, p. 5; "Boumédienne Analyzes France-Algerian Oil Crisis," *MEES Supplement*, June 18, 1971; also *Petroleum Press Service*, June 1971, pp. 204–5; *Washington Post*, July 28, 1971, p. A11; *Oil and Gas Journal* (Tulsa), June 21, 1971, p. 80; and Sonatrach, "Algeria-Petroleum," *Petroleum Times* (London), June 4, 1971.

[88] See U.S. Department of Commerce, *A Summary of U.S. Export Control Regulations*, revised September 1, 1972, pp. iii–v; and Gunnar Adler-Karlson, "The Teacher of the Oil Arabs," *Dagens Nyheter* (Stockholm), November 1973, reprinted in OPEC's *Weekly Bulletin Review of the Press*, November 30, 1973, pp. 2–4.

ates of U.S. enterprises were not allowed to sell to Cuba. In one such example, the U.S. directors of Litton Industries late in 1974 blocked the sale of $500,000 of office equipment—on the grounds that U.S. legislation forbade trading with Cuba, classified as an enemy country. This action triggered the passing of Canadian legislation which precluded the influence of foreign laws and measures on foreign-owned Canadian enterprises. The U.S. government stated that it would not lift its economic embargo on Cuba unless "Cuba pursued a more restrained international course." [89]

As mentioned earlier, Arab oil exporting governments have also resorted to the trade constraining approach, with their 1973–1974 reduction of oil supplies and boycott, particularly against the United States. Their reason was "self-defense," on the grounds that the United States was offering massive military and economic aid to Israel, helping it to perpetrate the occupation of Arab lands and people.[90] Even prior to the cutbacks and boycott, some 900,000 barrels per day of oil supplies were unavailable to Western Europe following Israel's destruction of oil terminals in Syria during the October 1973 war. The Saudi government, whose weight in any collective Arab oil decision is crucial, was reluctantly forced into the boycott approach as a "protest" action. As the Saudi minister of petroleum and mineral resources explained:

Saudi Arabia adamantly refused to use oil as a weapon to disrupt Western economies or as a punitive device. Therefore, the basis upon which the Arab producing countries reached agreement was that oil production should be reduced and not stopped altogether. As for the ban on exports to the United States, the late King Faisal's Government actively tried to avert it. However, the American military assistance to Israel during the war, unprecedented in its volume and nature, changed the course of the war and prevented the Arabs from achieving their legitimate goal—the recovery of their occupied lands. The natural reaction to this American action was the imposition of an embargo on oil exports to the United States." [91]

Obviously the "free trade" policy has had a hard time, and consumers worldwide, in developing and developed areas alike, suffer from the monopolistic or monopsonistic actions of governments or trade groups. Al-

---

[89] See *Business Week,* January 13, 1975, p. 42; and U.S. Secretary of State Henry Kissinger at a press conference, Washington, January 10, 1974.

[90] See, for example, Fuad Itayim, "Arab Oil: The Political Dimension," *Journal of Palestine Studies* (Beirut), vol. 3, no. 2, Winter 1974, pp. 84–97.

[91] Ahmad Zaki Yamani, "Oil and International Politics," *MEES Supplement,* April 25, 1975, p. 3.

though the U.S. government is still considered a world champion of freer trade and private-competitive enterprise, its actions in constraining trade are of particular importance owing to the pre-eminence of its economy. For illustrations of restrictive actions of international significance, the food and fuel trades offer an interesting field for analysis. In particular, the soybean episode of 1973 is most revealing. On June 27, 1973, the U.S. Commerce Department abruptly imposed an embargo on the export of soybeans, cottonseeds, and their byproducts. The embargo was replaced a few days later by a system of export licenses which prohibited new orders and limited exports of soybean to 50 percent, and soybean oil-cake and meal to 40 percent, of the amounts of the outstanding export contracts. Thus the United States proved that the government of the richest market economy in the world can afford with impunity not to honor contracts freely entered into between its businesses and other countries. The significance of the U.S. action was all the more important in view of the fact that the United States produces some 90 percent of world soybean output, and the fact that for Japan and several West European countries soybean has been a major source (90 percent) of protein and animal feed. *The Economist* demanded: ''But dare Japan and Europe continue to rest their agriculture and food supply on a product [or a producer country, this author adds] that may overnight be declared to be unavailable.'' [92]

The U.S. action was apparently prompted by the desire to curb the rising costs of U.S. livestock producers who rely on soybean for animal feed. But a leader of the American Soybean Association argued that the decision could mean ''less meat for the [American] dinner table and bring us to a rationing situation.'' Whatever the merits of the export restrictions on the domestic level, the fact that the U.S. government as a leader of private enterprise can feel free to renege on firm contracts entered into between its enterprises and other nations reflects sadly on the rules of open international trade. The French president commented that it would be unimaginable for Europe to remain dependent on outsiders for its food products. Notwithstanding the lifting of restrictions on October 1, 1973, the Europeans and Japanese had lost confidence in the United States as a reliable and cheap supplier. The U.S. agriculture secretary admitted: ''The

---

[92] ''American Trade: Carrying a Bean,'' *Economist,* July 7, 1973, p. 28; see also ''Le Soja nous tient!'' *Journal de Genève,* July 19, 1973, p. 1.

export controls we had on soybeans this year were disastrous in many repects." [93]

Food is undoubtedly an essential product for human survival, and many countries are unable to grow enough for their own requirements. Accordingly, security of food supplies is vital to their existence. The United States has for long been the leading exporter of food products, but U.S. food and fertilizer supplies have suffered from interruptions. This applies to both commercial and aid supplies. Though U.S. food aid has been shrinking in size, "political concerns have received a high priority." In 1974, over 50 percent went to political and military-related countries.[94] Quoting a press editorial of the *Alabama Star* to illustrate public reaction to the political use of food aid, the U.S. Senate Select Committee on Nutrition and Human Needs reported:

In the first place, we only give away surplus foods that aren't needed by the American people. Hardly a national sacrifice, but fair enough. Then we dispense the surplus foods not on the basis of where they are most needed, but on the basis of power-political considerations of foreign affairs. In other words, we use the food as ammunition. Very little of our Food for Peace has gone to Africa, where tens of thousands have perished from famine. But during the last year nearly half of it went to Cambodia and South Viet Nam. We stopped food assistance to the Chilean people when they elected Allende, and then resumed it when the military coup ousted the Allende government.[95]

Constraints on fertilizer exports were pronounced in 1973–1974, a year of energy shortage and hunger. Industrial countries (notably the United States and Japan) restricted fertilizer exports to meet rising domestic needs. Their actions contributed to accentuating the global maldistribution of fertilizer, and consequently to worsening food production. This is because the productivity of each additional ton of fertilizer in developing countries is twice as high as in developed countries. Moreover, there appears to be a maldistribution in the pattern of use of fertilizer. For ex-

---

[93] "The High Cost of Soybean Diplomacy," *Business Week,* July 7, 1973, p. 28; "Threat in U.S. to Soybeans," *International Herald Tribune,* July 10, 1973; "M. Pompidou: Il est inimaginable que l'Europe dépende de l'étranger pour les productions alimentaires," *Le Monde,* July 14, 1973, p. 28; *New York Times,* September 4, 1974, pp. 49, 51; and *U.S. News & World Report,* September 24, 1973, p. 24.

[94] George McGovern, chairman, U.S. Senate Select Committee on Nutrition and Human Needs, *Report on Nutrition and the International Situation,* 1974, pp. vii, viii.

[95] *Ibid.,* p. 28. See also "The Political Uses of Food Aid," *Washington Post,* reprinted in the *International Herald Tribune,* November 30, 1974, p. 4; and "Senate Unit Calls Food Aid Political," *New York Times,* September 10, 1974, p. 7.

ample, some 15 percent of the U.S. plant food (3 million tons in 1974) which goes for nonfarm purposes (lawns and other ornamental and recreational purposes) could yield some 30 million tons in additional grain production, a year's supply for 150 million people. One informed U.S. researcher commented: "We are caught in an absurd cycle in which a poor country is refused fertilizer, thus cutting its food production and raising its import needs (and quite likely famine-relief needs) by more food than the amount we rich countries produced with the withheld fertilizer in the first place, thereby inflating already high world grain prices. This will hurt rich and poor alike." [96]

Besides food and fertilizer, energy ranks in the same category of importance for humanity's welfare. Here also government actions of the energy-exporting countries impinge on global prosperity. Oil exporting countries' actions have already been reviewed. For non-oil exporters, U.S. actions are of equal significance, especially in the nuclear field. Concern for U.S. national interest seems to be paramount in the export of nuclear fuel, before concern for security of supplies to traditional buyers. Thus in March 1975 the U.S. government resorted to another "embargo," as described by *The Economist*. It consisted of halting all exports of nuclear fuel and reactors without prior consultation, pending the examination of handling and transport safety by the U.S. nuclear regulatory commission. The EEC protested vigorously and indicated its "serious concern regarding the security of supply from the United States." Previously, late in 1973, the U.S. had raised its prices unilaterally and exacted tougher delivery terms. To *The Economist,* "American suppliers, pushed by Congress, have proved unreliable in the past and are now turning awkward again." The suspension of U.S. nuclear exports lasted four months. [97]

Also prompted by regional interests, the EEC has asked member countries for the authorization to cut down on exports of grain through export

[96] James P. Grant, "Global Crises and Emerging Historic Discontinuities: What Role for UNCTAD," *Tenth Anniversary Journal* (UNCTAD), 1974, p. 45; "Your Lawn vs. Food for India: Both Sides of a Controversy," and "For the Hungry: Talk, but Not Much Help," in *U.S. News & World Report,* November 25, 1974, pp. 44–46. Also V. K. McElheny, "Rising World Fertilizer Scarcity Threatens Famine for Millions," *New York Times,* September 1, 1974, pp. 1, 34; and James P. Grant, "While We Fertilize Golf Courses," *New York Times,* August 28, 1974, p. 31.

[97] "Nuclear Fuel: Bear Hug?" *Economist,* April 19, 1975, p. 39; and "Enriched Uranium: Go, Stop, Go," *Economist,* July 12, 1975, pp. 35, 36.

levies. Such restriction of trade in an essential commodity does not take into consideration the needs of consumers outside the EEC.[98]

In fact, cutbacks in the production of certain basic commodities in order to sustain prices or for other purposes could very well hurt global welfare and have intolerable effects on the poor nations. This has been and remains a source of conflict and war. Large reductions in oil exports, for example, were considered by U.S. leaders to have a strangulation impact on industrial countries and to possibly invite military retaliation. In return, the president of Algeria, an oil exporting country, argued that reductions in oil availabilities were not brought about solely by the price-conscious policies of the oil exporting countries. They were also brought about by the consumer countries' actions, including the U.S. oil import duty of $2 per barrel. He also contended that developed countries "leave millions of acres fallow in order to avoid a fall in prices, while hundreds of millions of people go hungry in the underdeveloped countries." [99]

To lighten the burden of interruptions, production cutbacks, or similar actions, we could set up permanent multilateral mechanisms with set rules and standards of relief. Another approach would be to resort to ad hoc solutions for the mobilization of aid on a voluntary basis, as and when interruptions occur. A third approach would consist of having a standing committee which would convene at short notice to consider the problem at hand. The first approach has the merit of permanency; it also provides participants prior knowledge of what to expect in the event of interruptions and accordingly reduces uncertainty. The second approach leaves matters completely unstructured. The third approach is a compromise; it provides for the firm opportunity of discussing matters, with no commitment regarding the nature or size of relief to the suffering country.

In their search for greater security in obtaining basic commodities, several countries have adopted individual measures, such as building stockpiles or reserves of strategic and critical materials as the United States has done. Alternatively, the promotion of vertically integrated national enterprises with access to raw materials from various sources has appealed to some governments. Others, as shown below, have attempted to achieve intercountry cooperation and mutual assistance programs.

---

[98] See "La Commission européenne voudrait frainer les exportations de céréales en les taxant," *Le Monde*, July 13, 1973, pp. 1, 28.

[99] President Houari Boumédienne, in *MEES*, February 7, 1975, pp. 3–4.

Developed Market Economies

In the past two decades, the Western developed countries have taken steps individually and collectively to meet possible emergencies in supply interruptions. Thus, after the nationalization of the Suez Canal in July 1956 but two months prior to its closure, a planning mechanism to meet an interruption in oil supplies was agreed to by U.S. oil companies through the Middle East Emergency Committee, under the auspices of the U.S. Foreign Petroleum Supply Committee. A similar arrangement was set up by the Organization for European Economic Co-operation (OEEC). The two arrangements were unified within the oil committee of the newly created OECD, grouping the developed countries of North America, Western Europe, Oceania, and Japan.[100]

More specifically, the intergovernmental OECD Oil Committee collects and analyzes data on current and prospective conditions of demand and supply for petroleum and gas. It advises, plans, and administers the scheduling and apportioning of oil supplies for the benefit of member countries in periods of emergencies. Beginning at the time of the Suez crisis in 1956, all European OECD members except Finland have participated in the monitoring of a stockpile program and in apportioning domestic and imported oil supplies in periods of emergency, though not including stock accumulated before the crisis. Of total supplies to be shared, 90 percent would go to members in proportion to their recent consumption, and 10 percent would go to an emergency stockpile to be allocated to countries facing special problems.[101]

The OECD governments have authorized company representatives to organize themselves into an international Industry Advisory Body, and to meet on an ad hoc basis in the event that oil supplies are threatened. Periodic meetings are held between the Oil Committee and leading executives of oil companies in member countries to discuss the problems of the industry.

Besides the OECD Oil Committee, Western countries coordinate their domestic and international emergency preparedness planning within the

[100] See Schurr and Homan, *Middle Eastern Oil,* p. 14n.

[101] *Petroleum Intelligence Weekly* (New York), August 13, 1973, p. 4; and OECD, "Oil Supplies, 1970," *OECD Observer* (Paris), no. 54, October 1971, p. 29; see also "Energy Policy in the European Community," *OECD Observer,* June 1972, pp. 36–39.

International Energy Agency or IEA (see Chapter 2), and within their defense organizations. The leading example of the latter is the North Atlantic Treaty Organization (NATO), whose focus is not only on military emergency planning but also on civilian plans. NATO's Petroleum Planning Committee meets periodically, usually in Brussels.[102]

It has been suggested that "the most effective way to keep supply interruption from being employed as an instrument of policy is to render the use of such interruption futile." [103] The objective of assuring supplies, according to Western analysts, can best be achieved—assuming no military intervention or political coercion—by building inventories or keeping some domestic reserves unproduced in order to buy time for developing additional or alternative sources. European OECD countries agreed to a minimum stockpile of crude oil and products in 1973 equivalent to 50 days of current consumption, and sought to raise that to the equivalent of 90 days within a few years.[104]

The net benefits, if any, from reducing dependence on a few suppliers for key commodities are both economical and political. On the economic side, the importing country aiming at a higher degree of self-sufficiency or at building alternate supply sources can avoid the exploitation of its consumers through higher prices. On the political side, the importing country can reduce the leverage for political pressure exercised by major foreign suppliers.

Developed Centrally Planned Economies

East European countries, Mongolia, and Cuba are linked economically through the Council for Mutual Economic Assistance (CMEA). These countries constitute a reasonably self-sufficient economic area for several basic commodities, although deficits and surpluses do occur in a few. Supply-demand imbalances, coupled with freer international trade, have led to significant exchanges with countries outside the CMEA area after the mid-1960s. For example, USSR oil and gas exports from Siberian fields to West Europe are counterbalanced by gas imports from Afghani-

---

[102] U.S. Congress, *Twenty-First Annual Report of the Activities of the Joint Committee on Defense Production,* 92nd Cong., 2nd sess., p. 271.

[103] See, for example, Schurr and Homan, *Middle Eastern Oil,* p. 15; and R. L. Gordon, "Without Rudder, Compass, or Chart: The Problem of Energy Policy Guidelines," *Quarterly of the Colorado School of Mines,* vol. 64, no. 4, October 1969, p. 41.

[104] "Getting Together," *Petroleum Press Service,* June 1973, p. 203; and OECD, *Oil: The Present Situation and Future Prospects* (Paris, 1973), p. 83.

stan and Iran to the southern industrial centers of the USSR, and by East Europe's oil imports from the Middle East and North Africa.

CMEA countries agreed at their 25th session in August 1971 to pool efforts to insure adequate supplies of fuel and other raw materials. Their ultimate goal is integration, specialization, and balanced growth at the regional level. The leadership of the USSR and its capacity to carry out cooperative schemes in the CMEA will be crucial factors in its success. East European cooperation in fuel and raw material industries covers research and production of advanced equipment, long-term credits, intraregional trade, oil and gas pipeline networks, CMEA-wide search for minerals, and joint ventures to pool resources and achieve specialization and economies of size. Soviet sources have claimed that CMEA cooperation, for example in the oil trade between the USSR and Czechoslovakia, has resulted in lower-cost imports to the latter than would otherwise be the case.[105]

The principal areas of CMEA cooperation cover energy, chemicals, metallurgy, capital goods, transport, agriculture, regional trade, and science and technology. An illustration of cooperation in the area of energy is the July 1962 multilateral agreement to establish a united power grid known as *Mir* (peace). Its regional control center, located in Prague, started operation on January 1, 1963. It ensures that the electricity supplies of participating countries meet their demand most efficiently through a better utilization of generating capacities, interstate exchange of electricity, and coordination of the work of the national control centers on a day-to-day and also a long-term basis.[106]

Developing Exporting Countries

Primary exporting countries have taken public cognizance of the impact of demand interruptions on their economies. In fact, the OPEC Con-

[105] See "New Comecon Drive Banking on Oil, Gas," *Oil and Gas Journal*, August 30, 1971, pp. 26–27; A. Zubkov, "CMEA Countries' Cooperation in the Fuel, Power, and Raw-Material Industries," *International Affairs* (Moscow), December 1971, pp. 107–9; H. Ratnicks, "Development of Fuel and Raw Material Resources in the COMECON Countries," *Petroleum Times,* June 30–July 14, 1972; and B. Pokland and E. Shevchenko, *Council for Mutual Economic Assistance: Its Present and Future* (Moscow: Novosti Press Agency Publishing House, 1973); and O. T. Bogomolov and A. N. Barkovsky, "Economic Co-operation among the CMEA Countries," *Economic Bulletin for Asia and the Far East* (Economic Commission for Asia and the Far West, United Nations), vol. 21, no. 3, December 1970, pp. 11–29 (E/CN.11/1000).

[106] Pokland and Shevchenko, *Council for Mutual Economic Assistance,* pp. 51–53.

ference in 1972 instructed "the Secretary-General to convene a Working Party of experts from Member Countries at Headquarters in order to prepare a study on the establishment of a fund to assist any Member Country affected by actions taken against it by oil companies." [107] The matter was still under study in 1973.

There are, nevertheless, situations of one or more OPEC member countries coming to the rescue of another member country on their own initiative. For example, Libya came to the rescue of Algeria with a $100 million advance after Algeria was faced with a boycott from the oil companies in mid-1971; this followed its partial nationalization of French concessionaires. The Algerians managed to overcome their financial difficulties and settle with the French companies without having to make use of the Libyan credit. [108] And Iraq received credits from Kuwait and Libya following the boycott it faced in 1972 after its nationalization measures.

All primary commodity exporting countries are concerned about keeping demand interruptions from being employed against them and about rendering such interruptions useless. The most practical approach in the short run is to build international financial reserves (as some have done) and commodity reserves. In the longer run, they should aim at a balanced diversification of their economic resources, at a reduced dependence on primary exports, and at a joint insurance mechanism. With respect to the latter suggestion, Algeria, Iraq, and Libya agreed on May 23, 1970, to create a joint cooperative fund to aid any of the contracting states which "may suffer harm as a result of a confrontation with the exploiting oil companies." This fund has, as of 1975, not been set up. [109]

CIPEC countries have also attempted to face up to the boycott of their exports, and more generally to "economic aggression." The latter term was defined as "any act which impedes or hinders the exercise of the sovereign right of countries to dispose freely of their national resources in order to further their development." CIPEC countries agreed that members should not take advantage of the situation created by the aggression, such as replacing the markets of the victimized country. They also agreed to study methods of raising funds to assist such countries, and to

---

[107] See the OPEC communiqué in *MEES Supplement,* March 10, 1972, p. 5.

[108] "Boumédienne Acknowledges Libyan Support During France-Algerian Crisis," *MEES,* March 3, 1972, p. 4.

[109] *MEES,* May 29, 1970, pp. 2–3.

coordinate in this matter with other organizations of LDCs which export raw materials, notably OPEC.[110]

Developing countries, whether importer or exporter, share a concern for protecting the flow of trade and economic relations with their important traditional trading partners, the advanced industrial nations. This concern has prompted a group of twenty-one Latin American countries to place a resolution before the UN General Assembly's Political Committee urging the assembly to "take appropriate measures for the creation of a system of collective security to encourage sustained development and the expansion of national economies." This group of countries along with other LDCs are fearful of the economic blackmail which industrial countries can successfully resort to, in the same manner as they use military blackmail. As explained by a Latin American diplomat in forceful language: "We have tried to build safeguards against nuclear terror through a whole variety of disarmament measures in recent years. But our countries can be destroyed by economic terror as practiced by the industrialized countries—whether it is the United States or the Soviet Union or the Common Market—almost as severely as by nuclear terror." [111]

Developing Importing Countries

Unlike the developed countries, the LDCs do not have a multinational mechanism designed to protect them against unforeseen interruptions in the trade or supply of basic commodities. Consequently, this author suggests that a Commodity Insurance Fund (CIF) be set up for the purpose of assisting these countries during periods of interruptions. Help could be financial or in kind through compensatory supplies from alternative, and admittedly more costly, sources. The fund could also create an international stockpile agency to be financed by international organizations (for example, the IMF) and by assessments levied on participating member countries (probably based on their per capita income, population, and imports of raw materials concerned). The CIF could conceivably be supported by the richer countries as part of their aid program.

For several countries, sudden interruption of trade flows—especially of

[110] Santiago Extraordinary Conference of Ministers, Resolution of Measures of Defence and Solidarity, *Copper Market* (CIPEC), 4th quarter, 1972, app. 1.

[111] Society of International Development, *Survey of International Development* (Washington, 1971), p. 3.

certain commodities—is similar in its effects to a natural disaster. The world community has already recognized that hardships arising from the latter have to be alleviated. In fact, since 1972, there has existed a United Nations Disaster Relief Organization (UNDRO). Its functions are, among others, to "mobilize, direct, and coordinate the relief activities of the various organizations of the United Nations system in response to a request for disaster assistance from a stricken state." In addition, it coordinates UN assistance with assistance given by intergovernmental and nongovernmental organizations. Finally, it promotes the study, prevention, and control of disasters, and provides advice to governments on predisaster planning.[112] This assistance offered in natural catastrophes could be extended to other catastrophes, if the majority UN members were to agree to it. To get such an agreement is, admittedly, far from easy. The challenge of today and the future is therefore to create a body similar to UNDRO, with the capacity to provide an efficient and effective worldwide service to cater for manmade disasters. This new body could be referred to as the United Nations Emergency Stocks (UNES), and its functions could include holding reserves of key materials, or assured access to them, to meet such emergencies. These materials should include food, fertilizer, and leading minerals. UNES's reserves could then be used for sale or lending at fair prices in accordance to need. UNES's existence would protect the poor countries by fending off the pre-emption of supplies in emergencies by the affluent one billion of the world's people. It could also avoid manmade interruptions of demand or supply by encouraging long-term purchase-sales commitments, thereby giving a reasonable security to both exporting and importing countries.

Information and Cooperation

Technical managerial know-how has become a most important economic resource. The availability of relevant up-to-date information, its transfer and adaptation to local conditions, its effective and efficient use—all are crucial to progress.[113] To improve the flow of key information to LDCs—especially the small and poor countries not members of

[112] ECOSOC Resolution E/L.1438, reprinted in UN Information Service, *Round-Up of the 51st Session of the Economic and Social Council,* Geneva, July 30, 1971, pp. 31–32.

[113] See, for example, O. C. Herfindahl, *Natural Resource Information for Economic Development* (Baltimore: Johns Hopkins Press, 1969); and "Information as a key to Progress," *OECD Observer,* April 1972, pp. 6–8.

OPEC, CIPEC, or similar groups—the creation of a Resource Advisory Services (RAS) agency seems warranted. RAS could conceivably be run on a cost basis, with fees eventually paid by beneficiary countries out of profits derived from the information supplied. Payment for services could well turn out to be much less expensive than alternative courses of action, notably sole reliance on profit-making firms.

RAS's function could consist of centralizing the collection, storage, and dissemination of information to member countries and their agencies. The scope of the information should, in principle, be worldwide and cover: trade and freight figures; costs of various inputs; information on markets, credit, and technologies; fiscal charges, trade barriers, or incentives in the countries concerned; and a roster of firms, institutions, and experts dealing with various aspects of the resource in question.

RAS is likely to offer many interrelated advantages. It can preclude exploitation of ignorance, bring competitive forces to work, reduce uncertainty and facilitate decision-making, permit more efficient and effective use of opportunities, reduce losses from miscalculations or premature commitments, reduce the scope for bigotry, venality, misunderstanding or even conflict, publicize the relevant and valid experiences of other nations, and permit a wider and quicker access to technical knowledge, managerial know-how, credit opportunities, and tax information. Impartiality and speed in responding to requests from member countries and their enterprises are obviously essential to a successful operation of RAS.

There is, however, more information generated at present than the Third World countries can absorb. It is typically in English, but also in French, German, Japanese, and Russian. Developing countries lack the translation and publishing capacity and the trained minds to use a significant portion of the technical and managerial data already available. Accordingly, it will prove too ambitious for the proposed RAS to act outright as a central repository and disseminator of comprehensive information in the natural resources field. It is more realistic for an early stage of operation to have RAS act as an intermediary advising on the various sources for such information. Should individual countries, most likely LDCs, be unable to secure out-of-the-way information through their own means, RAS may then undertake to provide it, and advise on its authenticity and accuracy.

Moreover, it will be more manageable for RAS to start its activities with one or a few commodities (probably those for which information is comparatively inaccessible to LDCs) or one subject matter, say taxation.[114] The final scope of RAS' activities could be decided after surveying the needs of the developing countries concerned. Once proven workable and successful, RAS' functions could be enlarged to progressively encompass the whole field of natural resources. Such a scheme has already been favorably discussed by the UN Committee on Natural Resources and other UN forums.[115]

Availability of managerial and technical information in itself, though, is not sufficient for the transfer of know-how. For such transfer to be successful, there is need for person-to-person contact to make fruitful use of that information, and to adapt skills and technology to the particular environment and needs of the individual countries. In addition, feedback has to be arranged on a permanent and a regular basis in order to control, evaluate, and improve the relevance of the information made available. And further, to go beyond information availability into advising on its efficient use, there is need for effective links between the RAS and the beneficiary countries. These links can be established through experts who are prepared to assist in drafting legislation, in designing the relevant supervisory departments and agencies, in helping in plan formulation and in forecasts of demand and supply, and in pointing out up-to-date competitive terms of contracts and new market opportunities.

Resource advisers should not be expected to assume decision-making prerogatives in their dealings with member states. Their function should be limited to elucidating alternatives or options, and to analyzing and assessing elements of costs and benefits for various courses of action. They should also contribute to building the self-reliance of policy-makers in LDCs, and their capacity to make effective use of information in protecting and promoting national interests.

Before calling on foreign expertise, it would be logical for developing

---

[114] Dudley Seers recommended the creation of a similar international agency which would advise governments on tax and conservation matters, in "Big Companies and Small Countries," pp. 605–6. See also United Nations, *Science and Technology,* Report on the United Nations Conference on the Application of Science and Technology for the Benefit of the Less Developed Areas, vol. 2, *Natural Resources,* 1963, pp. 195–96, 200.

[115] See UN, ECOSOC, Committee on Natural Resources, *Report on the First Session,* February 22–March 10, 1971, New York, 1971 (E/4969; E/C.7/13), pp. 22–23; and *Report on the Third Session,* February 6–17, 1973, New York, 1973 (E/5247; E/C.7/43), pp. 12, 40. Also ECOSOC Res. 1761 B (LIV), and UN, ECOSOC, *Impact of Multinational Corporations,* pp. 36, 80.

countries to protect the outflow of their qualified nationals, and to win back those who have left, using the appropriate incentive system. The "brain drain" has significantly hurt the developmental opportunities of several LDCs. It was estimated that income transferred through the brain drain to the United States amounted in 1970 to roughly $3.7 billion. The United States total official development assistance to developing countries in the same year amounted to $3.1 billion. In this transfer, India was the biggest donor, and the United States the largest beneficiary. The contribution of developing countries through the brain drain amounted in 1970 to nearly 14 percent of the total U.S. expenditure on research and development, and about 38 percent of U.S. expenditures on higher education.[116]

Promoting greater global interdependence in a variety of fields, with fair sharing of benefits by all parties concerned, would certainly increase world harmony and welfare. There are already several examples of successful international cooperative ventures, and this chapter has attempted to suggest additional ones. The suggestions presented above vary in nature. Some are oriented toward competitiveness (for example, RAS), while others aim at exploiting market forces through group action. They can, however, be reconciled on the basis that they aim generally at promoting global harmony through improving the frameworks for the distribution of the gains from primary trade in favor of LDCs, and for averting or solving certain problems in the resource industries. All types of group action assume the presence of some measure of political goodwill for cooperation among nations, and a positive response on the part of transnational enterprises.

Of the suggestions presented above, the centralized exchange of information (RAS) is likely to encounter the least resistance, and accordingly appears more readily achievable. RAS can also promote communication, leading hopefully to improved mutual trust and cooperation. The development of new financial and guarantee institutions among or for LDCs is another practical move. Other promising fields include conservation of nonrenewable natural resources and the protection of the environment.

[116] "The Brain Drain," *Development Forum* (Geneva), March 1975, p. 8.

5. Resource Diplomacy: Sharing Gains through Cooperation

The economies of most resource-exporting developing countries are narrowly based on one or two commodities. Their foreign exchange and budgetary receipts and their national income are vulnerable to adverse changes in market and other conditions affecting their exports. Ironing out price fluctuations of primary commodities would in itself be insufficient, however. It has to be coupled with growth in real terms of export earnings. A leading U.S. legislator, Senator Frank Church, in a speech given on the Senate floor on October 9, 1971, advocated ''as an alternative to the palliative of aid, that we lend positive support to developing countries by entering into commercial arrangements that redress the terms of trade which are now rigged against them.'' [1]

Terms of Trade

To tackle the problem of protecting the export earnings of developing countries, the UN General Assembly, UNCTAD,[2] and other international forums have suggested the stabilization of terms of trade. Beginning in 1971, and for the first time in the history of international economic relations, this principle was applied, although in a fashion which later proved inadequate, by OPEC in agreement with the transnational oil companies.[3]

---

[1] *Congressional Record,* October 29, 1971, p. S1786; and *Washington Post,* November 7, 1971, p. B4.

[2] See, for example, proceedings of the UN General Assembly's Special Sixth and Seventh Sessions on Problems of Raw Materials and Development, April 1974 and September 1975 respectively; and the Secretary-General of UNCTAD, *Report of the Trade and Development Board,* October 14, 1970–September 21, 1971, New York, 1972, p. 236 (A/8415/Rev. 1).

[3] Discussed at length in Zuhayr Mikdashi, *The Community of Oil Exporting Countries* (London: Allen & Unwin; Ithaca: Cornell University Press, 1972), ch. 7; and Mikdashi, ''A

Stabilization of terms of trade purports to protect the purchasing power of a unit of exports in terms of imports, starting from a base year considered "reasonable" by protagonists. Even if this were administratively feasible, there is the risk that an automatic matching of the export price of a commodity with increases in the import price index will render that commodity less competitive, and eventually reduce the demand for it in favor of substitutes.

Demand for primary commodities is usually derived from demand for their final products. It is significant that the value of raw materials is generally a small portion of the price of the end products. By comparison, the share of labor (wages) and excise taxes in the developed industrial countries is more substantial and generally on the increase. Accordingly, it is unrealistic to charge those primary exporters attempting to stabilize or improve the purchasing power of their exports with sole responsibility for pricing the finished product out of the market. The small significance of primary commodities, including energy,[4] in the final price of manufactured products should generally lead to a correspondingly low incidence of price increases in primary goods on the manufacturers' final price.

It is conceivable that substitution of one primary commodity for another does not have a net adverse effect on the developing world exporting these two commodities, if both the beneficiary countries and the losing countries are developing. It is, however, possible that the net losers are the least developed, leading consequently to a decline in world welfare (omitting considerations of income distribution within these countries). Should the substitution favor higher-cost protected commodities produced in the developed countries—say, coal-based synthetics for packaging—at the expense of developing countries—in this case producing jute, tin, iron ore, or aluminum—world welfare would be lowered.

---

la recherche d'un accroissement des bénéfices économiques: les négociations par les termes de l'échange,'' *Etudes internationales* (Quebec), vol. 2, no. 4, December 1971, pp. 529–61.

[4] At the peak of oil price increases in 1974, the value of the oil input in the production cost of selected manufactured goods in industrial countries varied from lows of 2.6 and 3.0 percent for maritime construction and the car industry, respectively, to highs of 6.0 and 8.3 percent for construction materials and transport respectively. See Arthur D. Little and Co., Cambridge, Mass., as reported in a memorandum entitled "Le Pétrole, les matières de base et le développement,'' submitted by Algeria to the UN General Assembly's Sixth Special Session on Raw Materials and Development, New York, April 1974.

Alternatively, should substitution favor commodities produced in the developing countries at the expense of a higher-cost protected commodity produced in the developed countries, world welfare would be better off. The foregoing does not imply, though, that economically attractive inventions lower world welfare in the longer term.

The argument for protecting the purchasing power of their exports proceeds often advocated by LDCs is essentially an argument in equity. One should guard against using it indiscriminately in reshaping economic relations between primary exporter and importer countries. If it were to be applied to commodities with elastic demand, it might hurt exporters. Conversely, if applied to commodities with inelastic demand, producer countries could capture some of the consumer surplus. In addition, export gains do not hinge solely on the stabilization of the price terms of trade of LDCs; the diversification of the export trade and the expansion of its volume could prove of similar importance.

The United Nations has envisioned the introduction of a levy on commodities entering the world trade as a means of redistributing wealth in favor of the least developed poor countries. For such redistribution of wealth, some scholars have advocated taxing natural resources. One scheme called for arranging primary commodities into noncompeting groups, and used three criteria for tax levels: competing commodities within each group should be taxed at relative rates designed to minimize substitution, levels of taxes between groups should vary directly with their pollution impact and the risk of impending exhaustion, and tax levels should maximize the chances of political acceptance. Given the fact that the above first two criteria are not readily amenable to accurate determination, expediency would give the third criterion a more effective role.[5]

This scheme opted for a tax on exports—rather than on imports or on consumption of products—reportedly in order to avoid "considerable distortion" and reduce "expense in collection." It assumed that additional taxes on producer countries, given the inelasticity of demand (or absence of substitutions) for their products, should not hurt these countries. These contentions would have to be tested or guaranteed over the longer run for various internationally traded raw materials before producer countries would submit to taxes. Moreover, the enforcement of such a scheme

[5] See Ian Little, "International Tax on the Rich to Help the Poor," *Times* (London), May 9, 1972, p. 21.

would be based on the willingness of major protagonists to cooperate. This could hopefully be an initial step toward setting a worldwide central fiscal authority. One more question remains moot: why should the tax be limited to natural resources, and not be more comprehensive to cover all internationally traded commodities—the primary and the nonprimary? A comprehensive tax, though more complex to design and difficult to enforce, would represent a fair means of tapping world wealth for the benefit of the poorest countries.

LDCs are not only concerned about a deterioration in their terms of trade; they are equally concerned about the related problems of devaluation of major currencies (notably that of the United States) and access to major markets. The devaluation of a major currency can especially hurt those developing countries whose raw materials' exports are expressed in U.S. dollars. As one Western trade source argued:

From the standpoint of raw material producers and especially the developing nations, this is a major fraud. Seen in its simplest terms, the industrialized nations have revalued and the developing nations, dependent upon raw materials, have devalued and, with the United States as the dominant factor in major commodities, most metals and minerals will tend to follow the American currency. The result is that raw materials will be cheaper for Europe and Japan; for the developing nations, their mineral wealth, in the future, will buy fewer tractors, fewer hospitals, less food.[6]

This statement is, however, oversimplified. If primary producing countries upvalue their exports along with dollar devaluations, and in the absence of inflation in the U.S. economy, they could purchase cheaper goods from the United States—though not from other developed countries. Among LDCs, the OPEC countries managed in the 1970s to shield themselves against the adverse effects of price inflation on their imports through increases in oil export prices. The structure and conditions of the world oil industry permitted such increases.

Besides currency instability, access to the major markets of the developed countries is of crucial importance to the well-being of developing countries. Indeed, trade offers them their major opportunity for acquiring the resources they need for their progress. Trade impediments are, however, diverse and multiple. These can be broadly grouped into two: government-imposed trade and fiscal barriers, and market structure barriers. The first group covers governmental measures of a tariff and non-

[6] *Mining Journal* (London), December 24, 1971, p. 573.

tariff nature aimed at constraining the free flow of commodities. These measures include prohibitions and quotas, subsidies to domestic producers, duties and other indirect taxes, restrictive trade agreements, state agencies carrying out discriminatory government directives, national preference purchasing policies and regulations, import-export licenses, foreign exchange limitations, customs, and other administrative formalities.

The second group of impediments to free trade covers imperfections of industrial organization or market structure, barriers to entry of a technological, managerial, or capital requirement nature, and other restrictive tactics of private enterprise. These impediments may arise from conditions of economic size and business concentration, monopolistic practices, vertical integration, cartelization, interlocking arrangements, and geographical and functional diversification—with governmental inaction, permissiveness, or active support helping to sustain these conditions.

Indeed, cartels have been officially permitted in the industrial Western countries for a long time. And legislation protecting export cartels at the national, regional, or interregional levels has been enacted in the United States, Western Europe, Japan, and Australia. Areas of cartelization by transnational enterprises in the 1970s covered primary products, manufactured goods, and services.[7]

The benefits developing countries receive from trade could, therefore, be substantially enhanced if their major trading partners, the developed countries, would open up their markets and eliminate protective-cum-discriminatory measures favoring their domestic or regional producers.[8] In this regard, UNCTAD conferences called upon several industrialized countries to grant developing countries (numbering about one hundred in 1975) a Generalized System of Preference (GSP). This would grant unilaterally, and on a nonreciprocal basis, a partial or total suppression of tariffs on processed and manufactured goods exported by developing countries, subject, however, to important exceptions and safeguards. The EEC has been in the vanguard with respect to GSP schemes. Further-

[7] See OECD, *Export Cartels* (Paris, 1974); see also Heinrich Kronstein, *The Law of International Cartels* (Ithaca and London: Cornell University Press, 1973).

[8] These discriminations are analyzed at length in Zuhayr Mikdashi, "Influencing the Environment for Primary Commodities," *Journal of World Trade Law* (Geneva), vol. 8, March-April 1974, pp. 144–75.

more, in 1975 it set up a favorable trade association known as the Lomé Convention with a group of 46 African, Caribbean, and Pacific (ACP) developing countries.

More specifically, the Lomé Convention offered the following remarkable features: (1) Tariff-free and quota-free entry into the European community for all manufactured goods of the ACP countries, and for 96 percent of their agricultural products, including sugar. The remaining 4 percent were to be given preferential treatment. No reciprocity was required. (2) Stabilization of export earnings by the 46 to compensate for a fall in commodity prices: the 18 least developed nations would be compensated if their export earnings on major commodities fell more than 2.5 percent below those of a base period; the other 28 would be compensated if their earnings fell more than 7.5 percent. Commodities covered include bananas, cocoa, coffee, cotton, groundnuts, iron ore, leather and skins, palm oil, raw sisal, tea, and wood products. Compensation appropriated for the first five years was £156 million (sterling). For sugar, a key commodity accounting for 12 percent of exports from the 46, an innovative provision indexed the price of 1.4 million tons of sugar to the EEC's internal sugar beet price. Should the world market price be above the community's price, individual EEC countries—notably Britain—could bilaterally negotiate sugar import prices at levels above those obtaining in the community. (3) Financial aid to the 46 amounting to £1.412 billion, with over two-thirds in the form of grants. The major portion of this aid will go to develop small and medium-sized industries under the guidance of an Industrial Cooperation Committee, and a Center for Industrial Development.[9]

The EEC commissioner responsible for relations with the developing world commented on the European initiative as compared with that of other countries: "Countries infinitely more rich and powerful have not begun to look at the problem. It is Europe which has issued a challenge to the U.S., Japan, to the whole industrialized world." [10]

According to another EEC source, however, GSP schemes "are

---

[9] "Europe Aids the Third World," *European Community* (London), March 1975, p. 3. For a general analysis of stabilization of export earnings, see UNCTAD, *Compensatory Financing of Export Fluctuations in Commodity Trade*, Report by the Secretary-General of UNCTAD, Geneva, December 13, 1974 (TD/B/C.1/166/Supp.4).

[10] Claude Cheysoon, in *European Community*, March 1975, p. 5.

hedged about with conditions which greatly reduce their value." [11] Furthermore, developed countries can reverse trade liberalization at will. The U.S. Congress, for example, passed a law in 1974 denying OPEC member countries the conventional most-favored-nation clause generally applicable to members of the General Agreement on Tariffs and Trade (GATT). The legislation was designed to penalize the OPEC "cartel," even though U.S. legislation has tolerated export cartels of U.S.-based enterprises since 1918 (the Webb-Pomerene Act). The anti-OPEC legislation aroused opposition from Latin American and other developing countries.[12]

If a spirit of closer international economic cooperation is to guide transactions among nations, we must reduce the burdens (fiscal and otherwise) and trade restrictions which advanced countries place on those products based on raw materials largely exported by the developing countries, especially as these burdens and restrictions adversely affect the demand for these raw materials in favor of substitutes.

Producer Associations and the New Order

The governments of developing countries have generally faced difficult problems in overcoming poverty. In their endeavors, they have sought to assert control over their natural resources and to promote industrialization, expansion of foreign trade, and diversification of their export proceeds and their trading partners. It has become clear to a number of leaders from these countries that the foregoing objectives cannot be achieved single-handed; and that cooperation, ranging from exchange of information to policy coordination, could yield greater benefits.

The developing resource-exporting countries have several characteristics in common: they often rely heavily on a few commodities for foreign exchange receipts, fiscal revenues, and development; their resources have been controlled directly or indirectly, until recently, by foreign enterprises; their access to markets for their processed or industrialized goods has been hampered; and all strive to improve their socioeconomic benefits from the exploitation of their resources.

---

[11] Richard Bailey, "Aid through Trade," *European Community,* September 1974, p. 12. See also Peter Ginman, "GSP: Three Years of Progress," *International Trade Forum* (UNCTAD/GATT), October–December 1974, pp. 16–20, 31–33.

[12] See also Raymond Vernon, "The Oil Crisis and the International Distribution of Power," in *The Oil Crisis: In Perspective,* Fall 1975 issue of *Daedalus.*

An LDC's choice of policy or strategy invariably involves a "trade-off" of one package of costs-benefits against other packages. The choice is normally guided by the leaders' perception of net gain. Though supported by factual data, a perception of gain relies mostly on the value judgement of the decision-maker, based on largely subjective weights ascribed to nonmeasurable elements of costs or benefits.[13]

More specifically, resource-exporting governments have been faced with important and interrelated competing options with respect to the ownership, production, and pricing of their products. Most LDC governments have apparently opted for the policy of national ownership and control of their natural resources; a few with limited qualified manpower have not insisted upon this. In the latter situation, transnational enterprises are welcome to establish fully owned affiliates, though these host governments hope for joint venture relationships in due course.

Resource-exporting governments have also been faced with the dilemma of whether to produce as much as possible now or to conserve resources for the future. This is normally resolved by ascertaining the absorptive capacity of the national economy,[14] and the benefits derived from the current as compared with the prospective exploitation of natural resources. The higher the absorptive capacity of the domestic economy and the larger the profitable opportunities for current investments, the greater the production of resources today, and vice versa.

The third dilemma is lower versus higher prices. The higher the prices, the greater the conservation of the said resource and its substitution by alternative products, and vice versa. For mineral countries with vast reserves, their leaders' concern centers on obsolescence; whereas for countries with limited reserves, the primary concern is premature depletion.

Having convergent or broadly similar conditions, and being faced by groups of powerful international oligopolies and cartels, governments of

[13] See also "Exploring Energy Choices," a preliminary report of the Ford Foundation's Energy Policy Project, New York, 1974, p. 15.

[14] In the literature, absorptive capacity refers to the ability of domestic economies to utilize resources to produce capital goods. One study dealing with this subject has defined aggregate absorptive capacity (the aggregate ability to invest) as "the optimum aggregate amount of private and public investment opportunities that—given a time span of three–five years—can be undertaken, successfully implemented and subsequently productively operated under the assumption that adequate domestic and foreign savings are forthcoming and that the most appropriate choice of techniques is being used." See S. J. Stevens, *Capital Absorptive Capacity in Developing Countries* (Leiden: A. W. Sijthoff, 1971), pp. 51–52.

developing countries have sought redress. One approach used is the formation of state trading agencies with monopoly rights; another is the nationalization of foreign capital; a third is the creation of multilateral associations to cope more effectively with the bargaining power of foreign oligopolies or cartels, share the overhead cost of foreign trading, and build up and exchange information.

Under the influence of a majority of developing countries, the UN's ECOSOC, in its 1973 resolution on permanent sovereignty over natural resources, has come to favor collective action among developing countries in order to improve their economic position. More specifically, the resolution *"recognizes* that one of the most effective ways in which the developing countries can protect their natural resources is to promote or strengthen machinery for cooperation among them having as its main purpose to concert pricing policies, to improve conditions of access to markets, to coordinate production policies and, thus, to guarantee the full exercise of sovereignty by developing countries over their natural resources" (1737–LIV). The General Assembly, furthermore, in its May 1, 1974, resolution adopting a Program of Action on Establishment of a New International Economic Order, strongly supported producer-exporter associations aimed at improving the export income of developing countries (3202 S. VI). The scope for governmental consultation and cooperation among these associations was articulated at the Dakar Conference of Developing Countries on Raw Materials held on February 3–8, 1975 (Res. 6).

Producer associations of LDCs are therefore largely aimed at redressing the balance of international economic relations which now favors the industrial countries. Thus came the UN call for a new economic order. The secretary-general of UNCTAD explained that "one should not equate the efforts of producers of primary products so to organize themselves and to co-ordinate their policies as amounting to the establishment of cartels. There is already much concentration and sophistication, one should add, at the buying side of commodity markets and the joint efforts of producers could provide an offset or a countervailing power to this—a development which would result in a better rather than a monopoly price." [15]

The appeal of the cooperative approach to developing countries derives, of course, from the fact that it has proved relatively effective in the

---

[15] UNCTAD, *Monthly Bulletin,* March 1975, p. 3.

case of petroleum. But the subject is of equal importance to the developed countries because of their increased dependence on LDCs for imports of basic materials, and because of possible raw material shortages in years to come.

Ironically, though, the successes of OPEC have been costly for other developing countries too, since oil price increases have further burdened their balance of payments and raised the costs of their development programs. Yet most developing countries have been impressed by OPEC's achievements. Several saw in the OPEC model a fine example for emulation. As described by a perspicacious observer of the developing world scene: "In a tense world where the developing countries often feel like prisoners under commercial and monetary yokes, where they see their raw materials and primary products (energy and foodstuffs) transported to industrialized countries, this grouping on the basis of petroleum has become, for some countries, the symbol of their struggle to redress the imbalance." [16]

But could non-OPEC developing countries do the same? Table 7 outlines the major variables which influence cooperative arrangements aimed

Table 7. Variables positively influencing a producers' association

Economic variables
1. A large share of the world market
2. Low price elasticity of demand
3. Low price elasticity of supply outside the association
4. High demand growth
5. Few producers
6. Numerous and dispersed buyers
7. Low disparities in members' fixed-variable cost ratios, reserves, excess capacity, and social discount rates
8. High barriers of entry for competitors
9. Nonrecyclable product
10. Absence of major consumer stockpiles
Other variables
1. Common awareness of vulnerability of members
2. Common perception of *net* collective gain
3. Common perception of effective collective means of action
4. Cooperation or neutrality of transnational enterprises
5. Cooperation or neutrality of major industrial powers

Note: "Negative influence" obtains with variables of opposite value.

[16] Paul Gérin-Lajoie, president, Canadian International Development Agency, *Focus on Man* (Ottawa, 1974), p. 5. See also A. I. MacBean, *Export Instability and Economic Development* (London: Allen & Unwin, 1966), pp. 295–96; and B. Varon and K. Takeuchi, "Developing Countries and Non-Fuel Minerals," *Foreign Affairs,* April 1974, pp. 497–510.

at raising benefits from the export of a given commodity. The table is heuristic, and is not intended for empirical measurement. It is designed to reveal the key variables at work and to suggest the direction of their impact. It may serve as an aid, but not as a substitute, for individual judgments on methods of controlling possible gain from collective action.

To illustrate the impact of change in one variable—for example, supply elasticity of oil—let us assume an increased availability of competitive substitutes from non-oil sources in response to a higher oil price. The impact of such a price increase on cooperation is likely to be negative, since some member governments, especially the ones with ample reserves, would fear that non-oil competition would reduce their market share, render some of their oil reserves useless, and adversely affect their total benefits. These governments might consequently reconsider their support of a collective agency such as OPEC, bent on increasing the government taxes per unit of export. The reduction in such support could show up in the form of refusal to join in pricing or production programs, and in a decline in the scope or importance assigned to cooperation, probably limiting it to an exchange of information. Certain member governments, especially the ones with vast low-cost reserves and in need of additional sales, might then initiate a cut in export prices in order to maintain or improve their market position, and this in turn might trigger retaliation and the nullification of collective action.

In a nutshell, groupings of primary exporting countries aimed at market control have better prospects if certain conditions are simultaneously present: a generally low long-run price elasticity of demand for the association's product, a low elasticity of supply outside the association, the willingness and capacity of member countries to act jointly and to accept production control, little variations in production costs or in richness of resources among competing countries, broadly similar expectations from collective action, and uniform quality (or readily measurable quality differences) of the commodity in question.

Other favorable conditions may add to the prospects of success of commodity control, notably the unimpeded entry into major markets, the neutrality or support—explicit or tacit—of major importer governments, and the absence of importers' schemes such as stockpiles aimed at countering or reducing the impact of exporters' market intervention. Over time, the maintenance of similar interests and views among members is more significant than the sophistication of the collective structure they may design and evolve.

In reality, cooperation among developing countries has presented a number of hurdles. Chief among these are important divisions among the developing countries themselves. Divisions are both economic, mostly rivalry in the sale of the same or competing products, and political, arising from differences in regimes' and leaders' outlooks. Moreover, the countervailing power and the overt or covert opposition of the governments of industrial countries have often proved major obstacles, since LDC cooperation will increase expense to consumers and firms of the industrial world. In this respect, developed countries command potent weapons which have been both brandished and used more or less effectively. These range from direct political-military intervention to restrictions on the import or export of key commodities and the freezing of LDCs' foreign assets.

To the extent a primary commodity is a relatively small fraction in the consumer's budget, and to the extent growth in demand for that commodity is more related to growth in income, population expansion, changes in technology, or changes in the pattern of consumption, moderate price increases are not likely to have an adverse impact on volumes exported. Under these circumstances, "to ask the less developed countries to increase their export quantities of primary products (by reducing prices) in the face of a price-inelastic and not an upward-shifting demand schedule would be to ask, in effect, for an income transfer from poor to rich countries through a change in the terms of trade in favor of the latter." [17]

The problem for commodity exporters, assuming they can achieve collective action, is that by aiming at higher prices they will encourage the search for substitutes. For a commodity with close substitutes (for example, tin), a higher price strategy is not optimal if long-run maximization of export earnings is sought. It is not valid, however, to conclude that a price-raising or output-restricting commodity agreement should not be recommended, even if the long-run demand elasticity is substantially above short-run elasticity. Such a price increase would yield larger foreign exchange receipts in the short or intermediate run, which could be

[17] Gerald Meier, *Leading Issues in Economic Development* (New York: Oxford University Press, 1970), p. 503n.

put to good use in broadening the economic base and raising flexibility and productive capacity.

The case for higher immediate revenues for LDCs has been cogently argued by leading scholars of the subject: "Given that the less developed countries are anxious to industrialize as rapidly as possible, and in so doing expect to increase the flexibility of their economic structures, it might well be an optimum strategy for them to attempt to maximize their profits from primary production over the short run, at the expense of future earnings, in order to secure their development objectives." [18] Moreover, some developing countries have reason to fear that their natural resources could face market obsolescence resulting from technological change. This may well explain their desire to exploit the market fully now. According to available evidence, the optimum export tax a country can gainfully impose is higher the higher its social discount rate, the lower the long-term cross-elasticity of demand, and the lower the elasticity of supply. The social discount rate reflects the degree of urgency for availability of financial resources. The higher that urgency, the higher the social discount rate.

Assuming that demand for an industry's product is relatively inelastic in the short or intermediate run, the demand for the product of a single firm or country representing a fraction of the industry's output is, nevertheless, highly elastic. This situation calls for collective action if the aim is to exploit the global inelasticity of demand. Elasticity of demand, moreover, varies widely among primary commodities; and for the same commodity, the elasticity measures vary from one price range to another. For example, in mid-1970s' price conditions, intercommodity competition is keen between oil and nuclear power, copper and aluminum, and aluminum and tin.

If they wish to gain the most influence over their markets, producers of substitutable commodities which have a wide range of uses (such as aluminum, copper, tin, and steel in one group; hydrocarbons and uranium in another) should join together into supragroups. Prices of individual commodities in the group would then be raised in such amounts as to minimize intragroup substitution, and to exploit the inelasticity of demand for the whole category of these commodities. To achieve such cooperation, however, is difficult, as the parties involved are many and have diverse

[18] H. G. Johnson, *Economic Policies Towards Less Developed Countries* (Washington: Brookings Institute, 1967), p. 155.

interests, and the uses of the commodities in question change over time. It is naturally more workable to have a few countries agree on one commodity than to have several agree on a number of them.

It is not easy, furthermore, to segregate and seal commodities into separate groups of substitutable materials. It is possible that the major use of one commodity (say petroleum) is in a field (energy) which requires a long lead time for substitution (probably 10 to 15 years). However, non-energy uses of petroleum are of growing importance too, for example, petrochemicals, including plastics. And plastic products are also a close substitute for tin and aluminum. It is therefore likely that an increase in the price of crude oil would lead to an increase in the price of plastics, and thus adversely affect the latter's competitiveness vis-à-vis aluminum, tin, and other container materials. Moreover, the impact of a crude oil price increase is not limited to oil products, but will affect all commodities dependent on oil as a major input in their production. Since aluminum smelting is a heavy consumer of energy, a price increase in crude oil is bound to raise the cost of smelting aluminum more than copper, since the latter consumes less energy in its refining process. The end result is that copper will improve its competitive position, unless energy-surplus countries offer "cheap energy" to aluminum smelters to induce their location in their territories—as in fact some OPEC countries have done.

If price cooperation among several producers and several commodities encounters forbidding difficulties, fiscal cooperation is both possible and desirable. It is generally inadvisable for resource-exporting countries, a large number of which are developing countries, to outbid each other in offering vast concession areas, tax rebates, exemptions, or holidays, or to grant subsidies. It is even desirable, as some host governments have shown, to make foreign operators forfeit their concession rights over some areas, if certain known resources have not been developed and properly produced over a reasonable period of time.

According to CIPEC, the successes of OPEC in raising government revenues are worthy of emulation. CIPEC has argued that OPEC's achievements "have demonstrated how other producers of raw materials could satisfy their claims for an equitable compensation . . . offsetting the deterioration in the terms of trade which has resulted both from inflation in the industrialized countries and from changes in monetary parities." [19] But CIPEC, unlike OPEC, has failed so far to make a signifi-

[19] *Copper Market* (CIPEC), 4th quarter 1971, p. 3.

cant impact on copper prices. One major reason for this failure is the fact that the copper exported by CIPEC countries represents less than a quarter of the total world copper supply, while OPEC countries now supply over 50 percent of world petroleum and account for about 85 percent of world oil exports. Another reason is that copper scrap and copper produced outside CIPEC countries represent important alternate sources. Moreover, industrial users and the U.S. government keep sizable stocks to hedge against supply shortages and for strategic reasons. CIPEC countries are also faced with the threat of encroachments from close substitutes with potentially very large supplies, notably aluminum, which has grown in the last two decades at about 9 percent per annum, as compared to 4.5 percent annual growth rate for copper. No such large-scale substitute exists for oil, at least for a decade. Moreover, fuels are dissipated during consumption, and there is accordingly no scope for re-use.

A commodity in a similar position to that of copper, with respect to availability of scrap and to substitution, is tin. Tin uses, especially packaging, have seen encroachments from aluminum, steel, and synthetic substitutes. Tin demand has consequently grown at the modest rate of less than 2 percent per annum. Nevertheless, tin exporting countries have been able to influence the market, notably in reducing price fluctuations. This is due to their collective production control, and to the cooperation, explicit or tacit, of major importer countries. No similar cooperation has yet been possible between CIPEC and importer countries.

To make commodity agreements effective over the longer term, all significant exporters and importers must be willing to cooperate. Moreover, the collective agency should have at its disposal potent instruments of sanction for enforcing production control. In the case of tin, ITC can reduce a member country's production quota in future control periods and confiscate that country's share in the joint tin buffer stock, unless that country informs ITC of its decision to withdraw one year in advance.

Inspired by the experience of ITC, UNCTAD has proposed the establishment of international stockpiles in key storable commodities. The size of such stocks should be sufficiently large to absorb supplies in case of an unexpected shrink in demand, assure consumers of adequate quantities in case of unexpected interruptions or reduction of regular supplies, and iron out price movements. Along with the operation of such stocks, multilateral commitments of sales and purchases would improve the predictability of trade flows and rationalize investments. Compensatory arrangements to remedy fluctuations in sales proceeds and removal of trade barriers against processed products would furthermore help the producing developing countries.[20]

The factors that most facilitate the price stabilization function of a commodity agreement and the operation of its buffer stock are the uniform quality of the commodity, and the presence of one or several open markets for trading on a daily basis. Tin metal benefits from these two factors. It is a uniformly graded metal, whereas bauxite, iron ore, crude oil and other minerals have wide variations in quality. Moreover, the ITC has the LME and other open markets as forums for ascertaining readily the approximate value of tin, no matter how crude and imperfect its valuation is. Other minerals are not traded on exchanges for day-to-day valuations.

Of course, the fact that there are economic possibilities for, and advantages to, closer cooperation among developing countries does not mean that these possibilities are judiciously used. But the larger the perceived potential net gain from cooperation, the greater the willingness of governments to surmount resistance from within and from without to achieve it.

From the standpoint of the industrial powers, the success of collective action among developing countries could be negative or positive depending on the criteria used. It is negative if a strictly mercantile nationalistic standpoint is espoused, since the gain of developing countries would generally mean a parallel reduction in the gain of their major trading partners, the developed industrial countries. Viewed from the standpoint of promoting a redistribution of wealth from international trade in favor of developing areas, collective action among developing countries—coupled with other appropriate measures of aid via trade—should be on balance positive. Rarely, however, have wealthy nations willingly shared their power and wealth with the less privileged. Such an attitude is likely to remain, and developed countries will continue to be guided mostly by their national interest and to oppose groups which aim at nibbling at their gains.

Some officials and scholars of developed market economies have chided developing countries for their attempts at concerted action, often branding them as cartelists or exploiters. This is an exaggeration, even

[20] UNCTAD, *An Integrated Programme for Commodities*, Report by the Secretary-General of UNCTAD, Geneva, December 9, 1974 (TD/B/C.1/166), and Supplements 1 to 5.

for the relatively successful group of oil exporting countries.[21] Moreover, these critics usually overlook the fact that the developed industrial economies themselves are very far indeed from the model of competitive markets, and that oligopolistic-monopolistic market structures predominate in leading sectors with active or passive support of the home governments concerned. To call for a free play of competition on the side of raw-material-exporting developing countries, at a time when these countries face powerful industrial concentrations in the developed regions, reflects a total disregard for parity among all parties.

In an "enlightened" official view from a developed country, a French statement issued in December 1972 favored international collaboration in controlling commodity markets with a view to assisting developing countries:

Without an organization of the commodity markets giving producing states price and marketing guarantees, how can these countries acquire the foreign currency they need for their infrastructure and the preparation of precise development plans which appear to France to be essential for progress? That is why, in the teeth of the opposition of numerous industrialized countries favoring the law of supply and demand, which penalises the poorest of the developing countries even more, the representatives of the French Government have unfailingly supported the few agreements in operation for tin and coffee and recommended the conclusion of new agreements. . . . By making consumers in rich countries pay a higher price for these foodstuffs and metals than would result from the free play of competition, France is fostering the most acceptable form of aid—payment for human effort rather than charity pure and simple.[22]

The Australian Labour Government has also been sympathetic to LDC resource-exporters. Its minister for minerals and energy declared in 1975: "Australia should resist demands by the major industrialized countries to be lined up in their pressure groups against the under-developed resources-producing nations." [23]

For greater international harmony and speedier development, there is certainly a need for improvement in the framework of world economic relations. The restructuring of the world economic order as part of a global strategy for development and greater equality depends largely on

[21] See also Edward G. Mitchell, ed., *Dialogue on World Oil,* a conference sponsored by the American Enterprise Institute for Public Policy, Washington, November 1974.

[22] Quoted in *Tin International* (London), January 1973.

[23] R. F. X. Connor, speech at the Australian Labour Party Conference, Terrigal, 1975, p. 3 (mimeo).

the goodwill and cooperation of all parties concerned, notably the rich and powerful countries, and on the response of their transnational enterprises. In summing up his position at congressional hearings on U.S. foreign economic policy, one writer pointedly urged his country, the United States, to share with other countries its growing economic power:

We are at a point of history in which increased economic interdependence looks close to inevitable. But it is a lopsided interdependence, one in which the United States is seen as gaining most from the continuation of the trend, and losing least from its interruption. From a political and psychological point of view, that is a dangerous situation. If we are to mitigate the tension that the situation generates, it will be by action that comes hard to the nation state: by curbing the full exercise of our overwhelming economic power and by pooling that power with others. That kind of action will take a kind of wisdom and restraint which is rare in the history of nations.[24]

Resource industries have been undergoing remarkable mutations at a pace never anticipated. National control of domestic operations is now an established fact in several leading raw-material-exporting countries, and the benefits of some of the latter have increased beyond industry expectations. All this happened largely in response to the rising economic independence of LDCs and the impact of collective actions by host governments, with international market and political conditions helping.

The restructuring of power relations and trade gains between developing countries, developed countries, and transnational enterprises in the direction of greater equality need not lead to a similar restructuring among the developing countries themselves. Furthermore, the sharing of gain within developing countries need not necessarily move in the direction of greater equality among all segments of their population. Some authors, however, have cogently argued that external dependence supports internal inequality, and that by redressing external relations, internal socioeconomic development will benefit.[25] It is nevertheless obvious that in an increasingly interdependent world, the restructuring of economic relations in the direction of greater equality is of paramount importance to peace and prosperity in our spaceship Earth.

[24] Testimony of Raymond Vernon, in U.S. Congress, Joint Economic Committee, *A Foreign Economic Policy for the 1970's,* pt. 1, *Survey of the Issues,* Hearings before the Subcommittee on Foreign Economic Policy, 91st Cong., 1st Sess., 1970, p. 152.

[25] See Constantine V. Vaitsos, "Power, Knowledge, and Development Policy: Relations between Transnational Enterprises and Developing Countries," Dag Hammarskjöld Foundation, Uppsala, August 1974, p. 34 (mimeo).

Bibliographical Note

It is impossible to list here the numerous documents consulted, several of which have not been reported in the footnotes. The author would like, however, to emphasize the wealth of relevant information published by the following sources: the United Nations and several of its specialized agencies, intergovernmental organizations of the developing world (for example, the Group of 77, the Group of Non-Aligned, the Organization of African Unity, the League of Arab States, the Conference of Islamic Nations), and of the developed world (OECD, IEA, CMEA). Publications of producer associations and international commodity organizations have also been a useful source of information.

Most of the information available on natural resources is written by scholars in the developed countries. Developing countries have not had comparable means to support such research. Fortunately, in recent years, they have shown a rising interest in articulating their objectives and strategies in an area of vital importance to their well-being.

Index

Publications Written under the Auspices of the Center for International Affairs, Harvard University

Created in 1958, the Center for International Affairs fosters advanced study of basic world problems by scholars from various disciplines and senior officials from many countries. The research of the center focuses on economic, social, and political development, the management of force in the modern world, the evolving roles of Western Europe and the Communist nations, and the conditions of international order.

The Soviet Bloc, by Zbigniew K. Brzezinski (sponsored jointly with the Russian Research Center), 1960. Harvard University Press. Revised edition, 1967.

The Necessity for Choice, by Henry A. Kissinger, 1961. Harper & Bros.

Rift and Revolt in Hungary, by Ferenc A. Váli, 1961. Harvard University Press.

Strategy and Arms Control, by Thomas C. Schelling and Morton H. Halperin, 1961. Twentieth Century Fund.

United States Manufacturing Investment in Brazil, by Lincoln Gordon and Engelbert L. Grommers, 1962. Harvard Business School.

The Economy of Cyprus, by A. J. Meyer, with Simos Vassiliou (sponsored jointly with the Center for Middle Eastern Studies), 1962. Harvard University Press.

Entrepreneurs of Lebanon, by Yusif A. Sayigh (sponsored jointly with the Center for Middle Eastern Studies), 1962. Harvard University Press.

Communist China 1955–1959: Policy Documents with Analysis, with a foreword by Robert R. Bowie and John K. Fairbank (sponsored jointly with the East Asian Research Center), 1962. Harvard University Press.

Somali Nationalism, by Saadia Touval, 1963. Harvard University Press.

The Dilemma of Mexico's Development, by Raymond Vernon, 1963. Harvard University Press.

Limited War in the Nuclear Age, by Morton H. Halperin, 1963. John Wiley & Sons.

In Search of France, by Stanley Hoffmann et al., 1963. Harvard University Press.

The Arms Debate, by Robert A. Levine, 1963. Harvard University Press.

Africans on the Land, by Montague Yudelman, 1964. Harvard University Press.

Counterinsurgency Warfare, by David Galula, 1964. Frederick A. Praeger, Inc.

People and Policy in the Middle East, by Max Weston Thornburg, 1964. W. W. Norton & Co.

Shaping the Future, by Robert R. Bowie, 1964. Columbia University Press.

Foreign Aid and Foreign Policy, by Edward S. Mason (sponsored jointly with the Council on Foreign Relations). 1964. Harper & Row.

How Nations Negotiate, by Fred Charles Iklé, 1964. Harper & Row.

Public Policy and Private Enterprise in Mexico, ed. Raymond Vernon, 1964. Harvard University Press.

China and the Bomb, by Morton H. Halperin (sponsored jointly with the East Asian Research Center), 1965. Frederick A. Praeger, Inc.

Democracy in Germany, by Fritz Erler (Jodidi Lectures), 1965. Harvard University Press.

The Troubled Partnership, by Henry A. Kissinger (sponsored jointly with the Council on Foreign Relations), 1965. McGraw-Hill Book Co.

The Rise of Nationalism in Central Africa, by Robert I. Rotberg, 1965. Harvard University Press.

Pan-Africanism and East African Integration, by Joseph S. Nye, Jr., 1965. Harvard University Press.

Communist China and Arms Control, by Morton H. Halperin and Dwight H. Perkins (sponsored jointly with the East Asian Research Center), 1965. Frederick A. Praeger, Inc.

Problems of National Strategy, ed. Henry Kissinger, 1965. Frederick A. Praeger, Inc.

Deterrence before Hiroshima: The Airpower Background of Modern Strategy, by George H. Quester, 1966. John Wiley & Sons.

Containing the Arms Race, by Jeremy J. Stone, 1966. M.I.T. Press.

Germany and the Atlantic Alliance: The Interaction of Strategy and Politics, by James L. Richardson, 1966. Harvard University Press.

Arms and Influence, by Thomas C. Schelling, 1966. Yale University Press.

Political Change in a West African State, by Martin Kilson, 1966. Harvard University Press.

Planning without Facts: Lessons in Resource Allocation from Nigeria's Development, by Wolfgang F. Stolper, 1966. Harvard University Press.

Export Instability and Economic Development, by Alasdair I. MacBean, 1966. Harvard University Press.

Foreign Policy and Democratic Politics, by Kenneth N. Waltz (sponsored jointly with the Institute of War and Peace Studies, Columbia University), 1967. Little, Brown & Co.

Contemporary Military Strategy, by Morton H. Halperin, 1967. Little, Brown & Co.

Sino-Soviet Relations and Arms Control, ed. Morton H. Halperin (sponsored jointly with the East Asian Research Center), 1967. M.I.T. Press.

Africa and United States Policy, by Rupert Emerson, 1967. Prentice-Hall.

Elites in Latin America, ed. Seymour M. Lipset and Aldo Solari, 1967. Oxford University Press.

Europe's Postwar Growth, by Charles P. Kindleberger, 1967. Harvard University Press.

The Rise and Decline of the Cold War, by Paul Seabury, 1967. Basic Books.

Student Politics, ed. S. M. Lipset, 1967. Basic Books.

Pakistan's Development: Social Goals and Private Incentives, by Gustav F. Papanek, 1967. Harvard University Press.

Strike a Blow and Die: A Narrative of Race Relations in Colonial Africa, by George Simeon Mwase, ed. Robert I. Rotberg, 1967. Harvard University Press.

Party Systems and Voter Alignments, ed. Seymour M. Lipset and Stein Rokkan, 1967. Free Press.

Agrarian Socialism, by Seymour M. Lipset, revised edition, 1968. Doubleday Anchor.

Aid, Influence, and Foreign Policy, by Joan M. Nelson, 1968. The Macmillan Company.

Development Policy: Theory and Practice, ed. Gustav F. Papanek, 1968. Harvard University Press.

International Regionalism, by Joseph S. Nye, 1968. Little, Brown, & Co.

Revolution and Counterrevolution, by Seymour M. Lipset, 1968. Basic Books.

Political Order in Changing Societies, by Samuel P. Huntington, 1968. Yale University Press.

The TFX Decision: McNamara and the Military, by Robert J. Art, 1968. Little, Brown & Co.

Korea: The Politics of the Vortex, by Gregory Henderson, 1968. Harvard University Press.

Political Development in Latin America, by Martin Needler, 1968. Random House.

The Precarious Republic, by Michael Hudson, 1968. Random House.

The Brazilian Capital Goods Industry, 1929–1964 (sponsored jointly with the Center for Studies in Education and Development), by Nathaniel H. Leff, 1968. Harvard University Press.

Economic Policy-Making and Development in Brazil, 1947–1964, by Nathaniel H. Leff, 1968. John Wiley & Sons.

Turmoil and Transition: Higher Education and Student Politics in India, edited by Philip G. Altbach, 1968. Lalvani Publishing House (Bombay).

German Foreign Policy in Transition, by Karl Kaiser, 1968. Oxford University Press.

Protest and Power in Black Africa, ed. Robert I. Rotberg, 1969. Oxford University Press.

Peace in Europe, by Karl E. Birnbaum, 1969. Oxford University Press.

The Process of Modernization: An Annotated Bibliography on the Sociocultural Aspects of Development, by John Brode, 1969. Harvard University Press.

Students in Revolt, ed. Seymour M. Lipset and Philip G. Altbach, 1969. Houghton Mifflin.

Agricultural Development in India's Districts: The Intensive Agricultural Districts Programme, by Dorris D. Brown, 1970. Harvard University Press.

Authoritarian Politics in Modern Society: The Dynamics of Established One-Party Systems, ed. Samuel P. Huntington and Clement H. Moore, 1970. Basic Books.

Nuclear Diplomacy, by George H. Quester, 1970. Dunellen.

The Logic of Images in International Relations, by Robert Jervis, 1970. Princeton University Press.

Europe's Would-Be Polity, by Leon Lindberg and Stuart A. Scheingold, 1970. Prentice-Hall.

Taxation and Development: Lessons from Colombian Experience, by Richard M. Bird, 1970. Harvard University Press.

Lord and Peasant in Peru: A Paradigm of Political and Social Change, by F. LaMond Tullis, 1970. Harvard University Press.

The Kennedy Round in American Trade Policy: The Twilight of the GATT? by John W. Evans, 1971. Harvard University Press.

Korean Development: The Interplay of Politics and Economics, by David C. Cole and Princeton N. Lyman, 1971. Harvard University Press.

Development Policy II—The Pakistan Experience, ed. Walter P. Falcon and Gustav F. Papanek, 1971. Harvard University Press.

Higher Education in a Transitional Society, by Philip G. Altbach, 1971. Sindhu Publications (Bombay).

Studies in Development Planning, ed. Hollis B. Chenery, 1971. Harvard University Press.

Passion and Politics, by Seymour M. Lipset with Gerald Schaflander, 1971. Little, Brown, & Co.

Political Mobilization of the Venezuelan Peasant, by John D. Powell, 1971. Harvard University Press.

Higher Education in India, ed. Amrik Singh and Philip Altbach, 1971. Oxford University Press (Delhi).

The Myth of the Guerrilla, by J. Bowyer Bell, 1971. Blond (London) and Knopf (New York).

International Norms and War between States: Three Studies in International Politics, by Kjell Goldmann, 1971. Published jointly by Läromedelsförlagen (Sweden) and the Swedish Institute of International Affairs.

Peace in Parts: Integration and Conflict in Regional Organization, by Joseph S. Nye, Jr., 1971. Little, Brown & Co.

Sovereignty at Bay: The Multinational Spread of U.S. Enterprise, by Raymond Vernon, 1971. Basic Books.

Defense Strategy for the Seventies (revision of *Contemporary Military Strategy*), by Morton H. Halperin, 1971. Little, Brown & Co.

Peasants Against Politics: Rural Organization in Brittany, 1911–1967, by Suzanne Berger, 1972. Harvard University Press.

Transnational Relations and World Politics, ed. Robert O. Keohane and Joseph S. Nye, Jr., 1972. Harvard University Press.

Latin American University Students: A Six Nation Study, by Arthur Liebman, Kenneth N. Walker, and Myron Glazer, 1972. Harvard University Press.

The Politics of Land Reform in Chile, 1950–1970: Public Policy, Political Institutions, and Social Change, by Robert R. Kaufman, 1972. Harvard University Press.

The Boundary Politics of Independent Africa, by Saadia Touval, 1972. Harvard University Press.

The Politics of Nonviolent Action, by Gene E. Sharp, 1973. Porter Sargent.

System 37 Viggen: Arms, Technology, and the Domestication of Glory, by Ingemar Dorfer, 1973. Universitetsforlaget (Oslo).

University Students and African Politics, by William John Hanna, 1974. Africana Publishing Company.

Organizing the Transnational: The Experience with Transnational Enterprise in Advanced Technology, by M. S. Hochmuth, 1974. Sijthoff (Leiden).

Becoming Modern, by Alex Inkeles and David H. Smith, 1974. Harvard University Press.

Multinational Corporations and the Politics of Dependence: Copper in Chile, 1945–1973, by Theodore Moran, 1974. Princeton University Press.

The Andean Group: A Case Study in Economic Integration among Developing Countries, by David Morawetz, 1974. M.I.T. Press.

Kenya: The Politics of Participation and Control, by Henry Bienen, 1974. Princeton University Press.

Land Reform and Politics: A Comparative Analysis, by Hung-chao Tai, 1974. University of California Press.

Big Business and the State: Changing Relations in Western Europe, ed. Raymond Vernon, 1974. Harvard University Press.

Economic Policymaking in a Conflict Society: The Argentine Case, by Richard D. Mallon and Juan V. Sourrouille, 1975. Harvard University Press.

New States in the Modern World, ed. Martin Kilson, 1975. Harvard University Press.

No Easy Choice: Political Participation in Developing Countries, by Samuel P. Huntington and Joan M. Nelson, 1976. Harvard University Press.

The International Politics of Natural Resources, by Zuhayr Mikdashi, 1976. Cornell University Press.

Harvard Studies in International Affairs *

[*formerly Occasional Papers in International Affairs*]

† 1. *A Plan for Planning: The Need for a Better Method of Assisting Underdeveloped Countries on Their Economic Policies*, by Gustav F. Papanek, 1961.

* Available from Harvard University Center for International Affairs, 6 Divinity Avenue, Cambridge, Massachusetts 02138

† Out of print. May be ordered from AMS Press, Inc., 56 East 13th Street, New York, N. Y. 10003

† 2. *The Flow of Resources from Rich to Poor*, by Alan D. Neale, 1961.

† 3. *Limited War: An Essay on the Development of the Theory and an Annotated Bibliography*, by Morton H. Halperin, 1962.

† 4. *Reflections on the Failure of the First West Indian Federation*, by Hugh W. Springer, 1962.

5. *On the Interaction of Opposing Forces under Possible Arms Agreements*, by Glenn A. Kent, 1963. 36 pp. $1.25.

† 6. *Europe's Northern Cap and the Soviet Union*, by Nils Orvik, 1963.

7. *Civil Administration in the Punjab: An Analysis of a State Government in India*, by E. N. Mangat Rai, 1963. 82 pp. $1.75.

8. *On the Appropriate Size of a Development Program*, by Edward S. Mason, 1964. 24 pp. $1.00.

9. *Self-Determination Revisited in the Era of Decolonization*, by Rupert Emerson, 1964. 64 pp. $1.75.

10. *The Planning and Execution of Economic Development in Southeast Asia*, by Clair Wilcox, 1965. 37 pp. $1.25.

11. *Pan-Africanism in Action*, by Albert Tevoedjre, 1965. 88 pp. $2.50.

12. *Is China Turning In?* by Morton Halperin, 1965. 34 pp. $1.25.

†13. *Economic Development in India and Pakistan*, by Edward S. Mason, 1966.

14. *The Role of the Military in Recent Turkish Politics*, by Ergun Özbudun, 1966. 54 pp. $1.75.

†15. *Economic Development and Individual Change: A Social-Psychological Study of the Comilla Experiment in Pakistan*, by Howard Schuman, 1967.

16. *A Select Bibliography on Students, Politics, and Higher Education*, by Philip G. Altbach, UMHE Revised Edition, 1970. 65 pp. $2.75.

17. *Europe's Political Puzzle: A Study of the Fouchet Negotiations and the 1963 Veto*, by Alessandro Silj, 1967. 178 pp. $3.50.

18. *The Cap and the Straits: Problems of Nordic Security*, by Jan Klenberg, 1968. 19 pp. $1.25.

19. *Cyprus: The Law and Politics of Civil Strife*, by Linda B. Miller, 1968. 97 pp. $3.00.

†20. *East and West Pakistan: A Problem in the Political Economy of Regional Planning*, by Md. Anisur Rahman, 1968.

†21. *Internal War and International Systems: Perspectives on Method*, by George A. Kelley and Linda B. Miller, 1969.

†22. *Migrants, Urban Poverty, and Instability in Developing Nations*, by Joan M. Nelson, 1969. 81 pp.

23. *Growth and Development in Pakistan, 1955–1969*, by Joseph J. Stern and Walter P. Falcon, 1970. 94 pp. $3.00.

24. *Higher Education in Developing Countries: A Select Bibliography*, by Philip G. Altbach, 1970. 118 pp. $4.00.

25. *Anatomy of Political Institutionalization: The Case of Israel and Some Comparative Analyses*, by Amos Perlmutter, 1970. 60 pp. $2.50.

26. *The German Democratic Republic from the Sixties to the Seventies*, by Peter Christian Ludz, 1970. 100 pp.

27. *The Law in Political Integration: The Evolution and Integrative Implications of Regional Legal Processes in the European Community*, by Stuart A. Scheingold, 1971. 63 pp. $2.50.

28. *Psychological Dimensions of U.S.-Japanese Relations*, by Hiroshi Kitamura, 1971. 46 pp. $2.00.

29. *Conflict Regulation in Divided Societies*, by Eric A. Nordlinger, 1972. 137 pp. $4.25.

30. *Israel's Political-Military Doctrine*, by Michael I. Handel, 1973. 101 pp. $3.25.

31. *Italy, NATO, and the European Community: The Interplay of Foreign Policy and Domestic Politics*, by Primo Vannicelli, 1974. 67 + x pp. $3.25.
32. *The Choice of Technology in Developing Countries: Some Cautionary Tales*, by C. Peter Timmer, John W. Thomas, Louis T. Wells, Jr., and David Morawetz, 1975. 114 pp. $3.45.
33. *The International Role of the Communist Parties of Italy and France*, by Donald L. M. Blackmer and Annie Kriegel, 1975. 67 + x pp. $2.75.
34. *The Hazards of Peace: A European View of Detente*, by Juan Cassiers, 1975. $6.95, cloth; $2.95, paper.
35. *Europe in the Energy Crisis*, by Robert J. Lieber, 1976.

**The International Politics
of Natural Resources**

Designed by R. E. Rosenbaum.
Composed by Vail-Ballou Press, Inc.,
in 10 point VIP Times Roman, 2 points leaded,
with display lines in Helvetica Bold.
Printed offset by Vail-Ballou Press
on Warren's No. 66 text, 50 pound basis,
with the Cornell University Press watermark.
Bound by Vail-Ballou Press
in Joanna book cloth
and stamped in All Purpose foil.

Library of Congress Cataloging in Publication Data
(For library cataloging purposes only)

Mikdashi, Zuhayr.
  The international politics of natural resources.
  "Written under the Auspices of the Center for Inter-
national Affairs, Harvard University."
  Includes bibliographical references and index.
  1. Natural resources. 2. International economic
relations. 3. World politics—1965–   I. Harvard
University. Center for International Affairs. II. Title.
HC55.M54   1976   33.7   75-38002
ISBN 0-8014-1001-0